Instructor's Resource Manual

OB in Action:
Cases and Exercises

Sixth Edition

Steven B. Wolff
Marist College

Janet W. Wohlberg
The Rappay Group

HOUGHTON MIFFLIN COMPANY   BOSTON   NEW YORK

Executive Editor: **George Hoffman**
Senior Development Editor: **Susan M. Kahn**
Editorial Assistant: **Marie Bernard-Jackson**
Manufacturing Manager: **Florence Cadran**
Marketing Manager: **Steve Mikels**

Printed in the U.S.A.

ISBN: 0-618-05651-3

123456789-EB-04 03 02 01 00

To Users of *OB in Action*:

Thank you for using the sixth edition of *OB in Action*. Our goal is to make *OB in Action* a tool that is shaped by the users to best meet your teaching needs. We invite you to join us in this endeavor by providing feedback on the material that you use, offering general suggestions and comments for improving the book to better meet your needs, and providing material that you think would be a valuable addition to the book. Your input is welcome at any time; however, to be considered for the seventh edition, we will need it by January 2003. Please feel free to make copies of the following form and send in your feedback whenever it occurs to you. Mail the form to Steven Wolff, Marist College, School of Management, Poughkeepsie, NY 12601. You can also e-mail your comments to steven.wolff@marist.edu.

Contact Information (Optional—Necessary if you are sending in material to be considered for publication):

Name: ______________________________

Address: ______________________________

____

E-mail: ______________________________

Please let me know the material you use. This will allow me to keep the most useful material and cut the less useful. Also provide any suggestions for modifying the material.

I use the following cases and exercises (list case or exercise number) and definitely want you to keep them.	I use the following cases and exercises (list case or exercise number) but would not mind substituting others if you deleted them.

Please provide general suggestions and comments. For example, if you would like to see a case or exercise modified, provide its number and tell us the changes you would like to see. Are there types of exercises and cases that you would like to see included? Are there subjects that you would like to see included? Are there things that should be deleted? Are there things we deleted that you would like to see put back into the book? Are there ways the *Instructor's Resource Manual* can be made more helpful? Let us know your thoughts about the book in general. How can it be made to better suit your needs? Etc. (Please use additional paper if needed.)

Please let us know what goes into your decision to use a supplement such as *OB in Action*. For example, What are the make or break features of the book and instructor's manual? What do you look for in forming an opinion about the quality and usefulness of the book? Etc.

We welcome contributions to the book. If you have material that you think is suitable for the book and would like us to consider it for the next edition, please send it to Steven Wolff along with a teaching note. Teaching notes should include the following: group size, recommended time, what is provided, additional materials needed, required facilities, subjects covered, objectives, a synopsis, relevant background, theory and discussion of the case or exercise, discussion questions and answers where appropriate, and a suggested teaching plan.

CONTENTS

Part V: Organizational Processes and Characteristics

Appendix: Career Dynamics

PREFACE

The *Instructor's Resource Manual* for this edition of *OB in Action* has been designed to help you make the most efficient and effective use of the text materials. As you'll note, we have included comments from our own experiences with the various cases and exercises, all of which have been either classroom tested or used extensively and successfully in management training and adapted for the college classroom. In addition, we have continued our practice of seeking outside experts to act as commentators and to give us their reflections on the material. In this edition, we have also accepted a limited number of carefully selected cases and exercises from contributors.

Notes for exercises are formatted to let you know the approximate amount of time an exercise will take and the materials and facilities required. Time required, as you probably know, is a best guess. Some student groups complete exercises quickly, others go more deeply into the issues or are inefficient and thus require more time. In addition, some instructors—or some class-instructor mixes—generate lengthier discussion before, during, and after exercises.

International and multi-cultural aspects of organizational behavior, teams and group performance, management of change, and conflict management are continuing to be given ever greater emphasis.

The "Methodologies" section of the text includes guidelines for active listening, business writing, journal writing, and problem solving—all skills critical for getting the most out of a course that uses our student text.

Following this preface, you will find a listing of the cases and exercises by topic area. Many cases have more than one focus. While the listing is convenient, we urge you to read the case or exercise before you assign it to be sure it makes the point you want it to!

Section overviews are brief introductions to the key theories and concepts for each of the major areas of organizational behavior. We recommend using these in conjunction with enrichment readings, lectures, and a standard organizational behavior text such as *Organizational Behavior*, 6th edition, by Moorhead and Griffin (Boston: Houghton Mifflin, 2001).

We also recommend that students be required to write one or more case analyses over the course of a semester. For many students, writing helps clarify and focus ideas and learnings. We have found it useful to have students keep journals, write a paper based on their group's process (if they worked in groups for a project or for in-class exercises), and write short—usually 1 to 2 pages—reflection papers after finishing exercises.

We feel fortunate that many people have submitted material to be published in the new edition of *OB in Action* and have given us feedback and new ideas. It's exciting for us to have so many people continue to be enthusiastic about this book and its methods. This includes not just people teaching a course from this book, but students taking the courses as well!

A word about copyright: *OB in Action* represents the hard work of many people over a fifteen-year period. Besides being a violation of federal law, photocopying parts of the student text without obtaining written permission—or the *Instructor's Resource Manual* without adopting the text—means we get zero compensation for our labor and product. We hope you will take this into consideration before "borrowing" materials from this book. If you are concerned about the length of time it might take to receive permissions, please contact us directly, and we will try to expedite the process for you. Thanks.

Steve Wolff steven.wolff@marist.edu
Jan Wohlberg jan@treeage.com

ABOUT THE AUTHORS

Steven B. Wolff has over fifteen years of experience as an engineer in the high tech industry, seven years of which were spent as a manager, both project and line. He has conducted research in performance management of self-managed teams, peer reviews, organizational learning, and public-private partnerships for education. He has also provided training and consultation to a number of Boston School Site Councils. He holds degrees in electrical engineering from the Stevens Institute of Technology and Northeastern University, an MBA from Babson College, and a DBA in organizational behavior from Boston University. He is currently an assistant professor of management at the School of Management at Marist College in Poughkeepsie, New York.

Janet W. Wohlberg taught organizational behavior, mass communication, and andragogy at Boston University's Schools of Management and Mass Communication for more than a decade. She is currently vice president for public relations and advertising for TreeAge Software, Inc., in Williamstown, Massachusetts, and president of The Rappay Group, designers and sellers of corporate and organizational training materials. Her central area of research is in the uses and abuses of power in power-imbalanced relationships. Her recent publications have appeared in *The Bulletin of the Menninger Clinic*, *Psychoanalytic Inquiry*, *Psychiatric Services*, *The Clinical Supervisor*, and *The Journal of Sex Education*

TOPIC AREAS COVERED BY EACH CASE OR EXERCISE

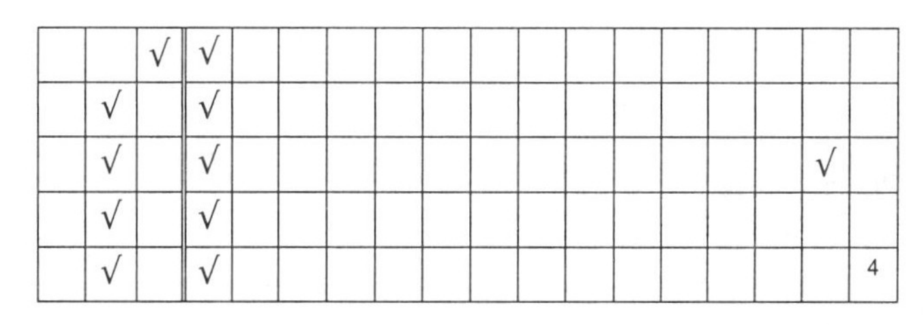

	CASE	EXERCISE	GENERAL INFO.	ICEBREAKER	MOTIVATION	LEADERSHIP	CONFLICT	CHANGE	DIVERSITY	GLOBALIZATION	GROUPS	PROBLEM SOLVING	DECISION MAKING	PLANNING	PERCEPTION	ETHICS/VALUES	COMMUNICATION	OTHER
Methodologies and Skills																		
Using Cases			√															1
Writing for a Business Audience			√														√	
Using Experiential Exercises			√															2
Active Listening			√														√	
Learning from Experience			√															3
Managing Confrontations			√				√											
Techniques for Problem Solving			√									√						
Force Field Analysis			√					√										
Icebreakers																		
Overview			√	√														
Networking		√		√														
Round Robin Interview		√		√													√	
The Realistic Job Preview		√		√														
The Nature of Today's Orgs.		√		√														4
Part I: Managing Global and Workforce Diversity			√						√	√								
1 Managing and Valuing Differences	√						√		√		√							
2 Disclosing and Predicting		√							√						√		√	
3 Observe and Predict		√							√						√			
4 Crossing the Chicago Highway		√							√								√	
5 The Dinner Party		√							√						√			
6 Mercury's Wings	√								√				√			√		
7 The Culture Quiz		√							√	√								
8 "When in Bogotá…"	√								√	√								
9 Who to Hire?		√							√	√			√					
10 Frederick International	√								√	√								
11 Tuckerman-Sawyer Advertising	√								√									

[1] critical thinking
[2] experiential learning
[3] using journals
[4] business environment

	CASE	EXERCISE	GENERAL INFO.	ICEBREAKER	MOTIVATION	LEADERSHIP	CONFLICT	CHANGE	DIVERSITY	GLOBALIZATION	GROUPS	PROBLEM SOLVING	DECISION MAKING	PLANNING	PERCEPTION	ETHICS/VALUES	COMMUNICATION	OTHER
12 Just-in-Time for Temporary Employees	√						√		√									
13 The Loch Ness Cotton Company	√						√		√									5
14 Nature or Nurture?	√								√									
Part II: Individual Processes in Organizations			√		√										√			6
15 What You See Isn't Necessarily What You Get		√													√			
16 Operation Transplant		√							√				√			√		
17 Family Values	√								√				√			√		7
18 Waiting Tables for Godot	√				√		√											8
19 Nude Dancing Comes to Wesleyville	√						√						√			√		9
20 Picking the Project Team		√									√			√				
21 Managing Performance					√	√					√							10
22 Another Sales Contest at Pattersons Department Stores		√			√													11
23 Linda Sifuentes	√				√				√									
24 Spanglemaker Publishing	√				√													
25 Queens Veterinary Hospital	√				√													12
26 Motivation at Bald Eagle	√				√													
27 The Sales Contest That Never Got Off the Ground	√				√													
28 Dr. Watson Gets Published	√				√		√								√			
29 The Issue of Equity		√			√													
30 The Workstation Bonus		√			√						√							
31 Dishonorable Intentions	√				√	√												
32 The Music Teacher from Hell	√				√	√												
33 United Dynamics: Downsizing		√			√						√			√				
34 Giving Negative Feedback Positively		√			√												√	13

[5] sexual harassment
[6] followership
[7] work-family balance
[8] reward systems
[9] organization as citizen
[10] performance mgmt., goal setting
[11] performance mgmt., goal setting
[12] followership
[13] substance abuse, performance mgmt.

	CASE	EXERCISE	GENERAL INFO.	ICEBREAKER	MOTIVATION	LEADERSHIP	CONFLICT	CHANGE	DIVERSITY	GLOBALIZATION	GROUPS	PROBLEM SOLVING	DECISION MAKING	PLANNING	PERCEPTION	ETHICS/VALUES	COMMUNICATION	OTHER
Part III: Interpersonal Processes in Organizations			√			√	√				√						√	
35 The Eyes Have It		√															√	
36 Karen Carlin	√				√	√	√				√							
37 A Straw Is a Straw Is a Straw		√				√												
38 Two Leadership Fishbowls		√				√											√	
39 The Great Post-It® Massacre	√					√												
40 Who Works Saturday Night?		√				√	√						√	√				
41 Trouble with the Team Project		√				√	√						√	√				
42 Meadowbrook Garden Center	√				√	√												14
43 Leadership at Prodigy Electronics	√					√												
44 Two Supervisors—A Study in Style	√					√												
45 The First Federal Bank	√				√	√												
46 The Eleventh Hour		√					√		√		√							
47 The Troublemaker	√					√												
48 The Outspoken Employee	√					√	√										√	
49 The X-Y Scale		√				√												
50 Danger: Radio Activity Hits Country in Long Island	√				√	√		√										
Part IV: Enhancing Individual and Interpersonal Processes			√				√						√				√	15
51 The Codfish Company		√									√			√	√	√		
52 Assigning the Team Project Tasks		√									√			√				
53 Managing Group Performance		√									√						√	16
54 Calendars and Clips		√					√										√	17
55 No Followers? No Leaders!		√				√											√	
56 Earthquake		√									√	√	√					
57 Three Brainstorming Exercises		√										√	√					18
58 What Do You Make of This Junk?		√										√	√					19
59 Doing the Impossible		√						√			√	√	√					20

[14] job design
[15] goal setting, job design, performance appraisal
[16] performance appraisal
[17] goal setting
[18] brainstorming
[19] brainstorming
[20] brainstorming

	CASE	EXERCISE	GENERAL INFO.	ICEBREAKER	MOTIVATION	LEADERSHIP	CONFLICT	CHANGE	DIVERSITY	GLOBALIZATION	GROUPS	PROBLEM SOLVING	DECISION MAKING	PLANNING	PERCEPTION	ETHICS/VALUES	COMMUNICATION	OTHER
60 Cyril and Edna: The Manager as Mediator		√					√										√	
61 Confrontation at Captain Cook's		√					√										√	
62 Five Conflict Management Role Plays		√					√										√	
63 A Place of Your Own		√					√										√	21
64 Rabbit Fever		√					√											22
Part V: Organizational Processes and Characteristics			√					√										23
65 The Craig Middle School	√							√				√						
66 Disability Services Disabled	√							√										
67 The Bureaucracy Game								√					√				√	
68 The Day Care Resource and Referral Agency	√							√										
69 Playing Footsy With the Family Business	√					√		√								√		24
70 The Providence Privateers	√							√										
71 The Seattle Ferry Company	√							√										
72 Dales Healthy Snacks	√				√	√		√										
73 The Deep-Water Harbor		√						√										
74 Issuing a Blanket Statement	√							√										
75 Insubordination or Structural Confusion at Omega House?	√					√												25
76 The Job Reference: An Ethical Dilemma		√														√		
77 Price Fixing at ADM	√															√		26
Appendix: Career Dynamics																		
78 Making the Ideal Job Come True		√																27
79 Ted Johnson	√																	28

[21] negotiation
[22] negotiation
[23] organization structure, culture
[24] family business
[25] organization structure
[26] followership
[27] career management
[28] career management

ICEBREAKERS
Networking*, Round Robin Interview, The Realistic Job Preview, and The Nature Of Today's Organizations

Group Size: Ideally no larger than 50, although all of these exercises will work with larger groups.

Recommended Time: 60 minutes.

Provided: All necessary background and instructions.

Also Required: Name tags, markers, and pins for attaching name tags are useful.

Facilities: A large room with moveable chairs.

Objectives

- To familiarize students with one another.
- To set the tone for the course.
- To help students identify and clarify their goals for the course.

Background

Other than setting the tone and going over the directions, instructors have little to do in icebreaker exercises; however, it is helpful to sit in on the different dyads or groups as they go through their introductions. Ask some of your own questions if you feel that students are not going into enough depth—students often become engaged in icebreakers only after they have gotten over their initial discomfort and dropped their defenses. When you have a sense that things are getting going, leave, having given the students some new openings. This is also a chance for you to get to know something about them.

As you go around the room, reposition students physically so that they are forced to face one another and establish eye contact.

It is important to be sensitive to the different cultural backgrounds of international students. Encourage domestic students to use their foreign language skills when paired with international students. This can add a whole new dimension to the discussions.

In the "Networking" exercise, while the students make the initial choice of partner, the composition of the groups formed by combining dyads can be yours. Try to mix groups, i.e., international students with domestic students, males with females, etc.

* The "Networking" exercise was written by Gail E. Gilmore.

In the "Round Robin Interview," try to give students from varying backgrounds the same topic area so that when they come together for consolidation, they represent many possible interpretations of what they have heard.

We are continually amazed at the degree to which these exercises determine with whom students sit over the remaining course of a semester and with whom they do final projects. We have had several long-term friendships arise out of the exercises and—from a class some years ago, a couple eventually married.

THE NATURE OF TODAY'S ORGANIZATIONS

Group Size: Any number of groups of four to six.

Recommended Time: Approximately 80–90 minutes.

Provided: Instructions in student edition.

Also Required: Large easel paper, markers, and tape or thumb tacks for posting results.

Facilities: One large room with movable chairs.

Objectives

- To explore today's business environment
- To connect characteristics of the business environment to employee and management skills
- To connect the skills required of a successful employee to what will be learned in an organizational behavior, psychology, or management class

Background

This exercise was developed to use as an icebreaker or a first exercise for groups that will be working together throughout the semester and/or to introduce the relationships that exist among business, the greater environment, and the individual. It helps answer the perennial question: "What is organizational behavior?"

Suggested Outline and Timing

1. Set-up (full class: 5 minutes)

Give each group a large sheet of paper and one or two color markers.

Explain the following:

a. This exercise asks students to think about today's business environment and the demands it places on managers and employees.

b. The demands placed on managers and employees require certain knowledge and skills if they are to be successful.

c. This exercise helps students begin to make this connection.

Divide the students into groups of four to six. Ask the students to name their groups or assign each a name or a number.

2. *Part I (small groups: 20 minutes. If this exercise is being used as an icebreaker, you may wish to give the students an additional 15–20 minutes to get acquainted.)*

Have the groups complete Part I of the exercise (Steps 1 and 2 in the student workbook).

At the end of 20 minutes, ask groups to begin part II.

3. *Part II (small groups: 20 minutes)*

In this step, students should think about the kind of people they will need to hire to meet the environmental needs they have identified, e.g., open and creative people who work well in teams to meet demands for innovation.

4. *Posting answers and generating questions (15 minutes)*

Ask groups to post their answers. Remind them to put their group name or number on the posting.

Groups should read the postings of the other teams (rotating from posting to posting in their groups), take notes, and come to a consensus on questions they wish to ask the other groups. Explain that time limitations will not allow each team to ask all of their questions.

5. *Class discussion (open-ended)*

If possible, have students arrange their chairs in a circle or semicircle.

Ask one group to volunteer by asking a question they have agreed upon, e.g., "We would like to ask Group 1 why they feel they need employees who are aggressive." Move from group to group, allowing each group to ask one or two questions and allowing the questioned group to respond. Encourage whole-class discussion after each question and answer.

Students often stray into areas that are important to organizational behavior but which do not specifically address the issue of skills required in today's business organization. It is often fruitful to allow them to follow their interests, particularly as you are striving to answer the question of what organizational behavior is all about and why it should be studied.

As the discussion progresses, take note of the issues discussed. Take a few minutes at the end of the discussion to show students how the issues they have surfaced are related to organizational behavior and where these issues may come up during the course.

1

MANAGING AND VALUING DIFFERENCES: A STORY

This case illustrates issues of managing and valuing differences that are based on learning and work styles, personality differences, and socioeconomic issues, rather than on culture, race, and religion. It asks students to consider how and why differences in the way group members work and think can lead to tension, loss of motivation, and unproductive conflicts. It also asks students to consider their own thinking, learning, and work styles and the ways they impact group efficacy.

The case has been written to stimulate reflection and discussion rather than to illustrate the right or wrong ways of group management. It is best used with students who are or have been engaged in group activities.

Questions for Discussion

1. What differences exist within groups that might potentially lead to unproductive conflict?

   In considering this question, students should reflect on and discuss their feelings on the following:

   a. The importance of knowing their group mates socially.

   b. Whether focusing mainly on the group's task is their prime motivator.

   c. Whether they need detailed facts and data to make decisions.

   d. Whether they use intuition in making decisions.

   e. Whether they prefer to work alone or with others.

   f. Whether they are more interested in getting a grade or learning.

   g. Whether change and uncertainty cause stress or whether they consider them to be challenges.

   h. Whether they need to have their point of view understood before they can listen to other points of view, or whether they like to listen to others before forming an opinion.

2. In what ways can groups effectively use the strengths of their members? In considering this question, students should reflect on and discuss their feelings on the following:

   a. How a person's strengths and weaknesses might complement another group member.

   b. How group members might learn from one another.

   c. What tasks and functions might be best/worst suited for each person.

3. Will differences in a group necessarily lead to tension before the group learns how to best use them—and if so, how should they be handled?

   In considering this question, students should reflect on and discuss their feelings on the following:

   a. How to recognize a problem early before it becomes a major source of tension.
   b. What a group can do to make sure the group becomes aware of concerns felt by its members.
   c. How a group can avoid overusing a strength.
   d. How a group can establish an environment in which it is safe to express concerns.
   e. How a group can avoid pressuring the minority voice to conform to the majority.
   f. Specific actions can be taken and procedures can be put into place for handling unproductive tension.

4. What happens when groups have good intentions but do not carry them out?

   In considering this question, students should reflect on and discuss their feelings on the following:

   What makes it difficult for many groups to actually follow through on their intentions, e.g., restraining forces, driving forces, and fears.

2

DISCLOSING AND PREDICTING

Group Size: Any number of dyads. (Use a triad when needed, but cut the number of statements by approximately 20%.)

Recommended Time: 120 minutes (5 minutes to set up; 5 minutes for each of 20 items; 15 minutes for discussion). This exercise may be done in less time by eliminating the first five to ten statements. It may also be used as an out-of-class assignment with students reporting their findings in class.

Provided: Instructions, grid.

Also Required: No additional materials are required.

Facilities: A large room with moveable chairs.

Objectives

- To explore the accuracy of first impressions
- To examine the bases on which we form first impressions
- To practice active listening skills
- To examine how getting to know someone through an open exploration of shared and differing values helps to change first impressions and bring perceptions more into line with reality

Background

For additional discussion of stereotyping, see the background notes on the exercise "Observe and Predict."

Suggested Outline and Timing:

1. Set-up (full class: 5 minutes)

Go over the instructions. Explain that the purpose of this exercise is to give participants insights rather than facts. Doing this keeps expectations realistic.

Ask students to select a partner who they do not know well.

Alternatively, (a) preselect the dyads, and assign students to them by distributing a list of the assignments, or (b) assign students to dyads randomly or by picking a number, closest birth dates, etc.

2. *Exercise (5 minutes per round)*

After each 5 minutes, ask students to go on to the next item. A minimum of ten statements should be used.

3. *Discussion (15 minutes minimum)*

Use the "Questions for Consideration" as a guide.

3

OBSERVE AND PREDICT

Group Size: Unlimited.

Recommended Time: 60 minutes (5 minutes for set up; 10 minutes each for Steps 1–3; 25 minutes minimum for discussion).

Provided: Instructions and worksheets.

Also Required: Chalkboards or flip charts for recording responses. The *Frontline* video "A Class Divided" is useful in illustrating the central points of this exercise.

Facilities: One large room with unobstructed views of front of room and other participants.

Objectives

- To explore the bases on which we judge other people
- To examine the way we stereotype people based on observational data
- To examine the benefits and dangers of stereotyping
- To examine how we use labeling to reinforce stereotypes
- To consider organizational issues that arise from stereotyping

Background

Stereotyping can be a convenient way to organize, manage, and control a universe that may otherwise feel too large and complex. Organizations, even the federal government, use stereotypes on which to base certain actions and decisions. Sometimes stereotypes are accurate, and making judgments based on stereotypes can save time and energy and maintain an organization's culture. But stereotyping is superficial and closes off or severely limits options and possibilities to benefit from new and different ways of thinking. In addition, stereotyping denies people their individuality and often unjustly limits their possibilities. In the workplace, stereotyping may create divisiveness and limit the ability of businesses to tap employee potential.

We often reinforce and continue stereotypes through the use of labeling. When a blond woman who wears tight skirts is called a "bimbo," we introduce language that allows us to perpetuate the stereotype conveniently without thought or further consideration of the individual being labeled. Often such labels begin to take on meanings that go far beyond original assumptions. The "bimbo" not only represents questionable intelligence but also becomes, by virtue of the label, a sex object.

Becoming aware of how we stereotype people is a first step in overcoming its negative effects. This exercise helps students begin to examine the stereotypes they hold and the impact of those stereotypes on their lives and in the workplace.

Suggested Outline and Timing

1. *Set-up (5 minutes)*

   Briefly review the background information given in the student edition and the instructions. The background information given above is for discussion purposes after the exercise has been completed.

2. *Step 1 (10 minutes)*

   Ask students to call out responses, and record these on a chalkboard or flip chart. Answers should be based on what students can tell about a person from four of their five senses, i.e., sight, touch, smell, and hearing. (While taste might apply, we'd suggest leaving this one off!) Responses may include race, weight, body type, body odor, hair color, clothing, posture, walk, facial features, shoes, accent, smoking, jewelry, hair style, hair type, height, cleanliness, glasses, facial hair, scars, physical malformations, effects of physical injury, age, gender, eye shape, items being carried, voice tone, speed of speech, physical surroundings, etc.

3. *Step 2 (10 minutes)*

   This step is slightly more difficult. Students should mix and match the list generated in Step 1 to look at what kinds of generalizations they might make about someone based on one or more of their observations. For example, they might make assumptions about someone's social class based on their clothing, items being carried and physical surroundings; employment based on gender, shoes, and cleanliness; religion based on jewelry and facial features; health based on posture and physical malformations, etc. Note that this list is general.

4. *Step 3 (10 minutes)*

   At this stage, students should be more specific in their answers. For example, they may conclude that someone wearing a six-pointed star and who has a large nose is Jewish; that someone is sickly because she or he doesn't stand up straight and is missing a leg; or that someone is wealthy because she or he is wearing the latest fashions, carrying a brief case, and dining at an expensive restaurant.

   In addition to developing this list, ask students to supply the one- or two-word label that might fit the description. Many students are uncomfortable with this part of the exercise, as they generally are aware that many labels are politically incorrect. However, the point is that we use language to sort and categorize people and hold them in place. Students who are uncomfortable using words like "nigger" or "honky" might feel perfectly comfortable categorizing people as "nerds" or "jocks" without thinking about the stereotype that such limiting terminology imposes.

5. Discussion (25 minutes minimum)

Begin by asking students if they know of exceptions to some of the items on their list from Step 3. In the examples given above, they might be right some or even most of the time. Explore what their expectations would be of the people on the list; for example, if they concluded that someone wearing a six-pointed star and having a large nose is Jewish, what would they then expect from that individual? How would that impact the way they behave towards that person?

Use the "Questions for Discussion" as a guide.

4

CROSSING THE CHICAGO HIGHWAY

Group Size: Any number of groups of three to five.

Recommended Time: 55 minutes (5 minutes to set up; 10 minutes for student preparation; 20 minutes for exercise; 20 minutes or more for discussion).

Provided: Instructions and exercise.

Also required: No additional materials required.

Facilities: One or more rooms with moveable chairs and space for approximately five feet between groups.

Objectives

- To explore the impact of personality on human interaction
- To examine how knowledge of another's personality aids in communicating and negotiating
- To examine how knowledge of one's own personality aids in communicating and negotiating
- To consider the usefulness of personality analysis

Background

The purpose of this exercise is not to promote the use of any particular testing instrument, including the Myers-Briggs Type Indicator (MBTI). Rather, the MBTI is used to illustrate the kind of information that such tests proffer. It is important to remind students that the usefulness of such instruments is limited and that in negotiating, as in other human interactions, considerably more data must be gathered and factored in. However, it is also important that students recognize and give credence to the impact of personality on conflict—its avoidance and its resolution.

In this exercise, conflict between the two characters over the planning and completion of a highway project is escalating. Cohen, a ward politician, is described in MBTI terminology as extroverted, intuitive, feeling, and perceiving. According to the exercise author, consultant Alice Jacobs, who has been certified to use the MBTI in her practice, people with Cohen's personality "want to talk about a solution in outline, not in detail. They'll want the people affected by their decisions to be happy." Says Jacobs, "If negotiations begin to drag on too long, people like Cohen need to be reminded that alternatives can't be examined forever. Show them the benefits of committing sooner rather than later."

Jones, described as introverted, sensing, thinking, and judging, is likely to want highly detailed, well-supported, and organized proposals well in advance of any meeting. This will give him time, says Jacobs, to go over the proposals privately and in depth so he will fully understand and appreciate suggestions. When dealing with someone like Jones, she adds, schedule meetings well in advance. Jones is likely to view phone calls and unscheduled meetings as unwelcome interruptions. At meetings, it is important to give Jones time to speak and make sure meetings don't run unnecessarily long.

Suggested Outline and Timing

1. *Set-Up (full class: 5 minutes)*

In setting up this exercise, briefly review the instructions and the learning objectives. Explore with students whether they have ever taken a personality inventory test and how that might have affected them.

Review the questions at the end of the case.

Remind students to familiarize themselves with the terminology before reading the case.

Divide the students into small groups.

2. *Student preparation (small groups: 10 minutes)*

During this time, students should read the background material and the short case.

3. *Exercise (small groups: 20 minutes)*

Working in their small groups, the students should come to consensus on the answers to the questions posed at the end of the short case.

Remind students to select a spokesperson for the report out.

4. *Report out and discussion (full class: 20 minutes, minimum)*

Use the exercise questions as a guide.

Ask students to consider how knowledge about themselves and their coworkers and friends helps them avoid or manage conflict. Many students will be able to share stories about personal experiences in which they treated another person in a specific way because of the knowledge they had about the other person's personality.

Explore the implications for the workplace.

5

THE DINNER PARTY

Group Size: Any number of groups of four to six.

Recommended Time: Up to 60 minutes, depending on the number of groups, plus discussion (5 minutes to set up; 30 minutes to establish the menu; 5 minutes per group for report out; open-ended discussion).

Provided: Instructions and menu grid.

Also Required: No additional materials required.

Facilities: A large room or several small breakout rooms.

Objectives

- To reflect on the numerous dimensions of diversity
- To consider the conflicting interests and needs of diverse populations
- To explore the meaning of diversity in interpersonal relationships
- To explore the challenges and benefits of diverse work populations

Background

This exercise uses food and food needs as emblematic of the diverse needs of populations in and out of the workplace.

Students are given a list and brief descriptions of six invited guests to a dinner party. Groups must come up with a menu that best serves the diverse needs of those who will attend. Conflicts between the interests and needs of each of the attendees have been built in. For example, the nine-year-old who hates vegetables may have differing interests from the Hindu graduate student who, based on her religion, may be a vegetarian. As a first step in tackling this exercise, students will need to identify the various needs and interests of the attendees. They will also have to consider whose needs will take precedence when conflicts arise that cannot otherwise be resolved. For added complexity, members of each group should factor in the impact of their own attendance at the dinner party.

Suggested Outline and Timing

1. *Set-up (full class: 5 minutes)*

    - Go over the objectives and instructions for the exercise.
    - Ask students to select a spokesperson to do the report out.
    - Divide the class into groups of four to six, making the groups as diverse as possible.

2. *Deciding the menu (small groups: at least 30 minutes)*

    If students elect to serve a buffet meal, they will still need to decide specifically what foods and beverages they will offer.

3. *Report out (full class: 5 minutes per group)*

    Use the "Questions for Discussion" that appear in the student text as a guide for this and for the class discussion. Students should be able to justify their menu plan based on the needs of the attendees.

4. *Discussion (full class: open-ended)*

6

MERCURY'S WINGS*

This case asks students to examine the difficult choices individuals constantly make between personal and work responsibilities, as well as the obligations of an organization to its employees and vice versa.

To analyze this case, students will need to consider the likely consequences of each choice available to Sarah. If she decides to go to London, Erin and Peter will be pleased with her willingness to sacrifice her beliefs to get the job done. If the show is a success—and every indication is that it will be-Sarah will likely have a solid career ahead of her with Mercury's Wings. However, the fact that she has been pressured to act in a way that is contrary to her deeply held religious beliefs may cause Sarah to feel angry and resentful. As a result, her productivity level and motivation may decrease.

If Sarah chooses not to go to London, she will be acting in concert with her religious beliefs. However, she may be forced to look for another job since it is likely that Peter and Erin will view a choice to uphold religious beliefs as indicative of Sarah's unwillingness to be a team player, particularly in a situation in which all are feeling under pressure. It is thus unlikely that she will attain upward mobility at Mercury's Wings.

Employee and Organizational Needs and Obligations

It is necessary to consider Sarah's obligation to Mercury's Wings, and Mercury's Wings' obligation to her. Class discussion questions should include whether an employee should be obliged to act in a manner inconsistent with her or his belief system if that is what getting a job done necessitates. To what or to whom is an employee ultimately responsible—to her or himself or to the organization? Does an organization have an obligation to respect the values and beliefs of its employees and, if so, to what extent?

In considering this last question, students should also think about what happens when the needs of an individual and an organization are in conflict. When this occurs, whose needs take precedence, and why? A likely response will be that the needs of the organization take precedence. However, this approach is not without costs.

An organization that continually places its own needs ahead of those of its employees may experience a higher turnover rate than an organization that attempts to meet its employees' needs. It may also experience lowered productivity, a higher degree of errors in employee work, and conscious or unconscious sabotage by employees who believe that the organization doesn't care about them.

* These case notes were written by Gail E. Gilmore.

Finally, students should discuss the extent to which it is possible for an organization to meet the needs of its workforce without compromising its own needs. As the workforce becomes increasingly diverse (a trend which will not be reversed in the foreseeable future), organizations will be faced with employee needs based on religious beliefs, cultural values, child-care issues, language issues, and dietary restrictions among others.

Discussion should focus on productive, creative, win-win solutions for organizations attempting to meet diverse employee needs.

7

THE CULTURE QUIZ

Group Size: Individuals, small groups, or full class.

Recommended Time: Open-ended.

Provided: Quiz and answers included in student edition.

Also Required: No additional materials required.

Facilities: Any size room large enough to accommodate full class or spaced small groups.

Objectives

- To stimulate awareness of cultural differences
- To promote consideration of the impact of cultural differences in a global economy
- To stimulate dialogue between domestic and international students
- To explore issues raised by culturally diverse workforces

Background

This is a self-scored quiz developed to encourage students to explore cultural differences from country to country and to do additional reading about conducting business outside their own country. It is meant to promote discussion and set the stage for the cases and exercises in the text's section entitled, "Managing Global and Workforce Diversity."

Occasionally students will argue that their country's practices have been misrepresented, and certainly any generalization is open to that criticism. We consider this to be an opportunity to question that student as to what she or he believes to be the practice, among what segments of society, and in what ways other practices of their country may differ from the United States.

Try this one on your friends and family.

8

"WHEN IN BOGOTÁ..."

Based on the actual experiences of the author, "When in Bogotá..." reflects four key dimensions of living and doing business in Columbia that differ significantly from those in the United States: social time, business time, family norms, and business relationships.

Family Norms

Jim arrives already aware that it is the custom of young couples to live with their parents during the early years of marriage. Thus, he's not surprised when his friend, Rodrigo, and his wife Eva, take Jim to stay with them at Rodrigo's parents' house. In addition, Rodrigo's assigning of his cousin, Diana, as Jim's evening companion, was done without discussion or preview. Not mentioned is the additional practice in Central and South America of hiring of relatives, something that is not only common but expected.

Social Time

Jim's description of the evening stretching into the morning is vivid. Ask your Central and South American students to describe their own experiences in this realm and how this affects their ability to work the next day. In Boston, as well as in other areas of the United States in which there are large numbers of students from Central and South America, late night and after-hours clubs proliferate. When these wind down, gatherings generally continue in private homes.

Eating in Central and South America is not restricted by the three-meals-a-day mentality common in the United States. As Jim describes, meals that resemble lunch or dinner but that take place in predawn hours are not uncommon. This is the situation that Jim describes as he and his friends stop at an outdoor grill at 5:30 a.m. for arepas con queso (grilled white corn pancakes with cheese) and mazorca (boiled or steamed large kernel corn). Aguardiente is a strong alcoholic drink made from aniseed. Breakfast is likely to be coffee and a pastry, taken around what we would consider to be coffee break.

Going out to dinner with friends in Central and South America tends to start late, and it is still not unusual for groups of men to dine out, leaving their wives at home. "If you're invited to have dinner with a friend at 8:30," says Ricardo Diaz-Zuloaga, vice president of human resources at Banco Provincial in Caracas, Venezuela, "and you arrive at 9:30, you can still expect to wait for an hour or more before your friend is ready. In the meantime, you will probably have coffee or a drink and chat with your friend's wife."

On the other hand, says Diaz-Zuloaga, business meetings start on time, and it's considered bad form to be late.

Business Time

Despite the previous statement, two of those expected at Jim's meeting arrive late with traffic as the explanation. While in the United States, business people are generally expected to consider the traffic and leave earlier for an appointment if traffic demands, traffic delay is an accepted excuse in Central and South America. This may reflect the historic "que sera sera" (what will be will be) attitude of this part of the world. It is also typical for such meetings to be largely social, at least the outset, and to extend through meals and into the evening.

Business Relationships

Here Jim learns an important lesson about the prevailing norms for business relationships—get to know and trust someone first, then do business. This takes time, sometimes even weeks or months to build the necessary relationship. Many a North American has foreclosed his or her options by pushing sales and even deals to buy too soon, too fast, and too aggressively. The norms here are clear and consistent, although some Central and South American business people have begun to acknowledge and accept what has long been considered the boorish behavior of their northern neighbors.

In discussing this case, look gently to your South and Central American students for their input. Some may be eager to share information about their culture; others may feel singled out and uncomfortable.

9

WHO TO HIRE?

Group Size: Any number of groups of four to six.

Recommended Time: 90 minutes (5 minutes to set up; 10–15 minutes for individual work; 30–40 minutes for group exercise; remainder for report-out and discussion).

Provided: Instructions and character descriptions.

Also Required: No other materials required.

Facilities: One large room with moveable chairs.

Objectives

- To explore the participants' cultural biases and expectations
- To examine cultural differences
- To consider the impact culture has on hiring decisions

Background

The characters described in "Who to Hire?" appear to present a no-lose situation. They have all been successful in marketing, and all appear intelligent and mature. Despite this, students often react almost violently to certain aspects of each of the characters.

When using this exercise with a broad mix of international and domestic students, the purpose for which it has been designed, the following trends have appeared: Students from Asian countries tend to oppose Zvi on the basis of his religious commitments because religion seems to take precedence over work; students from South American and Arab countries generally oppose Tex because of his "workaholic" personality, which they describe as deviant and antisocial; students from Asian and Mediterranean countries often object to Peter due to his apparent homosexual relationship and because of his outspoken political behavior.

Students from North America, particularly female students, express concern over the potential isolation of Mrs. Park; and students from countries such as Japan, Germany, Austria, Italy, and North and South America tend to discount Kiran, speculating that her obligations to her son will impede her ability to do her job. Some say they are offended by her basing her interest in the job on being able to provide for her son. It is important to point out that Kiran has been able to teach, conduct research, write books, and consult; therefore, the objection to the son is a phony issue. Students should probe further to find just what it is they are concerned about. Indian students have often expressed concern about her status as a widow and whether, as such, she should be in a business position.

Asian students tend to select Mr. Park as their candidate with regularity. Since they see the primary obligation of the employee as being to the workplace over and above the family, they generally deny that Mrs. Park's isolation is relevant; surprisingly, many of these same students object to Tex having been divorced. For students from European countries, facility with language is a key ingredient, yet students from North America rarely have considered this to be important.

Remember, these are just trends that we have observed; they are by no means universal. Still, the trends do appear to be consistent with a number of cultural norms. For Japanese students, for example, Peter's outspoken behavior is highly individualistic and therefore not congruent with their collectivist system in which "the nail that stands up gets hammered down."

South American and Arab societies are fairly high context;[1] that is, they depend on social relationships and hierarchies. Therefore, it is not surprising that people from these cultures would reject an individual with whom such a relationship would be difficult or impossible. Tex and Kiran are both experienced as too intense to enter into personal social relationships.

In countries such as Japan, Germany, Italy, and Austria, a woman's role is to take care of family and home.[2] In a number of Scandinavian countries, however, women are a more integral part of the workforce; students from countries such as Sweden, Denmark, and Norway are more likely to see Kiran as a viable candidate.

The Exercise

Students are often unaware of the role their own cultural backgrounds play in their decisions. In addition, they tend to underestimate or be unaware of the differences in cultural norms that exist from country to country. Before using "Who to Hire?," students should become familiar with at least some of the prevailing trends. "The Culture Quiz," found elsewhere in this section, is a good place to start the discussion; the resources cited in the quiz answers are all readily available for more in-depth reading. A partial list of additional resources is given below.

Students should be instructed to consider the ranking of the candidates based on their own cultural perceptions, those of the host country in which the manager will live, and those of the marketplace.

To save time, Step 1 may be done outside of class.

Suggested Outline and Timing

1. Set-up (5 minutes)

Go over the exercise and the learning objectives.

1. E.T. Hall, *Beyond Culture* (Garden City, N.Y.: Anchor Press, 1976.)

2. G. Hofstede, "Motivation, Leadership, and Organizations: Do American Theories Apply Aborad?" *Organizational Dynamics* (Summer 1980), 42–63.

2. *Individual rankings (10-15 minutes)*

Ask students to work individually to:

- read the background information and descriptions of each of the applicants.
- consider the job and the cultures within which the individual to be hired will be operating.
- rank the candidates from 1 to 5, with 1 being their first choice, and enter their rankings on the ranking sheet in the column marked "My Ranking."
- not discuss their rankings with classmates until told to do so.

Arrange students in groups. Groups for this exercise may be culturally mixed or culturally separated. Each possibility yields unique results. In using culturally separated groups, one method is to ask students to self-sort by what they consider to be their primary cultural identity—for example, Asian, Scandinavian, Middle Eastern, European, North American, and so forth. While this is not a finely tuned method, it is unlikely that a class of students will allow sorting by specific countries. By no means will this type of sorting result in uniformity of opinion, as significant differences will emerge from country to country within regions.

3. *Exercise (small groups: 30–40 minutes)*

4. *Report-out and discussion (full class: open-ended)*

Use the "Questions for Discussion" as a guide.

Suggested Readings

Adler, N. J. Pacific Basin managers: A Gajin, not a woman. *Human Resource Management* 26 (2) (Summer 1987), 169–192.

Adler, N. J. and Graham, J. L. Cross-cultural interaction: The international comparison fallacy. *Journal of International Business Studies* 20 (3) (Fall 1989), 515–537.

Barnlund, D. C. Public and private self in communicating with Japan. *Business Horizons* (March–April 1989), 32–40.

Dulek, R. E., Fielden, J. S., and Hill, J. S. International communication: An executive primer. *Business Horizons* (January–February 1991), 20–25.

Hofstede, G., and Bond, M. H. Confucius and economic growth: New trends in culture's consequences. *Organizational Dynamics* 16 (4) (1988), 4–21.

Ondrack, D. A. International transfers of managers in North American and European MNE's. *Journal of International Business Studies* (Fall 1985), 1–19.

Rugman, A. M., ed. *Research in global strategic management: International business research for the twenty-first century: Canada's new research agenda.* Greenwich, Conn.: JAI Press, 1990.

Tung, R. L. *The new expatriates: Managing human resources abroad.* Cambridge, Mass.: Ballinger, 1988.

10

FREDERICK INTERNATIONAL*

The main purpose of this case is to illustrate how a company's actions can become remarkably complicated when they are simultaneously trying to become successful in different countries; cultural values, the legal profession, governmental ideology, workers' rights, management practices, and competing technologies are all intertwined here, and it is difficult to separate which ones are most responsible for the respective successes and failures of Frederick International.

One way to make sense of this complex scenario is to break the case into some basic questions: What forces are contributing to success and what forces are contributing to failure in each of the three countries? Both questions are important, even though the French example seems entirely positive and the Japanese scenario is apparently quite negative.

For example, what forces are keeping Frederick from being more successful than it already is in France? We have no way of knowing if Laperrière has too many installations to handle or not. If that's not the case, consider the French inspector who has referred dozens of potential customers to Vachon and Laperrière; how many other inspectors know about Proxagard and might be inclined to recommend the product?

In the Japanese example, what positives exist? The Department of Trade is satisfied that the Proxagard is a unique product that could be useful to Japanese companies. Perhaps there are customers who would be glad to buy the product if they knew it was available. Japan is also heavily reliant on robotics, which are good applications for the product. Mitsui apparently sees a potential market for the product—otherwise it would not likely be inclined to send an engineer to the United States for training.

Some of the stumbling blocks with Mitsui are obvious: Japan is a less litigious society than America and, therefore, the impetus to invest in worker safety appears not as great as in the United States. Unions, which play major roles in protecting workers and enforcing safety standards, are also much more powerful in both the United States and in Europe than in Japan. In addition, Japan is at the other extreme from France in terms of federal safety inspection, while the United States falls between the two.

Students might speculate about the introduction of the Proxagard as a change issue in all three cases: Using a Force Field Analysis, what are the driving forces that are leading to widespread acceptance and purchase of the Proxagard in these three countries? What are the restraining forces that are inhibiting acceptance of the product in these three countries and cultures? Three Force Fields, one for each country, can be compared as a method for graphically illustrating why France is most successful and Japan is least successful in terms of sales. It may also become clear that many of the operant forces are firmly embedded in a country's culture or government.

Frederick executives may want to explore possible ventures in other countries—particularly in Europe—to determine if the laws and culture make them into viable options that might be worth pursuing with new sales representatives as an alternative to Japan.

* These notes were written by Scott Weighart. Used with permission.

11

TUCKERMAN-SAWYER ADVERTISING

This case requires students to identify such issues of diversity as tokenism, stereotyping, and the glass ceiling, all of which are common experiences for minorities in the workplace.

Suggestions for Bill Tuckerman should include, first and foremost, a thorough examination of the agency's attitudes towards minority employees and their expected role within the agency. The agency's pigeonholing and stereotyping of Andres, i.e., assuming that he can only work successfully with Latino clients and that he would be "better able to relate to his own people," very likely hinders Andres' professional growth and prevents the agency from realizing his full potential. Furthermore, it is probably discriminatory. The current expectation that Latinos hired at Tuckerman-Sawyer will work exclusively with Latino clients must be changed, both for the good of the agency and in order to retain minority employees.

Students should think of the extended implications of the present policy. Consistency would suggest that Tuckerman-Sawyer assign only Catholic clients to Catholic employees, blue-eyed clients to blue-eyed employees, and even only left-handed clients to left-handed employees. When seen this way, students might be better able to understand the problems inherent in Bill's thinking. On the other hand, serious arguments can be made that an employee is best used when assigned to do what she or he does and knows best. For example, would there be a problem with the agency assigning an employee who grew up on a farm to the farm-product clients?

Bill also needs to realize that having separate standards for evaluating the performance of minority employees may not only be unfair to all employees, but may significantly hinder minority employees' opportunities for professional growth and advancement. If Andres is being evaluated based on lower standards than those used to evaluate his colleagues, then he may not be being encouraged to work up to his full potential. This is not only a source of frustration and demotivation for Andres in his position at Tuckerman-Sawyer, but it may significantly hinder his chances of employment elsewhere. It is another aspect of the culture at Tuckerman-Sawyer that needs to be carefully examined and probably changed.

One key to the issue of whether or not discrimination is operant in this case is that while Andres says he has time and ability to take on more clients, his supervisor denies him the opportunity since the agency's other clients are apparently not Latino.

Despite what Andres and possibly the law consider discriminatory, this case opens possibilities for examining the rationale for affirmative action programs, minority hiring, and issues of reverse discrimination. There is considerable gray area between what constitutes legal and moral discrimination and what makes good business sense.

Bill Tuckerman is depicted as basically a decent person; there is no evidence to suggest that he is intentionally discriminating against Andres. Rather, the problems in the case seem

* These case notes were prepared by Gail E. Gilmore.

to stem mainly from ignorance and lack of sensitivity. Bill needs to realize that Andres, as a minority employee at Tuckerman-Sawyer, apparently feels he is not being treated equitably.

A companywide workshop on cultural differences aimed at helping eliminate the separatist attitude that appears to prevail may be useful. Hiring more minority employees and establishing mentoring programs would also be useful steps.

In discussing this case, ask students to share personal experiences of discrimination, how they felt, and what they did. Sharing this kind of information often helps students sensitize one another to issues of real and perceived discrimination.

12

JUST-IN-TIME FOR TEMPORARY EMPLOYEES*

Case Overview

The Just-in-Time (JIT) distribution center of Medical Supplies Corporation (MSC) was located in a large urban area near the hospitals it serviced. It was experiencing rapid growth, having doubled its annual revenues from $15 million to $30 million in the last twelve months. The number of employees also doubled from thirty to sixty in this same time period. The just-in-time distribution of medical supplies to the hospital was a 24-hour-per-day operation with three shifts of employees. The JIT distribution center's employees monitored inventories and replenished supply bins in each unit of the hospitals on a 12-hour cycle. Forty percent of the workforce were temporary employees, and sixty percent were permanent.

Sam Kellogg, general manager of the JIT distribution center of MSC, had just been informed by the corporate director of human resources that one of the temporary employees, a warehouse team member, had complained to the vice president of diversity management at corporate headquarters about discriminatory pay practices. Sam asked Jessica, the newly hired material services manager, to investigate this incident and report her recommendations.

Objectives

- To examine the management of employee diversity in the context of human resources management and the operation of a service business
- To gain an understanding of how to manage a temporary workforce that coexists with permanent employees in a service business
- To gain an understanding of how human resources policies impact perceptions of equity (i.e., procedural justice, distributive justice) and communication processes

Key Issues

- Valuing diversity
- Temporary employees
- Communications
- Perceptions of equity

* These case notes were prepared by David B. Balkin, Minnette A. Bumpus, and Wilfred J. Lucas. Used with permission.

Questions for Discussion

Here are some questions to consider when recommending a plan of action.

1. Why did Sam Kellogg think at first that the problem in the JIT distribution center involved pay discrimination? If in fact there is no pay discrimination, then is it appropriate to consider doing nothing after the investigation?
2. What was the true problem at Medical Supply Corporation's JIT distribution center?
3. How important are temporary employees to the JIT distribution center?
4. What should Jessica Jordan recommend to Sam Kellogg based on the investigation?
5. Explain why the temporary employee reported the pay discrepancy to the corporate officer rather than to the managers at the JIT distribution center.
6. In responding to Question 5, did you assume that the vice president of diversity management was African-American? Why or why not? Would your response to Question 5 have been altered if you had made a different assumption?
7. Does Speedy Personnel Services' wage policy of negotiating an individual wage rate have any implications for diversity management? Is there a potential for disparate impact? What actions should the JIT distribution center take to ensure a diverse supply of labor from Speedy Personnel Services?

Teaching Approach

This case can be used to stimulate discussion on how a manager might handle a diversity issue in a situation where the real problem is not what it initially appears to be; to explore the impact of human resources policies on perceptions of equity and communication processes, and to examine the management of a workforce that is a mixture of permanent and temporary employees. The instructor may elect to use some or all of the discussion questions depending on whether the focus is on valuing diversity (Questions 1, 5, 6, and 7), managing temporary employees (Questions 2, 3, and 4), perceptions of equity (Questions 4, 5, 6, and 7), and/or communications (Questions 2, 4, and 5).

The issues, problems, and solutions to this case can be discussed in small groups that present their findings to the larger group and then integrated with relevant course material by the instructor.

Discussion

1. Why did Sam Kellogg think that the problem in the JIT distribution center involved pay discrimination? If there is no pay discrimination, then is it appropriate to consider doing nothing after the investigation?

   A temporary employee, a member of a minority group, went over the heads of immediate supervisors and made a complaint to a corporate executive about pay discrimination. The corporate human resources director informed the local manager that he should investigate the matter to see if the complaint had merit. The problem was initially framed as one of pay discrimination. This problem could be classified as a crisis problem because, if not addressed immediately, it could lead to litigation.

To do nothing would be a low-quality decision.

If the investigation uncovers other issues, management should recommend making proactive changes to respond to the findings. If there are no other problems, and pay discrimination is not found, then Sam might choose to turn what he thought was a crisis problem into an opportunity problem. By addressing the issue, Sam would demonstrate that management is willing to respond to the concerns of its employees.

Management should at least inform all employees that a complaint of pay discrimination proved to be false. Pay policy information should then be shared with the employees. For example, management could inform all employees what the starting pay rate is for temps at both agencies and the policy of recognizing pay differentials for temps working late shifts or for operating forklift equipment.

2. What was the true problem at Medical Supply Corporation's JIT distribution center?

While the symptom of the problem was the complaint of pay discrimination, the true problem was much more complicated. It involved the challenge of managing an entrepreneurial business unit that was rapidly growing and had to operate within a corporate bureaucracy that was not always nurturing to entrepreneurship.

The JIT distribution center was on a fairly low point of the learning curve and did not have many established ways of doing things. Some things would fall through the cracks. Since management placed a very high priority on satisfying the needs of its customers, the hospitals, which required providing a complex service on a 24-hour-per-day basis, personal needs of temporary employees were not closely considered. Some administrative details were overlooked. In particular, the pay policies of the two different temporary agencies were not examined by management resulting in temporary employees doing the same work not receiving the same pay.

Some of the specific causes of the problem are as follows:

- Managers did not give a high priority to developing human resources policies for temporary employees. Temps had only a vague idea of the organization's culture and values.
- The center was highly dependent on temps to work with permanent employees in teams to provide services to the hospitals.
- The center was in a rapid growth mode and needed the flexibility in its workforce that temps could provide.
- While the center had considerable diversity in its workforce, the diversity was only within the hourly wage jobs. All management jobs were held by white employees. Some minority employees may have perceived barriers to communication. This may explain why none were consulted about the alleged instance of pay discrimination.
- There appears to be only one-way, top-down communication. Management does not seem to have an effective communication channel that provides useful feedback from temporary employees.

3. How important are temporary employees to the JIT distribution center?

Temporary employees are a key component of the unit's human resources management strategy. Without temps the unit could not provide the services that are required by the hospitals on a 24-hour-per-day basis. As long as the rapid growth rate continues, the temps provide the needed workforce flexibility.

Rapid growth makes human resources planning difficult. Quantitative forecasting techniques are of little use to the JIT distribution center, which lacks much of the historical data needed to predict future trends. Qualitative forecasting techniques might possibly be more useful for predicting human resources needs. Temps can help satisfy the customer's demands for services until permanent jobs are approved and filled.

4. What should Jessica Jordan recommend to Sam Kellogg based on the investigation?

The investigation showed that a discrepancy in pay was a larger symptom. While Jessica concluded that there was no evidence of pay discrimination from a legal standpoint, there was a perception among some of the temps that the pay policies were unfair.

For motivational purposes, perceptions of inequity need to be addressed. The African-American temporary employee concluded that he was being treated inequitably based on the comparison that he made of the ratio of his performance (inputs) and pay (outputs) to that of a white temporary employee. That is, he perceived that the white temporary employee was receiving more pay for performance that was identical to his own. The African-American temp made the phone call to the vice president in an attempt to increase his inputs and thus eliminate the pay discrepancy. Other actions that could be taken in an attempt to eliminate inequity include changing inputs (lower quality, lower quantity); distorting perception of self; distorting perceptions of the comparison other; choose a different comparison other, or leaving the job.

There are at least two recommendations that Jessica could make to Sam relative to perceptions of procedural and distributive justice. She could recommend that he hold a meeting to inform all employees that the investigation revealed inconsistencies between how the temporary agencies paid their employees—but not pay discrimination; hence, no changes would be made to the pay policies of either temporary agency. Alternatively, she could recommend that he inform employees that even though no pay discrimination was found, the investigation did reveal inconsistencies between how the agencies paid their employees, and therefore actions would be taken to correct the inconsistencies. Jessica could also suggest that Sam hire a person to coordinate the communication between the JIT distribution center and the temporary agencies, open effective all-way communication channels, and/or take steps to develop a clearer and more easily understood organizational culture.

If Sam and the other managers want the temps to be committed to the organization, at least some of the following quality solutions should be implemented:

- Standardize wage rates paid to temps by talking to the two temporary agencies and coming to some kind of agreement. Then inform temps of the pay policy.
- Evaluate whether two temp agencies are necessary. If not, move to one supplier—and therefore one wage rate—so that eventually all temps are paid on a consistent basis.

- Develop an in-house pool of temps instead of using temporary agencies.

The investigation revealed a broader set of issues that suggest some of the following recommendations:

- Develop an orientation program for new temps so that their role expectations are clear from the outset. Also, provide explanations about the mission and values of MSC's JIT distribution center so that the temps can identify with the goals of the organization.

- Hold meetings on a frequent basis so that information is exchanged and misinformation can be corrected before any problems arise.

5. Explain the temporary employee's possible reason for reporting the pay discrepancy to the corporate officer rather than the managers at the JIT distribution center.

The African-American temp may have felt uncomfortable complaining to a white manager due to cultural differences as well as because of perceived barriers to encouraging feedback from the temps. The temp might have learned that the vice president for diversity management welcomed feedback.

The perception that temps and permanent employees had a 90-day probationary employment period may have discouraged temps from behavior that could be interpreted by managers as grounds for ending their assignment. Further, the temp might have felt that the managers were part of the problem and not able to objectively evaluate it. Therefore it is not surprising that the temp complained to a corporate executive who was designated as the advocate for minority employees.

6. In responding to Question 5, did you assume that the vice president of diversity management was an African-American? Why or why not? Would your response to Question 5 have been altered if you had made a different assumption?

The instructor may want to use Question 6 to examine perceptions of the role of the vice president of diversity management. Must this individual be a member of a minority group to be effective in this position? Why or why not?

There should be a range of responses to this question. Some individuals will focus on the position and say that the temporary employee would have reported the pay discrepancy regardless of the VP's race because the job requires sensitivity to diversity issues (legitimate power, position power). Other individuals will focus on the person, not the position, and say that the temporary employee only reported the pay discrepancy because the VP was an African-American (referent power) and suggest that since they were both African-Americans, there would be fewer barriers to communication and greater opportunity for empathy.

7. Does Speedy Personnel Services' wage policy of negotiating an individual wage rate have any implications for diversity management? Is there a potential for disparate impact? If there is a potential for disparate impact, then what actions should the JIT distribution center take to ensure a diverse supply of labor from Speedy Personnel Services?

Speedy Personnel Services' policy of negotiating an individual wage rate may have implications for diversity management. There could be potential for disparate impact if African-American males with similar levels of experience and skills receive lower wages than white males due to the practice of requiring individual wage negotiation. This would be the case if an investigation revealed that, for example, African-American males received lower wages than white males due to stereotypes that put African-American males at a disadvantage. Thus, African American males may receive lower wages due to a factor that is not job related (job-related factors could be seniority or merit). To be more specific, when a white male negotiates for a favorable salary, the negotiation behaviors might be interpreted by the managers at Speedy Personnel Services as being assertive (positive and nonthreatening). When an African-American male negotiates a favorable salary, the same negotiation behaviors may be interpreted as aggressive and threatening to the managers. This may result in negative pay outcomes for the African-American males. One remedy could be to have a standardized wage policy for all temps.

There is also potential for disparate impact if the interviewer's ethnocentric views of appropriate negotiating styles interfere with his or her ability to objectively assess the interviewee's (temporary employee) negotiating skills. Ethnocentrism is the belief that one's own values, norms, and customs are superior. The communication style of the American corporate culture is based on the traditional white male workforce. This style is characterized by low-context communication. It is to the point; the words alone carry much of the meaning. Any deviations from this style may be discounted by interviewers who subscribe to and apply this communication standard to their negotiating process. In contrast, high-context communication involves relationships, and the context of the event carries much of the meaning. Many minority group members use the high-context communication style.

There is also potential for disparate impact if women and minorities are unfamiliar with the negotiating process. This would put them at a disadvantage compared to those who may have greater familiarity with negotiating tactics by, for example, virtue of longer participation in the workforce.

Prior to engaging in a contract with any temporary agency, the JIT distribution center should familiarize itself with and evaluate the agency's recruiting, interviewing, hiring and compensation policies. The JIT distribution center should also clearly define and communicate its expectations of the temporary agency on the issues of ethics and fairness.

Epilogue

Several steps were taken in the months following the investigation to address the true problem at the JIT distribution center. During the first month after the investigation, the following activities occurred: (a) Management at the JIT distribution center adopted a new pay policy for temps employed by both of the temporary agencies. This new pay policy involved paying all temps, regardless of talent or experience, $7.25/hour, plus a $.25/hour shift differential where applicable. All temps were immediately brought up to the new rate. (b) The area human resources manager visited the JIT distribution center for two days to conduct an employee feedback survey; and all employees were required to attend group discussions concerning job-related issues. (c) Management met after the human resources manager's departure to review the anonymous comments gathered in the employee feedback survey and to formulate an operating plan to address the concerns raised.

Comments were categorized as follows: racial, communication, teamwork, management, temporaries, environment, and schedules. The most critical comments were addressed post haste; for example, one temp claimed that a JIT distribution center's employee made a racial comment to him. After a thorough investigation, the JIT distribution center's employee was terminated. All items that could be corrected immediately were corrected; for example, more fans were purchased for the distribution center.

During the second month after the investigation, the following activities took place: (a) Weekly communication meetings were implemented. Based on a prioritized list developed by the employees (communication, racial, teamwork, management, temporaries, environment, and schedules), one topic per week was incorporated into the communication meetings. A topic at one of these early meetings was the corporate diversity movement and policies toward harassment. (b) Back pay was processed for the employees who were paid less than $7.25/hour as temps anytime during the seven months prior to the investigation. (c) In response to the employee complaints regarding the extended period of time that employees worked as temps before being hired as permanent employees, the management at the JIT distribution center began the process to requisition eighteen full-time employees to cover the temps who had been working at the JIT distribution center for six months or more.

During the third month after the investigation, the following activities took place: (a) Interviews were conducted and selections were made to hire eighteen new employees from the ranks of the temps. (b) A mandatory diversity training session for all permanent employees was conducted by the vice president of diversity management. The diversity discussion in this session led to the issue of how to improve the environment at the JIT distribution center. The two main areas that surfaced were training and communication. The group agreed that expectations needed to be defined. The vice president of diversity management agreed to return in three months for a follow-up session.

During the fourth month after the investigation, eighteen new employees were hired. In response to the need for more leadership and supervision, new team-leader positions were created for the night shift.

During the fifth month after the investigation, the day team leader position was divided into two positions in response to a need for more leadership and supervision.

During the sixth month after the investigation, the vice president of diversity management returned to conduct an employee follow-up session. During this session, the following corporate expectations were defined: communication, consistency, feedback, friendship, teamwork, pride, leadership, ownership, safeguard procedures, and results.

During the seventh month after the investigation, the employees were asked to sign a document confirming that the expectations and definitions had been communicated to them.

During the eighth month after the investigation, all the employees received a phone card that listed the phone numbers of the JIT distribution center's management and the ten expectations. These expectations were also painted on the wall of the distribution center and included in communication meetings.

The investigation and the follow-up activities enabled Jessica to further develop her management style. She learned several key lessons from this experience. She suggests that: (1) when establishing relationships with temporary agencies, make sure that consistency exists between and within the temporary agencies; (2) perceptions are indeed reality for some employees; (3) communication must be a two-way process between management and employees; (4) employee surveys are a useful means of facilitating communication; (5) ask for input in order to treat others as they want to be treated rather than automatically assuming that you should do unto others as you would have them do unto you; (6) to obtain 100 percent satisfaction from your customers, you must first have 100 percent satisfaction from your employees; and (7) evaluate your employees based on expectations that have been shared with them.

Suggested Additional Readings

Edwards, A. (1991) "Cultural Diversity: The enlightened manager, how to treat your employees fairly." *Working Woman*. January, pp. 45–51.

Kennedy, J., and Everest, A. (1991) "Put Diversity in Context." *Personnel Journal*. September, pp. 50–54.

Solomon, J. (1990) "As Cultural Diversity of Workers Grows, Experts Urge Appreciation for Differences." *The Wall Street Journal*. September 12, pp. B1, B15.

Songer, N. (1991) "Work Force Diversity." *B & E Review*. April–June, pp. 3-6.

13

THE LOCH NESS COTTON COMPANY
SEXUAL HARASSMENT? YOU BE THE JUDGE!

Although "The Loch Ness Cotton Company" is presented as a case, it may also be used as a small group exercise.

Group Size: Any number of groups of four to six.

Recommended Time: 60 minutes recommended minimum: 5 minutes for set up; 10 minutes for student preparation; 30+ minutes for small group discussion; open-ended report out and large group discussion).

Provided: Instructions, EEOC guidelines.

Also Required: No other materials required.

Facilities: Moveable chairs. Enough room for approximately five feet between groups.

Objectives

- To examine what does and does not constitute sexual harassment in the workplace
- To explore the process necessary for establishing the existence of sexual harassment
- To consider the impact of sexual harassment on productivity and morale

Background

A problem at one time pushed aside by many business leaders as not particularly significant, sexual harassment was rocketed into the public consciousness in 1992 when Law Professor Anita Hill challenged Clarence Thomas, in his bid to become a Justice of the United States Supreme Court, on the basis that he had used his position of power in their professional relationship to sexually harass her. On September 1, 1994, a jury in California awarded a former legal secretary $7.1 million for sexual harassment by a partner of the world's largest law firm, Baker & McKenzie. More recently, accusations of sexual harassment have ended the careers of military officers, teachers, and corporate officials such as the CEO of ASTRA-USA.

Sexual harassment is less about sex than it is about the use of power to make inappropriate demands of those in less powerful positions. Until laws were passed to regulate this kind of behavior, and some courageous victims took their cases to court and to the public, victims of this form of abuse had little recourse. Generally, it was give in or lose one's job and/or one's reputation. For most, if not all, job and reputation loss were unacceptable.

Today, while sexual harassment still takes place, victims have some ability to take action. Virtually every business and organization of any size has a clearly stated policy with regard to sexual harassment in the workplace, usually available through a human resources or personnel office, and a large proportion of training dollars and time are being devoted to educating employees about sexual harassment and its effects. Written policies and substantive responses to complaints are now recognized as not just needed to comply with the law, but also as good business. Sexual harassment can result in costly lawsuits, but it also interferes with employee morale and motivation and can severely and negatively impact productivity. When sexual harassment charges are brought, it is generally a matter for human resources departments.

Sexual harassment comes in two forms: *quid pro quo* ("I'll give you a raise, if you sleep with me," etc.) and *hostile environment.* The Loch Ness Cotton Company problem between supervisor Alex Lehmann and employee Dana Tibbetts may reflect some of both; i.e., employee whistles and comments and a lack of supervisor intervention create a hostile environment; direct comments from the supervisor, coupled with a seemingly subjective performance appraisal, may suggest quid pro quo harassment is taking place, but this is less clear. In fact, whether or not sexual harassment is actually going on in the Loch Ness Cotton Company case is inconclusive, and most of our experts felt that additional investigation would be necessary.

What Our Experts Said

We asked four experts to comment on the events at the Loch Ness Cotton Company: Detlev Suderow, human resources manager, Corporate Systems Engineering at Digital Equipment Corporation; Teresa M. Contardo, first vice president—Investments at Paine Webber; Darlene Nicgorski, education and training specialist for Ames Safety Envelope Company; and Robert L. Sanders, area director for the Equal Employment Opportunity Commission in New England. Here's what each had to say:

Detlev Suderow, human resources manager, Corporate Systems Engineering at Digital Equipment Corporation says that "the primary impact of Title VII has been to reduce the most blatant forms of sexual harassment or, at worst, drive them underground. However, the incidence of sexual harassment complaints that result from sharply differing interpretations of events has increased and can represent one of the thorniest employee relations problems, or worse, a liability issue, for the corporation.

"The Loch Ness Cotton Company case," he notes, "describes the more common and more difficult expression of sexual harassment that entails differences of perception, interpretations of behavior, assumed motives, and the sharp emotions that can come from events which are viewed in radically different ways."

Because of concerns about confidentiality, Suderow takes issue with the delegation of an employee committee to investigate Dana Tibbetts's charges. "Even companies that practice intense worker involvement and consensus decision-making processes," he says, "would run great risks of not protecting the rights of the parties by assigning a committee." Instead, Suderow places the responsibility for investigating the charges squarely on the shoulders of the human resources investigator who must "determine adherence to all formal company policies and procedures, both written or customary by practice and culture...." The role of the investigator, he notes, "is to minimize assumptions, determine the facts, and not rush to conclusions that will prejudice the outcome."

In addition to wanting to know what Dana Tibbetts did and did not say to Alex Lehmann about the porno pictures, the performance reviews, and concern over the behavior of Alex and the other employees, Suderow wonders what the existing policies and processes are for dealing with the issues presented. "The absence of written and formal policies," he says, "increases the risks for any corporation since the burden of proof rests with the company and not the employee."

However, Suderow continues, "... it is the obligation of employees to address their grievance by utilizing the available processes. It is a common assumption in the organizational behavior field that in the absence of clearly stated program and process boundaries, the full range of human behavioral dynamics will create interpersonal problems whose solution would elude Solomon. The most effective problem prevention process in sexual harassment cases is training both employees and managers in the rules and implications of Title VII."

"In many cases," he concludes, "the best resolution to various complaints is to clarify intentions by all parties, offer the accused the opportunity to apologize for having given the wrong impression of their actions, and allow both parties to walk away from the incident feeling that a fair solution has been reached. Only the most onerous cases require formal sanctions, punishment, or even termination."

Teresa M. Contardo, who successfully sued her former employer, Merrill Lynch, in the U.S. District Court in Boston in 1989 [Civil Action No. 86-1081-S, ruling dated 12/14/90] for sex discrimination, which included sexual harassment, says she feels that the "facts as stated are inconclusive" but that "Alex's actions are suspect. If they don't stop, the company should expect legal difficulties." She writes that "if there is no written company policy forbidding sexual harassment, one should be developed and implemented. It must be clear how the procedure works; e.g., for reporting specific violations, for maintaining records of complaints and responses, and for supporting statements. The company must commit and follow through." She adds, "If an employee has a complaint, it must be addressed."

While Contardo finds Tibbett's statements to be vague and suggests that more specifics are needed, she maintains that "whistling and crude comments must be stopped as they create an 'intimidating and offensive work environment' if allowed to persist by the supervisor." Contardo wonders whether the supervisor had made an attempt to find the source of the porno pictures. "If not," she says, "the message is clear that offensive sexual conduct is okay."

She also points out that in many ways Alex Lehmann has been remiss. "Recent tardiness and substandard work performance should have been addressed," and she asks, why Lehmann didn't "discuss the problems with Dana Tibbetts before writing them up." Contardo also questions what the specifics were of Lehmann's "effort to help Dana improve," and she points out that Lehmann's frequent comments on Dana's clothing, as well as discussing Dana's social life with employees, are both inappropriate and constitute sexual harassment. She notes, "If Dana wears inappropriate clothing, a statement with regard to acceptable dress needs to be posted for all."

Our third expert, Darlene Nicgorski, education and training specialist at Ames Safety Envelope Company of Somerville, Massachusetts, agrees that more information is needed before making an absolute determination of whether or not there was sexual harassment. Before launching a further investigation, however, Nicgorski says she "would arrange for training for the committee on how to investigate sexual harassment complaints." Next, she says, "the committee should discuss what they already know, what questions they have, and who will ask them." Among the issues she feels should explored with Alex are whether Dana expressed feelings of being upset and nervous over comments made about his/her appearance; whether Alex has received any training about sexual harassment; what Alex says when others talk about Dana's social life; whether Alex knew about the porno pictures in Dana's drawer; and what Alex has to say about Dana's response to the last quarterly performance appraisal.

Nicgorski also had a number of questions for Dana. "When, how many times, and in front of whom" she queries, "had Dana expressed discomfort, dislike, nervousness, and/or anger with Alex's comments and apparent condoning of the actions of others in the office?" Further, she asks, "Specifically what behaviors does Dana want to have stop in the work situation?"

Once the committee has completed its investigation, Nicgorski believes a list of resolutions can be drawn up. "One that I am sure will appear on the list of resolutions," she says, "is to provide training on sexual harassment prevention to all workers." At least one element of the training, she notes, should include some sensitization to cultural differences in gender attitudes."

"Without the information from an investigation," she concludes, "it is difficult to make a decision and recommendations. However, it does appear on the surface that Alex sexually harassed Dana, and Alex should have realized this. In addition, the whistling and comments created a hostile and intimidating work environment."

Robert L. Sanders, area director of the EEOC in New England, begins by giving us eight points to consider and use as guidelines:

- Employers should investigate complaints of sexual harassment no matter how trivial the circumstances appear.
- Employers must take timely and appropriate action.
- Employers should keep written records of their investigations.
- Employers should acknowledge the complaint in writing and have the Charging Party informed of the progress of the investigation and its outcome.
- The most credible witnesses are those who have no vested interest, are unbiased, have no motive, are consistent, and have direct knowledge.
- Title VII does not mandate that an employee determined to have engaged in sexual harassment be discharged.
- The EEOC and the courts look at the totality of the circumstances.
- Employers should determine if others were affected.

"Although the Loch Ness Company acted promptly," says Sanders, "much more needs to be done before the committee can fulfill its mandate. The investigation is incomplete. All you have on record is 's/he said,' 's/he denies,' supported by two unreliable witnesses." Here's what Sanders says is needed:

1. A detailed statement/affidavit from Tibbetts describing the behavior alleged to be sexual harassment; what occurred; who was involved; when it occurred; where it occurred; how often; whether it was verbal or nonverbal; the genders of those alleged to have been involved; identities of others working in the area where the alleged acts occurred or the names of employees who may have observed the alleged incidents, whether or not they will be witnesses.
2. Interviews with all employees in the front office and the stockroom regarding the interaction/relationship between the Charging Party and the alleged harasser and about the alleged harassment. Also, there must be an attempt to determine whether the alleged harasser's remarks were hostile and derogatory.
3. Performance evaluations of the Charging Party and others supervised by Lehmann for the two years preceding the filing of the charge. Investigators should compare the Charging Party's most recent evaluation to prior evaluations and those of others supervised by Lehmann.

"In hostile environment cases," Sanders concludes, "the Commission has adopted the 'reasonable person' standard for determining whether the harassment is sufficiently severe or pervasive to violate Title VII. If the alleged conduct would not substantially affect the work environment of a reasonable person, no violation will be found. A pattern of offensive conduct is generally necessary for a violation to be found."

Suggested Outline and Timing

1. Set-up (full class: 5 minutes)

In setting up this exercise, briefly review Title VII and the questions which appear at the beginning of the case.

Ask for and answer any questions on how to proceed.

2. Student preparation (full class: 10 minutes)

Have students, working individually, read the case and answer the questions that appear at the beginning of the case.

Divide students into their groups. It is interesting to use a combination of some all-male groups, some all-female, and some mixed. (Note that no genders have been given for either Dana or Alex.) Ask students to pick a spokesperson for their group for the report out.

3. Group discussion (small groups: 30 minutes)

4. *Report-out and discussion (full class: 20 minute minimum recommended)*

During this time, debrief the case in the larger group. Ask a spokesperson for each of the groups to first describe its findings. Next, ask each spokesperson to describe one or more of the elements of the group's plan.

The discussion might include or focus on such issues as:

- The difficulties in handling issues around sexual harassment.
- The need for clear and specific guidelines.
- The reliability of the witnesses.
- Personal experiences and reactions to sexual harassment.

Conclude the discussion by stressing the business benefits of having clear and unambiguous guidelines for investigating and determining the existence of sexual harassment, the importance of training around this issue, and the impact of sexual harassment on productivity and morale.

5. *Optional (full class: open-ended)*

Working in their small groups, ask students to develop a policy on sexual harassment for their workplace or college setting.

Ask each group to report their policy to the larger class, and discuss the strengths and weaknesses of each policy.

14

NATURE OR NURTURE?*

This case requires students to think about how organizations write and interpret their benefits policies, about what constitutes discrimination, and about the benefits that an organization can realize when its employees are able to successfully balance work and family needs.

Legal Concerns

Students will first need to decide whether Diana is being discriminated against. Some students may argue that the benefits policies are being applied as written and that, therefore, there is no discrimination. Other students may argue that Diana should have the same access to benefits such as maternity leave and flexible work scheduling as other employees, and that since her sexual orientation appears to be the only reason that she is not eligible for these benefits, there is discrimination.

Whatever stance students take, they should be able to logically support their positions with facts from the case, rather than with their personal opinions.

Balancing Work-Family Commitments

Regardless of the position students might take on the discrimination issue, it will be useful to discuss what an organization has to gain by enabling employees to balance their work and family commitments. Some areas for discussion might include employee satisfaction and loyalty, employee productivity level, turnover rate, and absenteeism.

From this discussion, students should begin to recognize the benefits of an organization's attempts, whenever possible, to meet their employees' needs to balance work and family commitments, particularly those of longtime employees in whom the organization has a significant stake.

Benefits Policies

Finally, the case asks students to consider what the bank, or any organization, might do to ensure that its benefits policies meet the needs of an increasingly diverse workforce. Students often think of diversity solely in terms of race and gender. It is therefore useful to discuss the increasingly broad way in which diversity is defined. The term diverse workforce includes employees of different genders, races, cultures, sexual orientations, marital status, caretaker status, religions, etc.

* These case notes were written by Gail E. Gilmore.

Once students realize the scope of diverse needs with which organizations must deal, it should be clear that forward-looking organizations will likely need to rethink many of their benefits policies. The recommendations students make should focus on assessment of needs as well as on the implementation of new policies.

15

WHAT YOU SEE ISN'T NECESSARILY WHAT YOU GET

Group Size: Any number individuals or small groups.

Recommended Time: 30–40 minutes (at least one hour if done in small groups).

Provided: Instructions and answer grid.

Also Required: No additional materials required.

Facilities: One large room.

Objectives

- To examine the relationship of perception to attribution
- To explore the impact of selective perception
- To examine the link between perception and behavior

Background

When completed individually, this exercise provides a quick way to stimulate thinking and discussion around perception, attribution, the meaning of first impressions—theirs of others and others of them—and stereotyping. When completed in small groups, the exercise helps students understand the bases for differing perceptions of the same phenomena.

Suggested Outline and Timing

1. Set-up (full class: 5 minutes)

Go over the instructions and learning objectives. Tell students they will have 10 minutes to decide and record their answers to the "Questions for Discussion."

2. Exercise (individually: 10 minutes)

Students should make careful notes on their decision and the reasons for it.

3. Debrief (full class: 15 minutes to open-ended)

Begin by asking students to indicate how many selected each of the possible choices as the person standing at their hospital room door. As each possibility is voted, ask students to explain why they did or did not select a particular choice.

Discussion about the relationship of perception to attribution to behavior should follow.

16

OPERATION TRANSPLANT

Group Size: Any number of groups of five to seven, preferably randomly matched or mixed for diversity. Do not seat students in groups until after they have completed their individual rankings.

Recommended Time: 120 minutes (can be completed in 90 minutes): 5–10 minutes to go over instructions, 20 minutes for Part l, 55 minutes for Part 2, about 40 minutes to report out and debrief (more or less depending on number of groups and desired length of discussion).

Provided: All instructions, descriptions, and answer grid are in the student edition. An optional "curve ball" is provided below. If you elect to use it, you will need as many copies as there are students.

Also Required: No additional materials required.

Facilities: One or more large rooms with moveable chairs. The rooms should be large enough to allow at least five feet between groups.

Objectives

- To explore decision making under conditions of uncertainty and complexity
- To practice the skills of group decision making by consensus
- To help participants explore the values and beliefs they hold that impact their interactions with others

Background

Operation Transplant© presents a situation in which rational thinking becomes blurred by emotionalism stirred by the participant's values, beliefs, and experiences. The exercise demonstrates the dilemma faced in disaggregating a problem in which it is virtually impossible to separate "facts" from feelings. It also demonstrates difficulties that arise when there are many points of view, some strongly held.

Discourage participants at the outset from using random choice (e.g., coin toss) or quantifying methods for rank ordering the transplant candidates, insisting instead that they reach agreement through discussion and consensus. Ultimately, however, students may develop a quantified list of criteria, reached by a consensus-making process.

Urge participants to do some reading on managing diverse work populations prior to doing this exercise and also to work at listening to the ideas of others.

Either before or after the exercise, ask participants to consider from where their ideas and perceptions of people come and how they believe those perceptions form the bases for behavior. After completing the exercise, it is useful to explore with participants whether their discussions and their personal perceptions, as well as those of their group mates, were surprising. This exercise often surfaces deeply held stereotypes that participants might otherwise avoid or deny. Assure participants that we are all subject to prejudging people based on stereotypes and that what is important is recognizing that we do this, understanding why, and learning how to deal with our tendency to stereotype people in work situations.

Occasionally, participants will protest that they don't like "playing God" or that this is an unreal situation. In fact, hospital groups make exactly these kinds of decisions every day, and the exercise was developed with the assistance and input of a number of physicians and hospital administrators to ensure its authenticity. However, the implications for this kind of decision making go well beyond hospital and life-or-death applications.

Decisions such as who will receive a necessary transplant operation are forced by financial, resource, and/or technical limitations, the very concerns that drive most business dilemmas and decisions. You might suggest in drawing this parallel, for example, that we could change the Operation Transplant© characters into people who must be fired or laid off in a corporate "down-sizing." Protests that someone can "always get another job" (as students are likely to argue that there will always be another liver or another major donor to support the transplant unit), are unrealistic when the worker is 55, is ill and loses health insurance, relies on an uninterrupted paycheck just to meet daily living expenses, has limited language ability, is handicapped, etc.

Trends and Findings

At this writing, this exercise has been used with more than 15,000 undergraduate and graduate students, primarily those pursuing managerial studies, and in numerous corporate, government, and nonprofit settings. A number of value-laden trends have emerged.

Clearly, the role of Peter sets up the most tension and cognitive dissonance. It is not uncommon for participants to argue that were this a "real" situation, Peter would probably have to be ranked first. Again, a corollary can be seen in laying off workers, i.e., your department is faced with downsizing, and your least productive worker is the nephew of the CEO (or the General, owner, major stockholder, etc.). Reducing the cognitive dissonance may take a variety of forms, including claiming that another donor will come along to save the unit. If this hasn't happened so far, why a miracle now?

Sandra (formerly described as Asian) and Sara are generally overlooked for their social functions, i.e., Sandra's role as a loyal employee in your hospital is ignored in favor of her caretaking functions as a mother. Generally, women are valued highest for this latter function. Often heard is, "Sara's kids are older; they don't need her as much," although asking students whether they feel their own mother is dispensable because they are now 18 or older generally brings an important perspective. Sandra's husband is rarely considered for his caretaking and parenting abilities, but Sandra generally ranks first or second, with the most common reason stated that "family values" have been given high priority in the decision-making process.

Ageism is often an issue in this exercise, particularly with Sara. Frequently we hear, "Sara is 42; she has already lived her life." In addition, her career as a teacher and writer are considered by most participants to have little social value.

What a person does is often a basis for assumptions about who that person is socially, economically, and even in gender; this exercise surfaces that point dramatically. While no gender is given for Chris, the character is overwhelmingly interpreted to be a male with the most frequently given reason, "He is a scientist." When Chris's lack of gender designation is pointed out, many students insist that it is irrelevant. Relevant, however, are the assumptions they have made about both Chris and Pat based on the descriptions. Most participants conclude that Chris's "same sex" partner, Pat, is female because Pat works in a shelter for battered women. Often they overlook the words "same sex marriage" in an unconscious attempt to reduce the cognitive dissonance set up. When we used this exercise with 25 women who self-defined as "militant lesbian feminists," all but one of their five-person groups concluded that Chris was male, and they did so for the usual reason. The fifth group spent considerable time arguing over whether Chris and Pat were two males or two females, again their attention being drawn by the characters' jobs. "They must be females," the group concluded, "because only females would work in a shelter for battered women."

Whether two males or two females, Chris and Pat present an opportunity to explore attitudes towards homosexuals in the workplace. Be prepared to deal with some strong emotions on this issue.

The original fifth character, Cuong Ti, has been replaced by Jean-Paul, a Haitian immigrant, in an effort to respond to some earlier limitations. Cuong Ti was a Vietnamese immigrant who had worked for the Americans during the war. We found that college-age students could no longer relate to the war in Vietnam and that overwhelmingly this character was rated low, fourth or fifth, with a "what has he done for us lately?" attitude often expressed.

We would be interested in hearing from you about your students' reactions to Jean-Paul. His character was developed to elicit current feelings about political asylum and the roles and rights of immigrants in our society. We have also given him a highly dependent and young family to test whether participants are able to extend and be consistent with their feelings about "family values."

Suggested Outline and Timing

1. *Set-up (full class: 5–10 minutes)*

In setting up this exercise, briefly review meanings for values, beliefs, attitudes, stereotypes, and cognitive dissonance. Ask students to consider:

- from where their values and prejudices come.
- what prejudices they believe they hold.
- the prejudices they believe their classmates have.

- how they feel their prejudices influence the way they treat others.
- how the prejudices of others influence the way they are treated.

Do the following:

- Briefly review the instructions for the exercise.
- Remind participants that they will have only 20 minutes to complete Part 1 of the exercise.
- Remind participants not to talk to other participants until they have completed their own rankings.
- Tell participants what group they will be in for Part 2 of the exercise and where their group will meet. (Ask them not to move into their groups until they have completed their own rankings.)
- Ask for and answer any questions about how to proceed.

Completing personal rankings first and without discussion locks in each participant's ideas and forces him or her to defend the rankings to the group.

2. *Part 1 (full class: 20 minutes)*

Have participants complete Part 1, marking their rankings on the scoring grid in the column titled "my rankings." Have participants list their reasons for their individual decisions in the column on the ranking sheet titled "comments/reasons."

Give participants a time check after 15 minutes.

(If you have students in the class who speak English as a second language, have a learning disability, or are known to be slow readers, you may want to ask them to read the descriptions in advance of coming to class. However, ask them not to discuss the characters with classmates or others, and ask them not to enter their rankings until the class meeting. At that time, ask them to briefly review the descriptions before entering their rankings.)

3. *Part 2 (Small groups: 55 minutes—although this can be completed in as little as 30)*

Do the following:

- Ask participants to move into their preselected groups.
- Ask participants to establish their collective values and responsibilities prior to beginning the rankings.
- Remind participants to enter their reasons for each ranking, using additional paper as needed.
- Ask each group to select a spokesperson to report its decision to the rest of the class.
- Draw an answer grid in a place visible to all (blackboard, overhead, etc.), labeled across the top with the group names or numbers and down the left side with the names of the potential transplant recipients.

Very often, groups that finish too fast haven't really looked at the candidates very carefully. As a facilitator, it may be helpful to ask the groups why they have made the decisions they have made and whether all group members agree. If they are unable to justify their decisions, or if there is a dissenting voice, insist that the group reconsider and get full agreement. Ask the dissenter the basis for his or her disagreement; then ask the group how they feel about that point of view.

Using the Curve Ball

When a group finishes too fast, tell the members that something has happened that may make them reconsider what they have done. Photocopy the description of Mohammed B. that follows this discussion, and distribute it. Ask students to enter his name in the vacant space on the grid, and walk away. It is not necessary to use the curve ball with all groups, although it will be necessary for the groups that receive the curve ball to explain it to the rest of the class during the report out.

Another Suggestion

Observe the groups and jot down comments that are the most value-laden, e.g., "Sara is 42; she has lived her life." A playback of these is often startling both to those who made the statements and to those who failed to question or protest them. (Be careful not to get drawn into the exercise during such observation.)

4. *Debrief and discussion (full class: open-ended; report out generally takes 5 minutes or less per group.)*

   Ask each group to report what they decided and why, and record their responses on the prepared grid. The discussion that follows might include or focus on such issues as:

   - The values and responsibilities they brought to this task.
   - Difficulties they found in being consistent in their decisions.
   - What they found easy about the task.
   - What they found difficult about the task.
   - What surprised them about their own attitudes.

   Next, ask the groups to describe how they reached their decisions and their group dynamics during the decision-making process. Did they listen to one another? Did they feel listened to?

   Conclude the discussion by stressing that there are neither right nor wrong answers to this exercise. Instead, it was developed to help participants understand that the way they think about people is likely to drive the way they treat them, and the way other people think about them is also likely to drive the way they will be treated.

Mohammed B., age 35, white, Moslem

After three months of political red tape, the Ecumenical Alliance, a group founded by all of the clergy in your town and with a membership of nearly 800, has finally succeeded in getting Mohammed B. evacuated from Bosnia and flown to the United States for desperately needed medical attention.

Since first being identified by the Red Cross as needing medical care not available in Bosnia, Mohammed's condition has steadily worsened. He is now seriously in need of a liver transplant if he is to survive. He will also need to be fitted for a prosthesis for his leg that was blown off in a bomb attack, and he will have to have considerable facial reconstruction due to damage from the same incident.

Mohammed is a gentle man who worked as a supervisor in a factory in Bosnia until the war brought production to an end. Since then, and until the bomb that injured him struck his neighborhood, killing his aged father and many of his friends and relatives, life was little more than a concentrated effort to stay alive. Virtually every tree within miles of Mohammed's hometown has been chopped down, and furniture or anything made of wood has been burned to cook and to supply heat during the cold Bosnian winter. Food shortages are critical.

After the bombing, Mohammed was taken to a makeshift hospital where there were few medical supplies, and treatment was limited.

There is considerable pressure on you from the members of the Ecumenical Alliance to move Mohammed to the top of the transplant list. The Alliance has raised more than $90,000 for Mohammed's care, and his arrival at your hospital made the national news. It is being hailed locally and nationally as a great humanitarian effort.

Enter Mohammed's name in the blank space at the bottom of the name column, and rank the transplant candidates from one to six.

17

FAMILY VALUES*

This case is designed to help students think about the values that are important to them in their private and work lives and whether it is important that the organizations for which they work shares their values. Additionally, the case will help students consider how they might go about learning whether and to what extent prospective employers share their values.

There are many things students can recommend to Brandi, the central case character, to obtain information regarding a prospective employer's track record on work-life linkages. In a 1997 "Managing Your Career" column in *The Wall Street Journal*, journalist Hal Lancaster suggests asking questions in interview situations that will elicit anecdotal answers rather than corporate rhetoric; asking questions of managers and employees; tracking down former employees, particularly the person who previously held the position; checking outside sources such as customers, recruiters, books, and articles; paying particular attention to the language used by the interviewers and the messages it implies; and asking to sit in on a team meeting.

This case also asks students to think about how they would view Brandi as a job candidate, and why. The discussion that follows may elicit some stereotyping; students may express beliefs that working mothers are less dependable, less flexible, and less serious about their careers than those without family obligations. These beliefs should be addressed and students asked to support them. Those students who view Brandi as more mature, experienced, and settled than her peers will most likely be very quick to argue with those who believe otherwise.

For students pursuing management careers, beginning to think about the ways in which an organization can benefit from being sensitive to and accommodating of the work-life concerns of its employees is an important step. Some benefits students should be able to identify include increased employee satisfaction, higher level of employee retention, greater employee loyalty, increased motivation, and a higher level of productivity.

Finally, students should consider what values they would like to see with regard to work-life concerns in either a company for which they work or one that they own. In discussing their answers and the reasons for them, students should consider the issue from the perspective of both the employee and the organization. When putting themselves in the place of the organization, students may feel very differently than when putting themselves in the place of the employee. This is a useful tool for helping students visualize work-life values that successfully address both employee and organizational needs.

* These case notes were prepared by Gail E. Gilmore.

18

WAITING TABLES FOR GODOT*

Students will likely be able to relate to the characters in this case and be very willing to share their own similar experiences. We have all had managers, supervisors, and even teachers who have ignored our good behavior and jumped on us the first time we have made a mistake.

A useful analogy to this case is what happens in some classrooms: The quiet, "good" kids get ignored and receive little positive reinforcement for their behavior; the "bad" kids get a great deal of attention from their teachers and positive reinforcement from classmates when they're disruptive.

Positive and Negative Reinforcement

In terms of positive reinforcement, Diane receives nothing from Godot. From her initial interview, Diane has the impression that Godot will demand a lot but will also give praise or recognition when deserved. She is mistaken. Godot uses reinforcement techniques only in their most negative forms, i.e., punishment and derision. Is this effective? Yes and no. While punishment may make an individual less likely to repeat the undesired behavior, when the punishment is perceived to be unfair and undeserved, the individual tends to exhibit fewer positive and negative behaviors.

Godot's use of negative reinforcement works initially. Diane's attempt to slow down and not drop anything is a behavioral response that leads to a reduction of something unpleasant, i.e., Godot's anger and criticism. The same is true when the waitstaff speeds up to avoid getting yelled at.

Ultimately, however, Diane returns to giving faster service. Why does she continue to engage in behaviors that may be punished? First, and probably the most obvious to the students, is the fact that the patrons of La Maison d'Essence give her positive reinforcement through better tips and occasional compliments when she gives prompt and personal service. More subtle, however, is that Diane works at a faster pace at the end of the case in part as a result of Godot's use of intermittent reinforcement; sometimes he punishes people who work too fast, and sometimes he punishes them for not working fast enough.

Cognitive Dissonance

This kind of schizoid behavior on the part of Godot, coupled with Diane's needs and interests, causes Diane to experience cognitive dissonance on a number of fronts: She wants to go as fast as she can to maximize her tips and to avoid incurring the wrath of Godot. She also needs to avoid being punished should she drop and/or break something as a result of being fast.

* These notes were prepared by Scott Weighart. Used with permission.

According to the theory of cognitive dissonance, individuals take steps to reduce dissonance and inner conflict. Consistent with the theory, by the end of the case Diane has moved toward reducing her dissonance. She decides that the extra money she earns for tips is worth the risk of occasionally breaking something.

From a management perspective, Godot has succeeded in alienating one of his employees, turning her away from his "vision," whatever that may have been that seemed to serve as an initial inspiration for Diane, and from any commitment to "teamwork." Instead, Diane reduces the cognitive dissonance that arises from her conflicting feeling about the restaurant by electing to concentrate on her needs only. Fortunately for Godot, these may be consonant with at least his short-term interests, but in other business settings, this is rarely the case.

19

NUDE DANCING COMES TO WESLEYVILLE—OR DOES IT?

Overview

This case describes a situation in which an individual, John Thompson, has been planning to open a nude dance club. He has spoken with a number of individuals in that business and has decided that it would be a profitable venture in his small town of Wesleyville. Because of his concern over probable negative public reaction to such a club, he makes all of the preparations for opening without being completely forthcoming about his intentions. At the time of the incident described in the case, he has already leased and remodeled his club, secured a liquor license, and hired dancers. However, the local ministerial alliance discovers his plans. Their representative, Reverend Beach, pays a visit to John Thompson to dissuade him from opening.

During the meeting, Reverend Beach threatens to organize around-the-clock picketing of Thompson's club, house, and other business (a used-car dealership). In addition, he threatens to run Thompson and his family out of town if Thompson proceeds with his plans. Finally, Reverend Beach asks Thompson to think about how he would like it if his own daughter were to dance in such an establishment. Thompson finds that question disturbing.

Objectives

This case provides a vehicle for student analysis and discussion of a number of important and timely issues, including:

- ethical or moral behavior versus legal behavior.
- the morality of picketing to protest a legal establishment.
- community decency standards.
- the plight of the unskilled, single mother in society.
- gender issues.
- concerns about the relationship and responsibility of a business to its host community.

Questions for Discussion

1. Should John Thompson proceed with his plans for the club? Why or why not?
2. How can you compare the apparent economic advantages of this venture with the possible damage to his reputation, family, and other business interests? Should his decision be made on purely economic grounds?

3. What do you think of John Thompson's attempt to conceal the true nature of his new establishment from the community? Was it the "smart" way to go about opening his new club?
4. How do you assess Mr. Thompson's argument that making a single mother try to survive on minimum wage is more degrading than dancing nude and being well paid for it?
5. What alternatives does an unskilled and poorly educated single mother have for employment? How can such a person support herself, much less children, with a minimum wage income?
6. What is your reaction to Reverend Beach's question, "Suppose it were your daughter?"
7. How should one judge whether an action is ethical? What standards should be used? Is legality an appropriate standard? An adequate standard?
8. If Mr. Thompson proceeds with this venture, how should he combat the opposition promised by Reverend Beach? Should he ignore it? Should he make public statements in support of his position? Do you think this matter will blow over quickly? Will the presence of pickets adversely affect his used-car business?

Conclusions

Because one's conclusions in this case are greatly influenced by personal value systems, we do not offer our own solution at any point in the discussion. We do conclude the class with an examination of the role that values play in determining attitudes and influencing business decisions. We hope that this case discussion imbues all students with an understanding that, as we put it, "good and decent people just like you can have quite different values."

If appropriate to the course in which this case is used, the value differences exposed in this discussion can be used as a jumping-off point for an in-depth examination of the origin of values, their role in attitude formation, the concept of the frame of reference, and the importance of tolerance in a diverse society.

20

PICKING THE PROJECT TEAM AT THE OZARK RIVER BANK

"Picking the Project Team" can be used as a case for class discussion, as a small group exercise, and/or as a case for written analysis. By way of background, students will need to know something about leveraged buy-outs in order to understand at least some of the issues presented.

In thinking about the problem presented, students should first consider the job to be undertaken in terms of the expertise needed and the demands and stresses that will be imposed on the team's members. Since the group will have to go through the stages of group formation to arrive at the functioning or performing stage, students should next look at the values and norms of the individuals available for the project team to consider the stumbling blocks to team functioning that each brings with him or her. They should also look at each individual's strengths. Making a list of these should help.

Arriving at the best solution is a little like putting a jigsaw puzzle together. Given the shapes and angles of each of the individual pieces, which ones fit together best?

The following are some observational notes on each of the characters. It is likely that students will come up with others.

Harold

Among the biggest issues with Harold are concerns over his health and stamina. The team faces a highly stressful situation. Harold's return after a lengthy absence may make other team members anxious and overly protective. In time, this could turn into resentment. In addition, teaming Harold with Jack, who pushes deadlines, may put Harold into an especially stressful situation. Teaming him with Cynthia, who was specifically hired to replace Harold, may be seen as threatening and uncomfortable to both parties.

Not assigning Harold to the team, especially since he has a solid track record, could further isolate him, something that is probably already a bit of a problem after his long absence. This could result in negative fallout over the long run.

Joan

Clearly Joan is likely to have problems with Joshua and his attitudes towards women. It also sounds like she might have problems with Jack both because of his personal habits and because of his tendency to procrastinate. She sounds somewhat compulsive, i.e., her attention to detail, while he sounds more casual.

Group norms have to develop not just around the job to be done but around the abilities of the workers to respect and trust one another. This must be considered when pairing Joan with either Jack or Joshua.

Conversely, Jack and Joan might serve as good balance for one another, with Joan serving the important function of tying up the pieces of Jack's innovations.

Cynthia

Having worked for the company that is the object of the team's project may be both a strength and a weakness. On the strength side, it is possible that she knows the people and the politics. Conversely, she has left the company and may either be compromised in her ability to function in an objective, arms' length manner due to relationships she maintains there or, if she left under strained circumstances, due to negative feelings towards the company that she might harbor.

Cynthia appears to be able to work well with Joan who may be more effective if teamed with someone she respects.

Students may raise concerns about Cynthia's obligations to her two young children, especially in the face of the time pressures of the job to be done. Using this as a basis on which to avoid using Cynthia on the team is discriminatory. The test students should apply is, "If Cynthia were 'Charles,' would the same standards be applied?"

Jack

Many of the problems with placing Jack on the team are noted above. These essentially involve his tendency to procrastinate and the impact this might have on the others. His tendency to put things off might also delay the healthy development of the group.

On the other hand, Jack is both knowledgeable and capable. His ability to be innovative would probably be considered an extremely positive trait in a complex situation such as the one presented.

Joshua

The biggest potential problem with Joshua mainly stems from his attitude towards women. It appears unlikely for him to be able to see much validity in the ideas and opinions of either of the women involved, whether or not they are offended by his comments. With such blind spots, conflict and inefficiency are both strong possibilities.

Joshua's knowledge of the politics of the organization could be important, however, and must be carefully considered.

The meaning of conflict and the ways in which it can be harnessed are rich areas for discussion with this case.

21

MANAGING PERFORMANCE BY SETTING GOALS

Group Size: Any number of groups of four to five.

Recommended Time: Part A, at least 60 minutes without a role play; Part B, 30 minutes, depending on number of role plays.

Provided: Instructions.

Also Required: No additional materials required.

Facilities: One large room.

Objectives

- To examine the use of goal setting in performance management
- To practice the techniques of performance management

Background

This exercise introduces the concept of formal goal setting as a way to manage performance. Part A presents a situation in which a teen is not meeting expectations at home, school, or personally. Part B asks students to apply what they have learned from the first scenario to a workplace situation. In Part A, the role play is optional; however, it is critical to Part B.

Suggested Outline and Timing

1. *Set-up (full class: 5 minutes)*

   Go over the instructions for Part A and the learning objectives. Before beginning, students should carefully review the procedural steps and the "Questions for Discussion."

   Decide whether students should use the optional role play. Adjust time accordingly.

   Ask each group to select a spokesperson for the report out.

2. *Exercise, Part A (small groups: 45 minutes without a role play)*

   Ask students to apportion their time in rough compliance with the times listed in Steps 1–4 in the student text, Pages 128–129.

3. *Report out and discussion (full class: 5–10 minutes per group with open-ended discussion)*

   Groups should report their responses to Steps 1, 2, and 4 in the student text.

4. *Exercise, Part B (small groups: 10–20 minutes)*

   Students may use brainstorming or other idea-generating models for selecting a work situation to role play. Ask each group to select two members to role play their problem.

5. *Role play (full class: 5–10 minutes each round plus open-ended discussion after each role play)*

   While students may complete the role plays in their small group, it is generally more useful to have the role plays completed in front of the full class with discussion about the effectiveness of the technique following. Make clear that role plays will likely improve in sequence as each performing dyad learns what to do and what not to do from the preceding dyads and discussions.

22

ANOTHER SALES CONTEST AT PATTERSON DEPARTMENT STORES*

"Another Sales Contest at Patterson Department Stores" illustrates the motivation issues of goal setting, participative management, achievement needs, and incentives. It explores the motivation of employees using participatively set goals versus assigned goals and the impact of management feedback toward goal accomplishment.

The case is useful as a basis for brainstorming about how to motivate workgroups toward assigned goals perceived to be impossible. It also asks students to assess how the second year of a contest might have been different if feedback after the first year had been more positive.

The case was developed for use in undergraduate courses in organizational behavior when covering motivational theories, especially goal setting. It is also appropriate for general management and human resources management courses. The case is a sequel to "The Sales Contest that Never Got Off the Ground," which focuses on expectancy theory; however, each case can be used independent of the other.

Case Summary

"Another Sales Contest at Patterson Department Stores" is about a young merchandise manager's experience in setting sales goals to win a company contest. After setting a very difficult goal and coming in second in the district contest, she receives only negative feedback from her store manager. When, in her second contest year a sales goal is assigned by management, it is perceived to be impossible, not accepted, and the contest ends with a decrease in sales over the prior year.

Kathy Lewis, a recent college graduate, takes her first management position with a store in a national retail chain. After one year of training, she becomes merchandising manager of the women's ready-to-wear department. The retail chain holds an annual pre-Easter two-week dress sales contest among its stores as a way to boost sales. Kathy and her sales staff, hoping to win the district contest, set a challenging sales goal of a 35% increase in sales from the previous year.

After putting forth extraordinary effort with an in-store fashion show, special window displays, drawings for gift certificates, cash awards to store employees, and purchases of extra merchandise, Kathy's department accomplishes a 30 percent increase in sales, the second highest in the district. While Kathy and her staff do not win the contest, Kathy is pleased with the 30 percent increase and a second-place finish, and she hopes to try again the following year.

* These case notes were prepared by Bonnie L. McNeely, Ph.D., Murray State University, and Mary Ann Watson, Ph.D., University of Tampa. Used with permission.

Kathy's store manager, on hearing the results of the contest, asks, "Do you know what they say about people who come in second?" He expresses disdain for the second-place outcome and walks away.

The following year, executives at corporate headquarters set the sales goals. Kathy's department goal is set at a 46 percent increase. After the negative feedback received following her first contest, Kathy has trouble feeling motivated to work toward a goal she views as impossible. She is also not particularly interested in working to motivate her staff.

Motivation Concepts Highlighted in the Case

Goal Setting

Goal setting states that specific goals increase job performance, and difficult goals, if accepted, result in higher performance than easy goals. It also suggests, however, that employees are less motivated when they are assigned a goal that appears unreachable or unrealistic.

This case illustrates the power of letting workers set their own goals. An ambitious goal of 35 percent set in the first year by the employees results in a 30 percent increase in sales.

Participation in Goal Setting and Goal Acceptance

The second year, when the goal is imposed by the district manager, goal acceptance is the critical missing component in motivating the employees to put forth much effort. "Going through the motions" is the behavior that is frequently seen in companies when goals are assigned that are perceived by the employees to be impossible. While difficult goals do increase productivity, goal-setting theory states that for goals to be motivating they must be perceived as realistic and attainable. Impossible goals cause individuals to give up and say, "What's the use trying? We can't possibly win." It is not surprising therefore that there was a decrease in sales in the second year.

Rewards and Incentives

One form of incentive illustrated by the case is the cash award given to the employees whose names appear at the bottom of the entry forms of customers who have won a drawing for gift certificates. Giving rewards to employees increased the number of customers visiting the dress department during the contest and thus increased the chance of sales.

Employees seek many types of rewards in the workplace. The paycheck is only one source of motivation and satisfaction. Recognition in the form of a trophy for winning a contest, for example, can be a powerful motivator as stated in:

- Maslow's Hierarchy of Needs—Esteem level
- Herzberg's Two-Factor Theory—recognition as a Satisfier
- Reinforcement Theory—reward any movement toward the goal

The winning store received a trophy and recognition from the district manager. While Kathy and her sales team did not win the contest, they did achieve a 30 percent increase in sales. That should have been deserving of recognition. An appropriate reaction by the store manager's reaction might have been, "For your first year, coming in second in a district sales contest is something to be proud of. I congratulate you and your staff on the 30 percent gain. You put in a lot of hard work. Next year we'll get them. We will win!" Had he been encouraging in this way, the second year's outcome might have been a great deal different.

McClelland's Need for Achievement

High achievers commonly share three characteristics. They prefer:

- moderate challenges.
- personal responsibility for tasks.
- rapid feedback.

The case describes Kathy as a high achiever. She is an individual who wants to succeed and win. As such, we would expect her to reject a goal that she perceived to be impossible, in this case a 46 percent increase in sales. High achievers perform best when they believe their probability of success as fifty-fifty. Whether she knew it or not, Kathy probably communicated, even non-verbally, her rejection of the goal to her staff. As we know from goal setting, if the goal is not accepted, it will not motivate behavior in the desired direction.

Expectancy Theory

The sales contest results for both years could be explained with expectancy theory. The motivational force in the first year was very high because: 1) Kathy and her sales staff believed that if they put forth a lot of effort they had a good chance of winning the contest, 2) Kathy and her staff believed that if they had the highest percent gain among the twenty stores in their district they would indeed receive the trophy, and 3) Kathy and her staff wanted the reward offered, i.e., the trophy and the recognition that it represented.

The motivational force the second year was very low. While the second two variables in expectancy theory remained strong, the first variable, effort-performance linkage, was close to zero. In her mind, the situation appeared hopeless. There was no amount of extra effort that she and her staff could put forth that they thought would produce the sales level that might win the contest.

Integration of the Motivational Theories

The above theories work together to improve our understanding of what motivates workers. Goals give direction to employees. Participation in setting the goals is important to goal acceptance.

Expectancy theory states that employees will exert a high level of effort if they believe there is a strong relationship between effort and performance, performance and rewards, and rewards and satisfaction of personal needs.

Needs theories, such as Maslow's Hierarchy of Needs, come into play with Kathy's need for recognition. As a high achiever (nAch), Kathy wants to excel and win the contest.

Reinforcement theory predicts that Kathy would have repeated her first year's efforts had she received positive feedback for the 30 percent sales increase. Instead, her efforts were scorned by the manager.

All of these motivational theories help explain what happened in this case. The theories also help explain how the sales outcome might have been different in the second year if management actions had been different after the first year's contest.

Teaching Strategies

1. Initial discussion of this case may be done in small groups of 4 to 5 students. After reading the case individually, groups should explore possible answers to the discussion questions and suggest strategies Kathy might have used to motivate her sales staff in the second year.
2. Using a role play of the manager and Kathy, students can recommend motivational methods that would lead to a better outcome in the second year.

Discussion Questions

1. What motivated Kathy Lewis to want to win her first dress contest?

   Given case evidence, Kathy appears to be a high achiever. As a high achiever, she probably likes moderate challenges, feedback, and personal responsibility for tasks. High achievers like to win and work to excel. The trophy would have been a tangible indicator of success and fulfilled her need for achievement and esteem. Kathy was also motivated by promotions that resulted in a higher salary. Her financial need to repay college loans and buy new furniture for her first home were strong motivators.

2. How was Kathy's goal determined for the first contest? What impact did that have on her behavior?

   Kathy and her sales staff set their own goal in the first year, one they thought was challenging but attainable. Having set their own target, they put forth a high level of effort to achieve their goal. Goal-setting theory states that the critical aspect of goal setting is *acceptance* of the goal. It matters little who sets the goal as long as the goal is accepted. Letting workers set their goals is one way to insure acceptance. In addition, research has indicated that some workers set personal work goals at a higher level than management.

3. What other motivators do you see in action?

   Money, in the form of a chance for cash awards, motivated store employees to send customers to the dress department to participate in a drawing for gift certificates. Some dress salespeople might have been motivated by thinking it was fun, participating in something different from the routine, anticipating the chance of winning, or having the sense of belonging to the sales team involved in the contest.

4. How did the motivational situation change in the second contest?

   Motivation in the second contest is very low. The group never accepted the goal that had been assigned and perceived it to be impossible. Not having received positive recognition from the first year's contest results, the dress sales team was not willing to put forth the effort required.

5. Is there anything the store manager could have said after the first year's results that might possibly have changed the second year's results?

   "Coming in second in a district sales contest is something to be proud of. I congratulate you and your staff on the 30 percent gain you produced through a lot of hard work. Next year we'll get 'em. We will win!"

6. What could Kathy do to motivate her sales staff to work toward the assigned goal the second year?

   Kathy might have asked her sales staff to disregard the assigned goal and focus on simply increasing sales. It was the sales increase that produced powerful results in the first contest, not reaching a particular sales goal. Winning or losing had more to do with how the other stores in the district performed, not Kathy's departmental performance alone. Kathy could also remind her staff that sales are influenced by many factors outside their store, such as the local economy, competitors' marketing efforts, and new competitors.

23

LINDA SIFUENTES

This case involves a number of OB concepts, most notably motivation. In analyzing this case, students should include a thorough description of Linda and Chris, and a more minimal analysis of Dersh Maven.

Motivation

Students should recognize the different stages of Maslow's hierarchy that Linda goes through as she works her way up the ladder. She begins by needing to fulfill her most basic physiological and safety needs and does so by going back to school and ultimately getting a job, moving from her welfare surroundings, etc. In her job, Linda begins to fulfill some of her social needs with relationships with her coworkers and her supervisor. However, it is also clear that she has esteem needs that are only fulfilled to a point, and it is here that she is thwarted as her coworkers are either promoted or leave for better jobs elsewhere. This also pulls the social needs rug from under her at her workplace. This may drive her to fulfill her social needs elsewhere, particularly with her fiancé. The instability of the real estate business may also be challenging her safety needs.

If you look at this case in terms of expectancy theory, Linda's need to move ahead is not met despite her hard work and diligence. In addition, the drone work of her job is greater, and even financial incentives have been curtailed. In equity theory terms, there is some questions as to whether Linda is being treated fairly—again, coworkers are moving ahead while she is essentially standing still. It is also useful to look at Herzberg's two-factor theory and recognize that while Linda is being reasonably compensated for her hard work, a hygiene factor, the motivator factors don't seem to be in place. Therefore, there is little in the job to motivate Linda to work harder or better.

Chris is harder to analyze. Apparently finding most of his or her motivation outside of the business, and seeing this as essentially a holding pattern until something better comes along, Chris appears to want to get the job done without a lot of aggravation from above or below.

The case makes clear that firing Linda is out of the question. If students suggest this, you might recommend that they reread the case and play out just what would happen should Chris follow that suggestion. With a no-hire policy, Chris puts himself/herself in an untenable situation by firing Linda—that is, the work needs to get done, and some help may be better than none at all.

Some students might suggest that Linda be promoted. Unfortunately, this may come across as rewarding failure to work. In addition, this may be unrealistic given the economic situation in which the company is operating. Rather, students should find some way to install motivational factors, i.e., job enrichment, training, more stimulating opportunities, and some meaningful support from Chris. Linda is clearly capable and has been motivated in the past.

Managing Diversity

You may get some stereotypes about single mothers, welfare recipients, Hispanics, and so forth. Certainly, Linda is all of these. Some students might wonder why she has not been moved ahead and might speculate that there is some bias involved. Given the facts of the case, however, this can only be speculation. Students who make the charge that she has not been treated fairly because she is a woman or a minority need to look at why this is not consistent with the career paths of others in the company—and probably should also consider the meaning of whether Chris is male or female.

24

SPANGLEMAKER PUBLISHING*

The goals at Spanglemaker Publishing are changing, and a key position becomes vacant and must be filled. While the case has been developed to help students understand some of the practical applications of motivation theories, issues of perception, leadership, Theory X, Theory Y, cognitive dissonance, organizational culture, and gender discrimination are raised as well.

Background

Marty Callahan has been asked to recommend a successor for himself. Despite his recognition that the goals of the job are changing, i.e., more innovation and a faster pace, and the realization that the organizational culture is changing to meet those goals, he recommends the one individual who is most like himself in the way he is motivated and the ways he motivates others. Because Marty's work style is not consistent with the new culture at Spanglemaker, this is probably not the right choice.

A widower whose social life appears to be tightly tied to his workplace and colleagues, Marty is moved toward retirement because he recognizes that his workplace will no longer fulfill his needs for affiliation, love, and relatedness. His thinking about the candidates reveals that he also sees others to be happiest and probably the most motivated when working for someone whose style is geared to fulfilling those needs. [See Moorhead and Griffin. *Organizational Behavior*, 5th edition (Boston: Houghton Mifflin,1998), Chapters 5 and 6.] For this reason, Marty immediately disqualifies Charles Langley from the job of executive editor.

Charles Langley, with his highly directive and controlling management style, appears to have needs for power, aggression, and impulsivity. He appears to overlook the achievement and growth needs of his employees, forcing those who work for him to seek fulfillment of those needs elsewhere. The rate of turnover among Charles's employees is high, and he seems to stifle innovation rather than take advantage of the growth needs of his employees by encouraging it. This is of special concern given the new goals of the company to be more innovative.

Dominique Bernays is an important character in this case, and it is she who appears to come closest to being able to fulfill the role that Guthrie has set out. She is an autonomous worker with an apparent awareness of the demand for innovation and a definite need for achievement, growth, and esteem. She appears to view her employees variously as Theory X and Theory Y and is willing to adapt her management style accordingly. She also appears to be flexible in her understanding of how to reward individual employees according to their needs, thus recognizing that not everyone is motivated in the same way.

* These notes were prepared by Scott Weighart. Used with permission.

Marty is apparently made uneasy by Dominique, primarily because her motivational profile is so very different than his own. In addition, he finds her to be "pushy." Research on gender attitudes has shown that the same characteristics which are believed to be favorable in men, e.g., being assertive and energetic, are described as "pushy" and "bitchy" when found in women. Students are often surprised by this, deny it, want to explore it, and find it a rich area for discussion. Tied to the issue of motivation, it is interesting to consider the impact of being called "pushy" on someone—woman, minority, young person—who is achievement or esteem oriented. If it is important to be respected and to have self-respect and/or it is important to move ahead and succeed, imagine the confusion of the individual who emulates the success behavior of a white male only to find her or himself deprecated.

Does Marty engage in gender discrimination when he does not recommend Dominique? It is certainly possible: He wonders how male workers will respond to "taking orders from a woman." What is likely to happen to Dominique's motivation should she not get the job, particularly if she believes that her femaleness is the reason, is rich fodder for discussion. Both equity and expectancy theories can be introduced at this point.

Lou Healy, who is essentially Marty's clone, definitely has needs for affiliation, love, and esteem. He is also strictly Theory Y, even when being so may not be appropriate. Despite Marty's recognition that he would not be happy with the new company goals and culture that would largely eliminate the opportunity to fulfill love, affiliation, and relatedness needs, Marty still selects Lou for the job. He minimizes his cognitive dissonance over this situation by finding as many reasons as possible as to why the other two candidates would not be appropriate.

Marty's decision is absolutely the wrong one for many reasons that can be proved effectively using Herzberg's Two-Factor Theory. When Marty asks Dominique how she would manage the copy editors, she emphasizes giving them interesting work, recognition, and rewards. Not only is this consistent with her need for achievement, according to Herzberg, these are all motivators. Meanwhile, Lou predictably emphasizes interpersonal relationships, close supervision, etc. These are hygiene factors and will lead only to higher levels of no dissatisfaction.

It would appear that Dominique is actually the right person for the job. Despite this, students often protest that her interpersonal skills are lacking. This then raises the issue of just what the role of a manager should be vis-à-vis his or her employees—an open-ended question that could perhaps best be explored within the context of a fishbowl exercise such as the one proposed on leadership elsewhere in this book.

25

QUEENS VETERINARY HOSPITAL: KEVIN'S STORY

Background

The Queens Veterinary Hospital hired Kevin for a new position as assistant manager. At first, Kevin seems motivated by the challenge of learning the various aspects of the job. Eventually he feels his job has become routine, and he lacks direction.

This case provides an opportunity to explore motivation from a traditional perspective as well as from the perspective that motivation is a shared responsibility. In this case, Kevin begins to feel "unmanaged and unchallenged" and begins to become discouraged. Although he has recognized a problem, he has not taken the initiative to address the situation. [See: Ira Chaleff, *The Courageous Follower* (San Francisco: Berrett-Koehler Publishers, 1995).]

The case may also be used to explore leadership, both Kevin's and the veterinary hospital's.

Alderfer's ERG Theory

Using Alderfer's ERG theory, Kevin appears to be motivated by both growth and relatedness needs. When Kevin begins working in the hospital, he is excited by the challenge and opportunity to learn new skills. He is also able to use his strengths to assist Hanna, the hospital manager. Kevin takes pride in his ability to master the tasks that are assigned to him and finds the challenge of learning interesting and motivating. These are indications of Kevin's growth needs.

Kevin relatedness needs are illustrated by his desire to be liked by those working for him. His social needs interact with his leadership style and lead him to feel uncomfortable assigning tasks to his subordinates. He says, "I wanted people to like me, and I was concerned that asking them to take on work would make them angry or make them feel I was being bossy."

Kevin seems to lack an understanding of what will motivate his workers. His social needs, coupled with his lack of understanding of motivation, lead him to feel tension as he is not sure how to encourage people to do their jobs without losing them as friends. Kevin begins to "feel a division" between himself and his workers, which thwarts satisfaction of his relatedness needs.

Job Design Theory

Kevin's situation can also be explained using job design theory. When Kevin begins his new job, he feels a sense of challenge. He learns new skills and experiences a sense that his job is meaningful as he is able to use his skills to help Hanna with computers. As time goes on, he no longer feels challenged, and he is not able to see the importance of the work he is doing. He begins to feel that his work lacks meaning. Furthermore, he is not given any direct feedback that would provide him with an indication of how he is doing. These factors contribute to a lack of motivation, lack of satisfaction, and a decline in productivity.

The Courageous Follower

As Kevin becomes more discouraged, he waits for someone to do something to make the situation better. Kevin has an opportunity to take responsibility for his own motivation but does not do so. If Kevin is feeling he lacks direction, he has at least two options: He could take the initiative to find something useful to do that would help the hospital, or at a minimum, he should explain his situation to his boss and provide her with recommendations for addressing the situation. To allow his energy to be drained by the situation while waiting for someone else to do something makes Kevin a contributor to the problems he faces.

Leadership

Kevin does not have leadership experience and needs to be coached by his superiors. However, he is left on his own. He occupies his time learning new skills and doing finite tasks. When he can't spend his time learning, he begins to become discouraged. Using Hersey-Blanchard's life cycle theory of leadership, Kevin could be considered an immature worker needing a telling style of management.

The lack of direction that Kevin receives seems to be indicative of the hospital as a whole. The job of assistant manager has been created without a clear role definition or expectations. According to House's path-goal theory of leadership, leaders need to define a goal and a clear path for achieving it. Both of these appear to be absent in this case. Not only does Kevin not know what he should be doing, he apparently receives no direction to help him figure it out.

Kevin's leadership is also problematic. Kevin indicates that he was torn between wanting to be friends with his workers and telling them to get to work. He also indicates that his workers, especially the technicians, are older and have had many years of experience. Using the Hersey-Blanchard model, it is likely that these workers are higher in job maturity. Although some of the kennel staff, who are younger, may need a telling style, the technicians probably need a more participating style. Kevin does not seem to be able to adjust his style to the maturity of his workers.

There is also no indication that Kevin has set clear expectations for his workers and provided the support needed for them to meet those expectations. Kevin may have good intentions when he does some of the work that he should have assigned to his workers; however, his workers are not likely to see it that way. It is more likely to be interpreted as Kevin's lack of trust in their abilities.

26

MOTIVATION AT BALD EAGLE SOFTWARE*

Martin Blanchard, vice president for research and development at Bald Eagle Software, fails to consider individual differences in motivation. Employee Hank Seaver is apparently motivated by his social and relatedness needs. Money and advancement seem to hold little interest for him. Martin, on the other hand, apparently needs to be respected by others, in particular his boss, and he seems to value the very things that Hank does not.

By insisting that Hank Seaver commit to Martin's personal framework for motivation, Martin Blanchard is more likely to diminish Hank's productivity than to increase it. Even worse, he is penalizing one of his best employees. Why does Martin pick on Hank when he ostensibly has many other employees who are less productive? This appears to stem from his inability to recognize what drives Hank. Instead, Martin interprets the differences in their motivational styles as threatening and undermining to his authority. It's a personality clash in which Martin has total authority to impose his personality on Hank. In addition, Martin's attack on Hank becomes personal—"You're at a standstill"—and punitive. Martin fails to see the potential negative consequences for the company. The irony is that he is cutting his own throat.

In a memo, Martin is told that productivity has to improve, and he interprets this as some sort of veiled message about Hank's socializing. Yet, the memo, which has been sent to all of the vice presidents, doesn't single out Martin's department. The action Martin takes will almost certainly cause productivity, at least for Hank, to drop.

Using needs theories, Martin can be seen as having a need for power, Hank as having a need for affiliation, and Olga as having a need for achievement. This last interpretation is suspect as we only experience Olga through Martin's eyes.

Students should recognize that Martin is a Theory X manager, his last words in the case—"Workers are like horses. Leave them alone, and they'll wander aimlessly. If you expect to get any work out of them, you have to keep them on a tight rein."—are a dead give-away.

Courses of Action

Some students will argue that Martin should never have spoken to Hank, taking a "if it's not broke, don't fix it" approach. There is probably some validity to this, and the tone of the case certainly sets one up to reach this conclusion. On the other hand, if productivity is a problem company-wide, Hank's social behavior might well be undermining the ability of others to work. This is something that students often overlook in their rush to defend the "good guy," Hank, from the "bad guy," Martin. Working after hours may be helping Hank to keep his own productivity up, but it isn't helping those with whom he chats at length during regular working hours.

* These notes were prepared by Scott Weighart. Used with permission.

Probably, Martin should not be taking the offensive position that he takes. This can only demoralize Hank, cause resentment, and ultimately backfire. Chances are Hank really cares about his "buddies" and would not want to jeopardize them. Martin needs to make Hank aware of the problem and suggest he find other means for social outlets. One possibility is social parties that reward reaching productivity goals; another is developing projects, such as community-based volunteer opportunities, that Hank and his friends could participate in outside of the workplace in the evenings and on weekends. These afford safer and more creative outlets for the expression of Hank's social needs and yet retain his connectedness to the company.

27

THE SALES CONTEST THAT NEVER GOT OFF THE GROUND*

Background

A department store manager is eager to try a new three-week employee sales contest to increase add-on and multiple sales. The employees who make the biggest sales of the day on each of the three levels in the store will receive a $10 bonus. The contest does not produce the desired results.

This case illustrates the expectancy theory of motivation using a real life example of what can go wrong when management fails to consider the three variables in this theory, i.e., effort-to-performance, performance-to-outcome, and outcomes and valences. [See: Moorhead and Griffin, *Organizational Behavior*, 6th ed. (Boston: Houghton Mifflin Company, 2001) Chapter 6.]

Questions for Discussion

1. Using expectancy theory, can you explain some reasons why little effort or energy was put into the sales contest by the majority of the sales employees?

   Each of the three variables in expectancy theory may help to answer this question.

   The effort-performance relationship: This is the probability perceived by the sales person that exerting a given level of effort will lead to performance. It is clear that employees selling in the low-dollar-value departments quickly realized that it did not matter how much effort they put into increasing each sale. Because of the nature of their department's goods, they were not going to have the high sale on their floor for the day to win the $10 bonus. It would take far too many baby items in the infant department to add up to one winter coat.

   The performance-reward relationship: This is the degree to which the sales person believes that selling at a particular level will lead to the attainment of the desired outcome, the bonus. Since this contest included competition among the sales associates, there was no certainty that a high sale would generate the bonus. Another sale of just one penny higher that day would give the bonus money to someone else. Therefore, there was no certainty that a very high sale would get the reward.

   The rewards-personal goals relationship: This is the extent to which company rewards satisfy the sales associates' personal goals or needs and the attractiveness of the $10 bonus to the employees. In this case, $10 did not seem to be enough to overcome the negatives related to the contest, i.e., wearing the gaudy ribbon, responding to customer inquiries about the ribbon, and having to take the ribbon from a fellow sales associate.

* These case notes were prepared by Dr. Bonnie L. McNeely, Murray State University. Used with permission.

2. Could the contest be modified in any way to create the results the manager was hoping for?

   Student responses may vary for this question. Perhaps instead of dollar volume for the winning sales person, the criteria for winning could be number of items sold (to encourage add-on sales and multiple sales) or some other measure.

28

DR. WATSON GETS PUBLISHED*

This case presents an anonymous letter to the editor in the local newspaper written by a disgruntled faculty member in a college of business at a state university. The college is apparently in transition, changing from a teaching-oriented institution to one that is more focused on research. The state is experiencing very difficult economic times, and the professor's letter to the newspaper attempts to arouse public (taxpayer) sentiments against the reallocation of scarce resources away from teaching and towards research.

On a personal level, it would appear that the professor feels his/her contributions and those of others who have set teaching excellence as their primary goal have not been rewarded. This is confirmed in the conversation among the administrators. Dr. Watson's letter, in tone and in the fact that it has been sent anonymously, seems to be written in retaliation against this perceived unfair treatment.

Many issues can be explored through the use of this case, including one or more of the following:

1. The changing mission of an organization and management of that change
2. The mission of higher education in America
3. A possible trade-off between teaching and research
4. The role of the taxpayers' needs or desires in determining goals for a state university
5. Reward systems
6. Retaliation by a disgruntled employee
7. Consequences of perceived inequity
8. The ethics of submitting an unsigned letter to the editor designed to pressure one's employer
9. Actions to be taken by the university:
   a. Developing a public response
   b. The desirability of identifying the author
   c. Reconsideration of the university's objectives
   d. Reconsideration of the university's performance appraisal and reward system

Analysis of the Case

The problems presented in this case are quite common in organizations and most specifically to a college or university attempting to improve its regional or national reputation by means of encouraging faculty research.

Editor's note: Dr. Watson's gender has not been specified in the case and is important only to the degree that students jump to conclusions about the gender based on perceptions and stereotyping.

The College of Business at The Regional University, in changing from a teaching-oriented to a research-oriented institution, must concomitantly change its reward system. Formerly, teaching excellence was the primary factor by which rewards were allocated. Now, the research-oriented faculty have reduced teaching loads, fewer students, and greater financial rewards.

Students react very strongly to this situation since it is one with which they are involved on a daily basis. The question of the roles various individuals and groups should play in establishing the organization's objectives is a good way to begin. The state legislature, board of trustees, university president, faculty, students, alumni, business community, and taxpayers are all stakeholders with valid interests in the problem at hand. Students should consider ways to resolve the problem that will allow input from all concerned groups.

The general question of the role of teaching versus the role of research in the American educational system generates a great deal of student interest. Many students tend to be in sympathy with the disgruntled professor and feel that the only goal of a university professor should be excellence in the classroom. Discussion about the appropriateness and value of research needs to be guided before it finally gets recognized.

Once students come to grips with the value of both teaching and research, the question of performance appraisal and reward allocation can be brought into the discussion. Here it might be useful for the instructor to bring in the actual performance appraisal program used at his or her institution and others. Students are generally quite surprised at the number of factors considered and the weights given each.

Equity and expectancy theories may be used to examine the impact of Dr. Watson's university's performance appraisal and reward system on his/her future performance.

Students should also look at the position of Professor Watson in this situation and the alternatives available to him/her or any disgruntled employee. The ethics of sending the letter and the issue of loyalty are both topics to be raised.

Finally, students should consider and make specific recommendations of a course of action for the university administrators now that Dr. Watson's letter has become public.

29

THE ISSUE OF EQUITY: SECTIONS 1 AND 2

Group Size: Any number of groups of four to five.

Recommended Time: Section 1, 45 minutes; Section 2, 45 minutes (for shorter time periods, omit the small group work).

Provided: Instructions.

Also Required: No additional materials required.

Facilities: One large room.

Objectives

- To examine the relationship of inputs to outcomes in organizational settings
- To explore the role of perception in employee motivation and satisfaction
- To reach a better understanding of equity theory and its application

Background

This exercise provides a quick way to stimulate thinking and discussion around equity theory and its relationship to employee motivation and satisfaction.

In Section 1 of the exercise, students are asked to consider how they would feel, on an absolute basis, about their job, salary, and career path based on given information. In Section 2, students are given comparative information and asked to consider how they feel based on this new information.

Students should not look at Section 2 until they have completed Section 1.

Suggested Outline and Timing

1. Set-up (full class: 5 minutes)

Go over the instructions and learning objectives.

2. Exercise (individually: 10 minutes)

Students should make careful notes on their answers to Questions 1, 2, and 3 under "Procedure" on Page 152 of the student text.

3. Debrief (full class: 15 minutes to open-ended)

4. Section 2 (full class: 5 minutes)

Students should read Section 2 of "The Issue of Equity."

5. Small groups of 3 to 5 (20–30 minutes)

Working in small groups, students should explore answers to Questions 1, 2, and 3 under "Procedure" on Page 153 of the student text.

6. Report-in and debrief discussion (open-ended)

30

THE WORKSTATION BONUS

Group Size: Any number of groups of four to seven.

Recommended Time: 120 minutes (5 minutes to set up; 20 minutes for individual preparation; 40–60 minutes for group decision; 15–30 minutes for report out; open-ended discussion)

Provided: All instructions, descriptions, and forms.

Also Required: No additional materials required.

Facilities: A large room with moveable chairs or several small break-out rooms.

Objectives

- To consider the relationship of performance appraisal, feedback, and reward to motivation
- To consider the interdependency of team members
- To explore the difference between bonus rewards and salary

Background

This exercise requires students to make the connection between performance appraisal, feedback and reward, and motivation. In addition, they must consider the meaning of teamwork and the implications of the interdependency of team members. Often, students who are assigned group projects express dismay over the idea that their product and their grade, at least in part, are going to depend upon the efforts and talents of others. Like it or not, however, teamwork is increasingly the norm in business today. Therefore, students who hope to work in management positions had best learn how to motivate teams as well as work in them.

The Problem

The CEO of the company has authorized $35,000 in bonus money to be allocated among the individuals who worked on a creative project. Participants must decide whether to allocate this by team or individual, how much should be awarded to each, and why. Some of the options are to divide the $35,000 equally among the six employees ($5,833.33 each); to give a larger share to one team than to the other; to award larger amounts to those who seemed to exert the most effort, etc.

The members of each of the two teams, A and B, are presented. Participants are given three kinds of information on each of the six individuals: personal, professional, and level of team performance and contribution. In addition, information is given on the outcome of each team's efforts. Before doing this exercise, students should understand the various theories of motivation such as equity and expectancy theories, Maslow's Hierarchy of Needs, Alderfer's ERG, and so forth. They should also have some grounding in group dynamics. [See: Moorhead and Griffin, *Organizational Behavior*, 6th ed. (Boston: Houghton Mifflin Company: 2001) Chapters 6 and 7.]

Responses of the Experts

The exercise was given to four experts: Joseph Auerbach, a practicing lawyer and professor emeritus at Harvard Business School, whose expertise is in corporate governance; Dr. Lloyd Baird who has taught at Boston University for 18 years and who is an expert in the study of organizational effectiveness, performance management, and human resources management; William A. Krein, who has served as CFO for a number of Fortune 500 companies and is a consultant to developing high tech companies; and Stephen A. Stone, former CEO of Converse, Inc. (a marketer of athletic shoes) and a corporate director. The following is a synopsis of their responses.

According to Joseph Auerbach, rewarding on a team basis indicates a recognition that "no man is an island" and acknowledges the "specific contribution of each team." He suggests that this method would avoid a perception of favoritism, cultivate the sublimation of the individual to the common effort, and establish a record for the future of team reward.

At the same time, he suggests that giving individual rewards encourages individual efforts, recognizes the 24-hour responsibility an individual has to a team and honors that individual for his or her efforts, confirming the position of the individual on the team.

His solution: Give 65 percent to Team A ($22,750) and the remainder to Team B, dividing it evenly so that each member of Team A receives $7,583.33, and each member of Team B receives $4,083.33.

Dr. Lloyd Baird concurs. "The actual work output is the result of a team effort," he says. "Therefore, it is the team that should be rewarded. You want them to work well together in the future and not get into politics trying to upstage each other..." in an effort to reap more of the rewards. "If you reward individuals, you run the risk of not being able to explain the rewards, because the only measurable product is the completion of the design, which was a group project."

Dr. Baird suggests that bonuses should be given in recognition of short term outcome performance. In this case, he says, "you want to encourage cooperative behavior." In the future, the team members will recognize that the way to increase their rewards is by "helping each other improve the total performance of the whole group. This, of course, is based on the assumption that they will be working together again in groups and know that they will be rewarded based on the group's performance."

William Krein also agrees, and he offers a hands-on approach. "I would want to personally present the bonus payment to each individual," he says, "because that would allow me to comment on some element of their particular contribution. I think it is important that each member of the team has the sense that the bonus award is tied at least in part to their unique contribution.

"I probably would present the bonus awards to each of the groups separately, but to all the members of the group at the same time. This would allow the opportunity to reinforce the 'successful outcome' and 'team performance' points that I believe are important—that is, only successful projects earn bonuses and teamwork is the keystone of success." Mr. Krein adds that he "might want to counsel members on strengths and weaknesses, but that would be done after the bonuses are presented and on a one-on-one basis."

His solution: Give $21,000 to Team A and $14,000 to Team B, and allocate equal shares of the total team award to each member. "I am comfortable with each member of the team receiving an equal share, particularly as I want the emphasis to be the team performance and not any single individual." Mr. Krein also notes that "a modest premium" might be added to the bonuses of the team leaders if they had been designated.

Stephen A. Stone makes it unanimous. "I chose the team basis," he writes, "because I had already determined that the task would be performed by two teams...presumably because the creative work contemplated could most productively be done by cooperation among diverse personalities and talent.... I must have recognized the diversity and variation when I made the original selections, so I cannot fairly penalize attributes that I knowingly hired and assigned to work together."

"It is impossible for me to assess the relative importance of individual contributions in a creative effort. I believe that an attempt to do so would destroy any chance to elicit cooperation from teams of my selection in the future, and therefore adversely affect motivation henceforth."

Mr. Stone suggests "that the decision to use two teams, competing with each other as well as with other bidders, acknowledged the stimulus of internal rivalry. That justifies an award to both teams. One team did produce the winning design, but the firm and department were winners as well."

His solution: Give $20,000 to Team A and $15,000 to Team B, and allocate equal shares of the total team award to each member.

Mr. Stone also suggests two other areas for discussion: "Before accepting the CEO's offer, I would have secured his clear agreement that his action constituted a precedent which he is committed to follow in similar circumstances in the future." Given that bonuses often ultimately are perceived to be entitlements, Mr. Stone's question raises an important issue of motivation over the long run.

"Second, what is he doing for me? Surely, it would be destructive for me to skim the pot for myself in the absence of the boss's clear directive." This question raises two important considerations: As manager of this department, you have also achieved success. In the absence of reward, what happens to your own motivation? Additionally, what, as manager, is your ethical and moral responsibility in this situation?

Addenda

Students will often get caught up in the amounts to be rewarded and the personal needs and traits of each of the individuals. Many will have the instinct to give more to some individuals who are perceived to be "good guys" or needing it and to be punitive towards others who are perceived to be lazy or not represent acceptable values. As you will note from the comments of the experts, the personal information given is not considered germane.

Stephen Stone also writes, "It is interesting that in the automobile assembly field, certainly no breeding place for such socialist ideas as cooperation, the new Japanese plants in the United States using these team, cooperative approaches are topping the productivity per man hour of American-managed plants by a factor to 2:1 (Robert Reich) and doing it with traditional American workers!"

Suggested Outline and Timing

1. Set-up (full class: 5 minutes)

Go over the learning objectives, background, and instructions.

2. Individual Scoring (20–30 minutes)

Ask students to read the background information and the profiles of each of the team members, calculate the amount of the bonus they would give to each, and to give the reasons for their decision.

3. Exercise (small groups: 40–60 minutes)

Ask students to discuss the problem and come to a group consensus on how the bonus money should be divided and why.

Ask students to select a spokesperson for their group.

4. Report-out (full class: 15–30 minutes)

Ask students to report their decisions to the class and explain why. Record each group's response in a visible place.

5. Discussion (full class: open-ended)

Use the "Questions for Discussion" as a guide.

31

DISHONORABLE INTENTIONS

Sean Lavelle, director of product design and development at Artemis Software, seems to show no recognition of what he has done to undermine the motivation of Dale Carini and Dale's coworkers. Nor does Sean seem to understand just what it is that motivates Dale and how that differs from his own motivational needs.

To analyze this case, students must recognize that Dale appears to be motivated primarily by the social needs as described in Maslow's Hierarchy, McClelland and Atkinson's affiliation needs, and the relatedness needs described by Alderfer's ERG Theory. Dale's statements, such as "It just isn't the same anymore...," along with his/her rejection of the promotion to Andrea's former position, indicate that Dale values relationships with fellow workers and that his/her needs are largely social. However, students should not overlook the fact that Dale liked the work, the ability to be creative, and the opportunity to see his/her work in public places. These suggest the presence of strong secondary ego, esteem, growth, and achievement needs.

Needs Theories

Students often wrongly conclude that only one level of Maslow's Hierarchy can be operant at a time. It may be necessary to point out that Maslow suggested that varying degrees of each need may be present at any one time. Therefore, it is possible for Dale to be motivated primarily by social needs and secondarily by ego and esteem needs. Students may also be confused that the case character who seems so unlikable, Sean, is motivated by needs higher on Maslow's Hierarchy than Dale. This is important, as students tend to conclude that one is somehow superior if one is motivated by higher-order needs and that, for example, assembly-line workers can't be driven by higher-order needs. If this were the situation, how would one explain the motivational needs of an out-of-work banker whose mortgage has been foreclosed? Another useful example was the need for achievement, affiliation, and other higher-order needs among concentration camp inmates.

Sean, in contrast to Dale, seems to be driven almost exclusively by ego and esteem needs. In talking about his parties, to which he does not invite his coworkers, he indicates that he fulfills his social needs outside of the workplace. As a worker starting out, he shuns group activities, and even as a director of a department, he largely avoids contact with coworkers and subordinates. On the other hand, he takes Dale's idea and runs with it, knowing exactly whom to approach in order to achieve his desired outcome. This, along with the appearance of a friendly relationship with Dale when Dale was the boss, give an indication of Sean's need to gain and hold power (McClelland), either by affiliation or position.

Case questions specifically point to needs theories, and the case is most easily analyzed within a needs-theory framework. Therefore, equity and expectancy theories are probably a stretch, although Dale clearly sees Sean's promotion as unfair (equity theory), and Sean appears to believe that he is reaping the benefits of his own hard work (expectancy theory).

Dale appears to recognize the individual motivational needs of his/her workers. Dale managed Sean correctly by recognizing Sean's need for power and giving him a great deal of autonomy, but he/she was apparently naive as to the possible outcomes. Other workers are motivated at the social levels (after-work get-togethers) and at the ego and esteem levels (telling them when a job is well done or not). Sean appears not to recognize the motivational needs of his workers, but rather "gives orders" and threatens their job security and thus safety needs—"I've told those people in design... they probably ought to start looking for other jobs." In blaming the workers for anything that goes wrong, rather than praising them for work well done, Sean also undermines their ability to fulfill ego and esteem needs (Maslow) or achievement needs (McClelland) or growth needs (Alderfer).

Motivating Dale

In considering what can be done to help Dale become productive again, students will have to explore the problems with Sean, both in terms of Sean's difficult management style and in terms of Sean as a symbol to Dale of things gone awry. Dale has been undermined by Sean's actions—prior and present.

Discourage the idea of firing Sean: This is facile. Instead, encourage more creative thinking that also reaches into impacting the morale of the entire unit. After all, Dale is clearly tied to his/her coworkers and they to him/her. If it is possible to work on motivating them as a group by recognizing the group's primary needs, results are likely to be better and/or faster. This could, for example, mean more hands-on involvement on Andrea's part and more autonomy for Dale, bypassing Sean for at least a period of time. It might also mean recognizing Dale's contributions in a way that supports his/her need for social relationships within the work place, e.g., a special project, social get-togethers, a problem-solving retreat, etc.

In dealing with remotivating Dale, students may primarily consider their own motivational needs. In the interest of helping them become introspective, self-understanding adults and managers, students should be pushed to think about and describe just how they would be in Dale's situation and what would move them along. But they should also engage in class discussion since their answers to what would help them as individuals are bound to differ. Exploring the range of responses and the reasons for them should help students understand that what drives them personally is not necessarily universal.

Ethical Issues

It appears, superficially at least, that Sean has stolen Dale's idea. However, this is difficult to support. Dale has said that he/she really doesn't have time to work on the idea and probably never will. Students may argue that Dale has passed the idea on, but they may also argue that Sean owed it to Dale to share what he was doing and give Dale a chance to participate.

"Dale" was purposely chosen as a gender-neutral name to allow students to better identify with his or her dilemma.

32

THE MUSIC TEACHER FROM HELL*

Unfortunately, everything in this case is true—except for the part about "excessive flossing"—and the scenario is not wholly uncharacteristic of the way any number of public school systems are run.

Social Powers

Principal Joe Swanson has virtually no reward power. There is essentially nothing he can do to get "The Music Teacher from Hell" fired or to cut her salary, no matter how many other teachers, parents, students, and administrators attest to her incompetence. In the Dacron school system, salaries are based solely on seniority and have nothing to do with performance. As long as Vandeberg doesn't do something really horrendous, such as punch a student or offer drugs to the children, she has a job somewhere in the school system for as long as she likes.

Swanson also has no referent power. Due to the music teacher's previous experiences with school principals, Vandeberg casts him as the villain from day one. Obviously, he does nothing that will make her respect or like him during the school year.

Swanson has legitimate power. Because he is the principal, he can assign Vandeberg to do various mundane tasks. She doesn't dare to be directly insubordinate, so she complies by doing the bare minimum necessary to avoid being fired.

Swanson also has coercive and expert powers. He knows from experience that there is no point in trying to get the music teacher fired, and he knows the school system well enough to know that the only way to get rid of a tenured teacher is to make him or her miserable through the use of coercive power. He uses this frequently during the case, tenaciously doing all he can to make her so sick of the harassment that she will request a transfer.

Equity and Expectancy Theories

Equity and expectancy theories are both demonstrated in "The Music Teacher from Hell." The system does not reward effort or performance. In fact, Vandeberg's lack of effort and poor teaching performance lead to the positive outcome of getting paid a lot for doing very little.

In terms of equity theory, the other teachers are angered at the great discrepancy between their salaries and that of the music teacher. The younger teachers could attempt to restore equity by lowering their work efforts to that of Vandeberg's, or by doing what often happens—quitting the public school system to find jobs where their efforts and strong performance are more likely to be rewarded.

* These notes were prepared by Scott Weighart. Used with permission.

33

UNITED DYNAMICS: DOWNSIZING—FIRING BY ANY OTHER NAME

Group Size: Any number of groups of five to seven.

Recommended Time: 120 minutes (5 minutes to set up; 35 minutes for individual decisions; 40 minutes for group decisions; remainder for report out and discussion).

Provided: Instructions, descriptions.

Also Required: No additional materials required.

Facilities: A large room with moveable chairs or several small breakout rooms.

Objectives

- To examine the responsibilities that go with managerial power
- To examine the short-term effects of layoffs on group cohesiveness, morale, and productivity
- To examine the long-term effects of layoffs

Background

Although based on some of the events that occurred at General Electric in 1991 when a contract for building a new generation of jet engines went to a competitor, United Dynamics could be virtually any company at any time.

That managers have power has long been a significant element in the attraction of a business school education and managerial careers for many students. Sometimes, however, students overlook the responsibilities that go with having that power. In addition, they may fail to see that being a manager can mean having to make decisions that may be unpopular with those above, are certain to be unpopular with those in subordinate positions, and are likely to be personally uncomfortable. Making the decisions along rational lines is not always easy or even possible, but working towards that goal may at least help reduce cognitive dissonance. Therefore, students should be encouraged to weigh carefully the pros and cons of keeping or laying off each engineer. This requires first understanding the role of business. Here, the various philosophies of what constitutes the appropriate role of business in society may be explored.

Students are given three kinds of information about each engineer:

- personal (i.e., family and personal financial information)
- professional (i.e., how technically able they are as engineers)
- group role (i.e., how they fit into the "team" and into the organization)

Deciding on the weight to give each of these areas of information is among the difficult tasks facing the student. Many management gurus suggest that little if any consideration should be given to personal issues, such as the impact of loss of health or retirement benefits, and that decisions about whether or not to retain an employee should be made on the basis of performance alone. During a difficult period at IBM, Chairman John F. Akers told attendees at a small group seminar, "Our people have to be competitive, and if they can't change fast enough, as fast as our industry...good-bye" (*WSJ*, B1-2, 5/29/91). Says *The Wall Street Journal* reporter Paul B. Carroll, Akers "is telling managers to fire far more marginal employees" (ibid.).

Students must grapple with the impact that laying off a marginal member of a cohesive group could have on the functioning of the rest of the members. Issues of the meaning of loyalty and seniority must also be considered from both long- and short-term perspectives.

Some answers to this problem are more right than others, but there are few absolutes, and students will have to examine not just the individual employee's qualifications, but how she or he interacts with others as well. Keeping a mediocre employee on for fear that she or he might sue, for example, is not appropriate. However, keeping an average employee who is able to bring out the best in others in a team situation may have considerable merit. Poor performers ought to be fired.

The following should be noted.

Harold Aldrich

Reasons for retaining: Seniority, his contacts in government and private industry, his reliability and loyalty, his willingness to put the company's concerns above his own, his commitment to the team approach, his role in the socialization of the group, he is in the middle of a project, and he will lose his retirement benefits.

Reasons for laying off: His skills are apparently average, his impending retirement forecloses long-term participation.

Special considerations: Typically, students might suggest that Harold is "over-the-hill." Nothing in his profile suggests that this age bias has validity. Laying Harold off with that in mind might well result in the company being sued for age discrimination—and losing. In terms of loss of benefits, early buy-out of personnel nearing retirement age is often far less costly in dollars and goodwill than simply firing. Harold might be a good candidate for such an early buy-out. This would reward his commitment and loyalty.

Jane Calloway

Reasons for retaining: Related to your boss, is valued by the group, has a positive influence on morale, has personal relationships with many in the unit, is socially conscious.

Reasons for laying off: Is only an average engineer.

Special considerations: It would be foolhardy to overlook Jane's political connections, i.e., her brother-in-law is your boss, and the next cut could include you. Like it or not, this is not a good reason to keep her on. What is more important is that she has a positive impact on morale. Whether to keep or cut Jane may be a toss-up decision.

Lloyd Hunt

Reasons for retaining: He will probably sue, seniority; he appears to have social concerns and some ethical standards.

Reasons for laying off: He is not an integral part of the team; skills are average.

Special considerations: Anyone can sue anyone for anything. Lloyd's style seems to be to hold people hostage until they settle to get rid of him. This could be both costly and time consuming. However, anyone can be fired for any reason except for those few areas specifically prohibited by law, i.e., discrimination, revenge for whistleblowing, issues covered by the Americans with Disabilities Act, and not much else. Hopefully you have done regular performance appraisals on your employees that make clear just what their shortcomings are. Getting rid of Lloyd now might save additional aggravation in the future.

Zelda Karas

Reasons for retaining: Her skills are excellent; she supports and cultivates younger workers; she adds gender diversity to the workplace; she is a team player.

Reasons for laying off: She doesn't need the job; she takes long vacations.

Special considerations: The fact that Zelda doesn't need the job is irrelevant. By delaying her vacations to coincide with the completion of projects, Zelda has clearly demonstrated that her first commitment is to her job. In addition, her contributions as an informal leader go far in sustaining the group. She is a focal point and might well be the one able to rebuild the group's cohesion after the layoffs have been completed. Zelda is probably a keeper.

Murray Mangino

Reasons for retaining: He is well connected throughout the company; he has determination; he has lots of bills to pay.

Reasons for laying off: He does not handle time pressures well; he is not a "star."

Special considerations: Murray apparently plays an important role in tying the unit to the rest of the company. However, Murray's problems with time pressures are not likely to get any better when the workforce has been cut and fewer engineers are going to be sharing the load. Whether to keep or cut Murray is a toss-up decision.

Matt Peebles

Reasons for retaining: He is becoming a star; Zelda values him; he has special skills (detail-oriented/troubleshooter/on-site skills); he has good relationships with clients; he needs the income to support his mother.

Reasons for laying off: He is HIV-positive (although he will lose his long-term health benefits); fear of reaction of Matt's colleagues.

Special considerations: Having tested HIV-positive certainly makes Matt a health risk and a potential drain on the company's health insurance plan, but he doesn't have AIDS and information on the relationship between the test and the onset of AIDS is unclear. Moreover, firing someone because she or he has AIDS is a discriminatory practice. A New York Appeals Court, in a case in which a waiter was fired, said: "We note that the discharge of the complainant immediately after his condition became known supports findings of impermissible discrimination..." (*The Boston Sunday Globe*, 6/2/91, p. 80).

Matt is performing a number of specialized functions for the unit—and performing them well. In addition, laying him off could have serious implications in terms of Zelda and her productivity and position as informal leader.

Robert Anderson Selkirk

Reasons for retaining: He is a star; he is a minority; he is in the middle of a project to which he is important; Zelda is impressed by him; he will need the money to support his new child.

Reasons for laying off: He does not have seniority; his wife is professional and probably earns a good income; you have other minorities in the unit (Asian, female).

Special considerations: While Robert is important to maintain government-mandated diversity, far more important are Robert's skills as an engineer. The fact that Zelda, as the informal leader of the unit, is impressed by him, is important. As with Zelda and the others, the need for the job should not be a consideration. Robert probably should be retained.

Eugene Stapleton

Reasons for retaining: He is a good engineer; he has an important specialty; he helps win contracts; he depends on the childcare benefits offered.

Reasons for laying off: He is apparently not a star; he can't work nights and weekends.

Special considerations: Eugene seems like a really nice guy in a tough spot. His expertise in the design of cooling systems for boats makes him a valuable employee, but his inability to work nights and weekends at a time when the workload is going to be concentrated may result in some resentment from the rest of the group. Whether to keep or cut Eugene is a toss-up decision.

Wei Tan

Reasons for retaining: He has excellent skills; he is willing and able to work nights and weekends; the group has protective feelings towards him; he needs the money; he is a minority.

Reasons for laying off: His language skills cause problems; he has no seniority.

Special considerations: Tan's communication problems could become an issue in stressful times such as those which appear to be coming. The fact that he needs the money should not be a consideration. However, the fact that Tan's skills as an engineer are well above average, and the fact that he has demonstrated a willingness to commit himself to whatever needs to be done, probably make him someone who should be kept on. Tan might be a candidate for the next round of layoffs—should that come.

Adam Twersky

Reasons for retaining: Someone in the executive office has an interest in him; promises were made to him; he is hard working; he has expertise in planning; he let you use his car.

Reasons for laying off: His skills are average; he does not have seniority; he doesn't have a family to support.

Special considerations: Since you have no way of knowing just what the plans are for Adam, chances are he should be on your cut list. His skills as an engineer are apparently below average, and his special expertise is severely limited.

Additional Thoughts and Areas for Discussion

In looking over the reasons for retaining and for laying off, students should begin to pare the list. However, they need to do so based on uniform criteria. To make the decision to keep one employee because she or he has seniority and to keep another who does not have seniority but who needs the job is both inappropriate and unfair. More pragmatically, it can open the organization to suits for wrongful dismissal because uniform standards were not applied.

Among the common issues on which the engineers could be retained or laid off are seniority, need for the job/money, personality considerations, and engineering skills. While some students might argue for a decision made along the lines of seniority, solid engineering skills probably better meet the needs of the organization. This issue is rich fodder for classroom discussion.

At least one additional issue needs to be considered—that of future layoffs. Here the manager might do well to agree to make more cuts at this juncture. William A. Brandt, Jr., president of Development Specialists, Inc., consultants to distressed companies, suggests that cutting more than need to be cut from the outset results in less insecurity and a better recovery. "Once you're done," he says, "call a meeting of those you've chosen as your recovery team. Tell them why you made the cuts you did, that there won't be anymore, and that you're counting on them to see you through" (*WSJ*, B2, 5/29/91).

Suggested Outline and Timing

1. Set-up (full class: 5 minutes)

Go over instructions and learning objectives.

2. *Individual scoring (25 minutes)*

Have students:

- Read the background information and the profiles on each of the engineers.
- List the reasons for retaining and for laying off each of the engineers.
- Note who they will lay off and who they will retain.

3. *Exercise (small groups: 40 minutes)*

Divide the class into groups of five to seven students.

Ask groups to discuss the characters, and come to a group consensus on who they will retain and who they will lay off.

4. *Report-out and discussion (open-ended)*

34

GIVING NEGATIVE FEEDBACK POSITIVELY

Group Size: Any number individuals or small groups.

Recommended Time: 90–120 minutes (5 minutes for set-up; 10 minutes for initial role play; 5–10 minutes for discussion; 20–25 minutes for second role play and discussion; 20–30 minutes to prepare action plan; 5 minutes per group for report out; open-ended discussion).

Provided: Instructions.

Also Required: No additional materials required.

Facilities: One large room with moveable chairs.

Objectives

- To explore the managerial task of giving feedback to employees
- To consider how to make feedback useful
- To practice the skills of giving helpful feedback

Background

This role play is designed to help students practice the skills of giving feedback, particularly when the feedback is negative. The role play should be used at least twice, as each time it is completed and analyzed by the full class there are learnings for the subsequent role players. Class discussion should include how effectively the manager handled Chris's anger.

The role play is meant to take place in front of the full class.

Suggested Outline and Timing

1. *Set-up (full class: 5 minutes)*

   Go over the instructions, learning objectives, and the "Questions for Discussion."

2. *Role play (full class: 10 minutes)*

   Select role players either from volunteers or at random.

3. *Discussion (full class: 5–10 minutes)*

   Examine what the role players, particularly the manager, did well, and what could have been improved.

4. *Repeat Steps 1 and 2 above (20–25 minutes)*

   Additional time is given for the role play and discussion, as more information on how best to conduct the steps is now available.

5. *Preparing an action plan (small groups: 20–30 minutes)*

   Working in small groups, students should prepare an action plan to help Chris improve. Each group should select a spokesperson to report their plan to the class.

6. *Report out and discussion (5 minutes per group, plus open-ended discussion)*

   Be sure to explore how students feel the manager should proceed as Chris meets or fails to meet the goals set out in the action plan.

35

THE EYES HAVE IT

Group size: Any number of dyads.

Recommended time: 90 minutes (35 minutes for the exercise; 15 minutes for discussion within the dyad; 40 minutes for report out and open-ended discussion).

Provided: All instructions and descriptions.

Also Required: No additional materials required.

Facilities: A large room with moveable chairs or several small break out rooms.

Objectives

- To emphasize the value of face-to-face communication
- To examine the cues and information that body language provides

Background

This exercise is designed to help students recognize and appreciate the value of face-to-face communication.

With communication increasingly limited to voice- and e-mail, many individuals have come to prefer these more impersonal methods of communication. Such electronic communication largely eliminates having to deal with emotions and/or responses.

By working through this exercise, students are able to see that face-to-face communication can provide important cues regarding the receiver's response to the sent message that more impersonal, "blind" methods of communication cannot.

Discussion

Discussion should focus on having students compare their experiences between the back-to-back and face-to-face communications. Areas to explore are:

- How did it feel to communicate blindly with someone else?
- Did the speaker feel heard and/or understood?
- Was the receiver engaged in the communication?
- What is one able to learn via body language and facial expressions?

- Why might the information learned be advantageous?

Students should be able to identify instances in which it would be appropriate or inappropriate for a manager to use each method of communication.

Suggested Outline and Timing

1. *Set-up (full class: 5 minutes)*

   Briefly review the learning objectives. Assign students to dyads by any method. The student instructions are self-explanatory and should be reviewed in the dyads.

2. *Exercise (dyads: 30 minutes for exercise, 15 minutes for discussion within dyads)*

   The exercise is broken into two parts: 10 minutes for remote communication and 20 minutes for face-to-face communication. See student instructions for an in-depth explanation.

3. *Report out and discussion (open-ended)*

   Students should explore the benefits and drawbacks of remote and face-to-face communication with regard to time required, depth of understanding, clarity of message, and general relationship areas and their short- and long-term implications.

36

KAREN CARLIN

Even though we have included the Karen Carlin case in the section, "Interpersonal Processes in Organizations," it can also be useful for exploring issues of motivation, leadership, group decision making, participative management, conflict, change, and ethics. However, in teaching this case, it is probably important to focus on only one or two areas. Students often find it most helpful to begin by doing a symptom analysis rather than a character analysis as they attempt to "crack" this case.

Analyzing the group dynamics of the schedule typists' office can identify several problems, e.g., the existence of an informal group that overlaps the formal group and that is deliberately restricting production; the establishment and enforcement of group norms that hinder rather than help the organization; and the social, security, and identity needs that belonging to this group affords to its members. Many examples of each of these are cited throughout the case.

Students are generally quick to pick up the group norm that actively discourages group members from working too hard and too fast. They also note that the group members are cohesive and cover for one another with a kind of "us against them" mentality. Be sure that students are aware of the symbols which both form the group's self-identification and help assure its separation from the rest of the organization. The group's embracing of the label "black sheep," for example, turns out to be both impetus and inspiration for group members who find clever ways to beat the system. For example, the use of the elevator telephone is an almost diabolical means of circumventing imposed restrictions on telephone use.

The counterproductive dynamics of the group are reinforced by other influences: Frazier's insistence that the group do things his way may be the key source of discontent and unwillingness to cooperate. There is evidence in the case that the group members have several ideas on how to improve performance: Frazier has ignored their suggestions. Students should consider what Frazier is doing to cause the behavior presented and what he ought to be doing to change the work ethic.

Group Development

This group has gone through the stages of formation and has become highly cohesive. They "cover for one another," as well as support one another in their escapades. Karen's introduction into the group is as a deviant who ultimately conforms to the counterproductive norms and thus becomes a full-fledged member. Her appointment to a leadership role has the potential to once again make a deviant of her. Virtually any management approach that she uses will probably send the group back through the stages of formation.

Sources of Conflict and Change

Understanding the conflict management problems in the case requires students to identify the sources of conflict such as perceptions—correct and incorrect—that the key players have about one another, and to identify their roles and responsibilities.

Students could also examine the forces that are operating at Hepplewhite and Boyce that drive and restrict the necessary changes for the entire organization and for the schedule typists' group. A Force Field Analysis based on what Karen Carlin's goals ought to be might highlight low productivity and high wages as driving change and perceptions by group members of their place in the organization, the high cohesion level of the group, and the negative work ethic as resisting.

Leadership and Sources of Power

The leadership styles exhibited by Frazier (the formal leader), Carlin (the newly appointed leader), and Pauline (the informal leader), also are worth analysis. There is a shift in power relations as Carlin, younger and less experienced than the other workers, is granted legitimate power over the others. Carlin will need to use her bases of power, other than those granted to her formally by the organization, if she is going to be allowed to lead. Rather than using coercive power, which most likely will result in more acting out, she might try using reward power (praise, recognition, and a restructuring of incentives) and perhaps referent power (articulating a vision for the group through expressions of her personal magnetism).

Motivation

Expectancy theory might also be applied to this case. The workers currently expect to receive more work, not praise or valued rewards, for being efficient. Alternatively, if they work slowly, they are rewarded by having their excess work given to others.

Recommendations

The quality of recommendations for this case will vary depending on how effectively students have been able to define the problem. (See "Techniques for Problem Solving and Heightening Creativity" on Page 14 of the student text.) "Changing Frazier" is not an acceptable recommendation. He is not going to go away—nor does the case give Carlin the ability to change him. However, she might change his role, becoming a buffer between him and the group.

Possible recommendations to Carlin include:

1. Find out what it is that the workers value and provide these as rewards based on performance. Stop rewarding negative behavior.

2. Ask group members, either individually or as a group, for their ideas and suggestions for generating solutions to current problems and work with them to implement their suggestions.

3. Work with the informal leader, Pauline, to alter detrimental norms and to develop beneficial group norms that will increase the group's effectiveness.

4. Develop positive ways to meet the group's social/identity needs to replace the negative "black sheep" identity they now have. Find ways to integrate the group, now alienated and isolated both physically and psychologically, into the rest of the organization.

Ethical Considerations

Karen's ethical dilemma with Jane Thorley should not be overlooked. She cannot go back and remake her original decision to lie in order to get her job. Students should consider their perceptions of her initial decision to accept the job, the consequences they believe she and others may have suffered as a result of her decision, why they think she is now having difficulty with that decision, and how the decision fits into their own ethical framework. Because there is probably no "right" answer to what she should do now, it is rich territory for discussion. In addition, the ethics of the new suggestions by Jane Thorley should be considered.

37

A STRAW IS A STRAW IS A STRAW – EXCEPT IN THE HANDS OF A HIGH PERFORMANCE TEAM

Group Size: Any number of groups of six to eight.

Recommended Time: 60 minutes (5 minutes to set-up; 25 minutes to complete the model building; 15 minutes for small group discussion; 15 minutes for large group report outs and discussion).

Provided: Background and instructions.

Also Required: About 100 plastic or paper drinking straws per group. Flip charts, white boards, etc., are useful for report outs. We have found a video of the *60 Minutes* program "Pinchas Zukerman and the St. Paul Chamber Orchestra" useful in illustrating the learning points of this exercise.

Facilities: A large room, with moveable chairs and sufficient space to ensure at least six feet between groups. Tables for holding models.

Objectives

- To provide students an opportunity to objectively analyze the impact a leader's behavior has on their individual performance
- To demonstrate the impact of leadership on team performance
- To help students understand the leadership elements that make a leader succeed or fail

Background

Being an effective leader requires conveying a clear vision, helping one's followers reach a shared understanding, and coaching the followers to perform at optimal levels. It requires recognizing the needs and special talents of each individual in terms of what that individual is best able to bring to the task. It also means using the individual's talents to the fullest and in the best interests of the team.

In most situations, natural tensions of the workplace deny employees opportunities to objectively analyze the elements of leadership. Instead, time pressures, concerns about success, concerns about job security, and so forth, generally result in emotional rather than clear and rational understandings of what works and what doesn't work for leaders and followers. This exercise gives students a chance to step back and analyze what succeeds for them and what kinds of leadership behavior get the best results.

Suggested Outline and Timing

1. Set-up (full class: 5 minutes)

Briefly review the learning objectives; ask students to get into their groups. Distribute the straws. The instructions are self-explanatory and should be reviewed in the groups.

Stress that participants should read the discussion questions and "What to Look For" prior to starting. Stress that this exercise is about the roles of leaders and followers in high performance teams and understanding, meeting and exceeding customer needs—not about how well they can erect buildings from straws. The latter is merely a vehicle.

Tell the participants at what time they must stop building (approximately 25 minutes), and give a signal to begin.

2. Exercise (small groups: 25 minutes)

Students will ask whether they may use additional materials. Do not go beyond saying "yes." Avoid making suggestions or helping students locate materials. As part of the class discussion at the completion of the exercise, explore with students how they discovered their personal and material resources.

When the time is up, give a clear signal to stop all construction.

3. Debrief (small groups: 15 minutes)

Ask the participants to debrief in their groups, using the discussion questions and "What to Look For" as a guide.

Have each group select two reporters—one to present the building and how it meets the needs of the customer, the other to describe the leadership and process.

4. Discussion (15 minutes minimum: not more than 4 minutes for each group)

Ask the reporters from each group to:

- display their models.
- briefly describe what their goals were, as defined by their leaders.
- briefly describe how they went about carrying out their leader's missions.
- briefly describe one leadership behavior that worked well and one that didn't.

Encourage applause after each report out.

38

TWO LEADERSHIP FISHBOWLS
Fishbowl #1

Group Size: Ideally not larger than 25.

Recommended Time: 90 minutes (5 minutes for set up; 15–20 minutes for fish discussion; 15–20 minutes for observations; and 10–15 minutes for general discussion; 10–15 minutes for completion of definition).

Provided: Instructions.

Also Required: No additional materials required.

Facilities: Room large enough for students to sit in a circle.

Objectives

- To examine the elements of poor and good leadership
- To examine the participants' experiences with good and poor leadership
- To practice the important leadership skill of active listening

Background

While students sometimes groan at having to "be quiet and listen" to what their peers have to say, they are invariably surprised by just how much they are able to hear and learn. The fishbowl technique has a duel purpose—practice in listening skills along with practice in articulating what they have heard. (See "Using Experiential Exercises in the Study of Organizational Behavior," Page 6, and "Active Listening," Page 9, in the student text.)

In using fishbowls, it is important to put students on notice at the outset that everyone will be required to participate, that they are not to take notes, and that they are not to speak unless given permission to do so.

Generally, the best discussions have evolved from descriptions of bad leaders. (See Step 1, Option 2, below.) Virtually every student has had experience with someone who has been aloof, nonresponsive, abusive, moody, or has failed to give clear directions. One student reported working digging holes and laying foundations for a swimming pool company. He told his horrified classmates that the site superintendent found it amusing to kick dirt into the hole and onto the backs of the workers. Another student reported working for a kitchenware store in which he was told to stack glasses, but when he asked where and how, he was told to figure it out for himself. Turning the descriptions of actions into descriptions of poor leadership characteristics, and then reconstructing them to develop an understanding of good leadership is a useful first step to uncovering just what leadership is all about.

French and Raven's sources of social power can sometimes provide a useful framework for understanding what the fish have described. Theory X and Theory Y also provide useful models for analyzing the leaders.

A few helpful hints:

1. Avoid the temptation to jump in during awkward moments in the fish discussion. Generally, one or two of the fish will jump in to organize the others and get them going. This is leadership, the evolution of which has probably just happened before the students' eyes.

2. Do not allow students, other than the fish, to speak during that fish phase of the exercise. Monitor this carefully. When those outside the fishbowl are speaking, do not allow the fish to speak. This forces the groups to listen to one another.

3. Warn students that as you go around the room it will get harder to think of something new to say.

4. Do not allow note-taking, as it is virtually impossible to write and listen at the same time.

5. This is a good opportunity to put those students who have difficulty speaking in class in a more comfortable position for participation since everyone is doing it. We try to get to those people within the first ten speakers in the round robin phase, but not first or last.

6. Long-lasting results among students who have been chosen as fish are evident. Because both instructors and peers pay close attention to the fish, students who play fish often find this a point of validation. It has not been unusual for those who have been the "fish" to go on to be leaders in their group projects despite earlier, more passive or reticent roles. At the very least, there is a marked change in classroom behavior.

7. During the reporting of observations, it is useful for the instructor to repeat, in different words, what she or he believes the student to have said and then ask that student for corrective feedback, e.g., "So you are suggesting that good leaders listen to what their workers have to say?" This models active listening and affords an opportunity to praise the student briefly for having made an important observation.

   Restating a student's observations can also be an opportunity for an instructor to interpret to the class what an international student who speaks English as a second language has said. Our method for dealing with not being able to understand what it is the student has said has been to say, "Tell me more." This often gives validation to the student that his or her ideas can be understood and are meaningful. Students who speak English as a first language are often more willing to listen to the international students after this has taken place.

8. Photocopy the various definitions or lists, and use them as a basis for later discussion.

Suggested Outline and Timing

1. Set-up (full class: 5 minutes)

- Go over instructions and learning objectives.
- Remind students that they are not to take notes.

- Explain to students what will be expected of them after the fish discussion. This helps keep them alert while the fish are talking.
- Select the five fish and arrange the remainder of the students around them.

2. *Fish Phase (20 minutes)*

Ask students to:

Option 1. Think about people for or with whom they have worked and who they felt were good leaders.

Option 2. Think about people for or with whom they have worked and who they felt were poor leaders.

Students on the outside of the fishbowl are not to speak while the fish are speaking. Their job is to observe, listening for common threads as well as differences in what they are hearing. Those outside the fishbowl should listen carefully but not take notes.

If there is a lag in the conversation, it is important for everyone, including the facilitator, to resist the temptation to jump in and help. It is not unusual for such lags to occur at the very beginning of the exercise and again before the onset of the general discussion that takes place among the fish after each has told his or her story.

3. *Observer report-out (15–20 minutes, depending on size of group)*

Going around the class, every student on the outside of the fishbowl should report on one thing that he or she has heard about the elements of leadership discussed by the fish. During this phase, the fish are not allowed to talk. These common elements should be listed in a visible place.

4. *Observer-fish exchange (10–15 minutes)*

When the observation list has been completed, exchange and general discussion between the fish and the observers may take place.

5. *Defining leadership (small groups: 10–15 minutes)*

When the first four steps have been completed, the class should be divided into groups of five or six. If possible, there should be at least one fish in each group. Working in these small groups, students should do one of the following:

Option 1: Develop a 25 to 50 word definition of leadership that begins with the phrase "A good leader is…" and incorporates at least three to five elements of good leadership.

Option 2: Develop a list of the personal and interpersonal traits, skills, and abilities you would like to see in a leader.

6. *Report-out and discussion (open-ended)*

Fishbowl #2*

Objectives

- To observe the process of leadership as it emerges in a group discussion
- To examine the elements of poor and good leadership
- To practice the important leadership skill of active listening
- To explore cultural differences in how effective leadership is perceived

Procedure

1. *Set-up and debate (20 minutes: 5 minutes for set-up; 15 minutes for debate)*

Give students a topic to debate for 15 minutes. Select six students, at random or from volunteers, to debate each side of the issue (three on each side). These students will be the "fish" and should sit in a small circle in the center of the class (or in a central place where they can be seen and heard by the other members of the class). During the debate, the fish may only speak with the other fish.

Students on the outside of the fishbowl are not to speak while the fish are speaking. Their job is to observe the debate. Tell the observers that they will be asked to comment on what they have observed regarding leadership.

They should listen carefully but not take notes.

Note: If there is a lag in the conversation, resist the temptation to jump in. Such lags tend to occur at the very beginning of the exercise and again before the onset of the general discussion that takes place among the fish after each has voiced his or her opinion.

2. *Observations (15–20 minutes, depending on the size of the group)*

Going around the class in order, every student on the outside of the fishbowl should comment on one thing that she or has observed with regard to leadership. During this part of the fishbowl exercise, the fish are not allowed to speak.

List the observations in a visible place.

* These case notes for "Fishbowl #2" were written by Sandi Deacon Carr. Used with permission.

3. *Discussion of observations (5–10 minutes)*

When the observation list has been completed, exchange and general discussion between the fish and the observers may take place. The discussion should focus on the comments and observations made, not on renewing the debate.

4. *Class discussion of leadership observations (open-ended)*

Drawing from the comments made, a focused discussion of the elements of leadership should take place. Discussion points might include:

- Examining the issues of power and influence in the group as they relate to leadership.
  Who had the most influence? Why?
  Who talked the most?
  Who sounded most like an expert? Did that person have more or less influence? Why?
  Was anyone able to change or sway your opinion on the issue? Why?
- Examining cultural differences.
- Examining the importance of active listening and its role in leadership.
- Examining the process of the discussion.
  Who started the discussion?
  How and/or by whom was it determined who would speak and when?
  Did the fish listen to each other, talk over each other, or interrupt each other?

5. *Small group exercise (10–15 minutes)*

When the first four steps have been completed, divide the class into groups of five or six. If possible, there should be at least one fish in each group. Working in these small groups, have students do one of the following:

Option 1: Develop a 25 to 50 word definition of leadership that begins with the phrase "A good leader is..." and incorporates at least three to five elements of good leadership.

Option 2: Develop a list of the personal and interpersonal traits, skills, and abilities you would like to see in a leader.

6. *Report-out and discussion (open-ended)*

Have students report their results to the class. Discussion should follow.

39

THE GREAT POST-IT® MASSACRE

Leadership

The Hersey-Blanchard Life Cycle Model suggests that as workers become more "willing and able" to do their jobs, they can be given increased amounts of autonomy, whereas learning a new job generally requires more direct supervision. [See Moorhead and Griffin, *Organizational Behavior*, 6th ed. (Boston: Houghton Mifflin Company, 2001), Chapter 13.] The theory refers to workers who do not know how to do jobs or new job tasks as M1 workers who need a telling style of leadership, including task-related directions. As a worker begins to learn the rudiments of a task, the leader must do more selling or encouraging of the worker to continue in the learning path. As a worker has begun to master the task and needs fewer instructions and handholding, high levels of encouragement should continue. Finally, when the worker has mastered the job, she or he needs both minimum direction and minimum prodding and/or encouragement to continue learning.

Followership and Motivation

Beverly Sadowsky appears to be well able to understand the followership needs of Bob Scanlan. With most new tasks, she appears to take him through the stages of the Life Cycle Model at varying rates, using telling, selling, participating, and delegating according to Bob's needs. In turn, Bob seems to do the same with his employees. (There are many examples of Bob's and Beverly's use of the various stages of the life cycle throughout the case, which students should be able to cite in support of their arguments.)

George Fishman, on the other hand, micromanages Bob's every move. Bob has needs for growth—he welcomes challenges and the opportunity and encouragement Beverly gives him with regard to taking courses—and he is driven largely by ego and esteem needs. He appears to find George's highly telling style of leadership demeaning, and his motivational needs are thus undermined. Bob's ego and esteem needs, however, are partly fulfilled by the pride he appears to take in receiving compliments from others in the organization. ("He prided himself on making his boss and the department 'look good.'") To achieve this, Bob treats his employees the way he himself wants to be treated, i.e., he follows them through the life cycle, adjusting his leadership style to their individual needs in order to get the optimal performance out of each.

George's leadership style appears to be driven by ego and esteem needs and an apparent need for power. ("Follow the instructions I give you. When I want your input, I'll ask for it.") It appears that it is important to him to look good to the outside world ("If you make a mistake, I'm going to get blamed for it, and I don't want that.") and to maintain control over his environment. This means looking over the shoulder of any subordinate and closely monitoring his or her work.

Beverly's needs are a little less clear. She does not appear to be as driven to fulfill her ego and esteem needs through her position as COO as does George in his position as first vice president, and she appears instead to be willing to take risks that others might make mistakes that could reflect on her. Whereas George appears not to be willing to take the risk inherent in delegating responsibility, Beverly seems perfectly comfortable with doing so once she has set the stage. Bob's need for autonomy meshes perfectly with Beverly's willingness to relinquish and/or share control and her interest in not being bogged down by the day-to-day workings of the office.

It would not be surprising to find some students arguing that Beverly should fire or otherwise take action with regard to George, although it is unclear whether he is still within her span of control. Chances are, George isn't going to change, but he might benefit from some support from Beverly who has already done the job that he is just learning. As a mentor, Beverly might act as an informal leader for George, walking him through the tasks of the job and moving him through the stages of the life cycle until he is more able to do his job. As part of this, Beverly might gently suggest using Bob as a resource and promote an understanding of the ways in which Bob can be the most productive.

As for Beverly's advice to Bob, chances are she might urge him to keep looking for and preparing for other opportunities. After all, she encouraged him to take courses and also encouraged him to acquire additional skills. In doing so, she seemed to recognize that Bob would need to move along into new challenges. In the meantime, she might well suggest that Bob do his best and follow George's directives exactly.

Questions 3 and 4 in this case are largely for students' personal opinions, many of whom will have bosses who use the wrong style of leadership with them.

40

WHO WORKS SATURDAY NIGHT?

Group Size: Any number of groups of five to seven.

Recommended Time: 90 minutes (5 minutes to set up; 10 minutes for individual preparation; 30 minutes exercise; 10 minutes to score manager; remainder report out and discussion).

Provided: Instructions and Observer Sheets in student text. Role descriptions for managers and workers in the *Instructor's Manual* to be photocopied and distributed in class.

Also Required: No additional materials required.

Facilities: One large room with moveable chairs or a number of small break out rooms.

Objectives

- To explore leadership styles—autocratic, democratic, and laissez faire
- To examine the effectiveness of the different styles in decision-making situations
- To examine the impact of leadership styles on subordinates

Background

This exercise was developed to help students understand the complexities of decision making and the responsibilities of a leader in making decisions; explore their own styles in the management of decision making processes and the possible responses to those styles; and consider the role of participative decision making in managing change.

There is no single "right" solution to this exercise. Any solution may be complicated by concerns for the integrity of the project, the company, the group, and the individuals. The health of the company, job security, and team and project success are some of the areas that will be impacted by the quality of the decision made. It is the manager's job to be sure that the individuals participating in the decision-making process are aware of these implications.

There are some cultural issues to be considered in this exercise. Japanese students, for example, often point out that in Japan, work—and allegiance to one's work group—take precedence over family and other obligations. South American students, however, often argue that family comes first. This can be a rich area for discussion in a diverse classroom.

Be sure to make enough copies of each role so that each member of the class has one role description.

Suggested Outline and Timing

1. Set-up (full class: 5 minutes)

- Go over the background, instructions, and learning objectives.
- Remind students that they will have 30 minutes to reach a decision.
- Divide students into groups, and distribute roles to all but the managers. It is a good idea to have decided who will play the managers in advance of the class.
- If your groups are larger than five, assign some students the role of observer or double up on roles.

Optional: After distributing the roles to the members of each group, divide the class into groups of same role members, i.e., all managers together, all employees with the employee one description together, etc. This gives individuals a chance to identify with and better understand their roles. Give groups about 10 minutes to discuss their roles and plan out their possible strategies. (Make clear that individuals may play their roles as they wish and are not bound by the group's suggested strategies.)

2. Exercise preparation (small groups: 10 minutes)

- Ask students who have been handed roles to read them carefully and think about how they will justify their positions.
- Ask all students to carefully read the questions on the "Observer Sheet" and the "Questions for Discussion."
- Ask those who have been selected to be managers to leave the room and wait for you outside the classroom.
- Meet briefly with the managers. Distribute their roles to them, having approximately equal numbers of autocratic, laissez-faire, and democratic managers. Give them clear instructions on how they are to play their roles.

  Highly autocratic: Those who play autocratic managers may listen to the employees but should make clear from the outset that the decision is going to come from management. Autocratic managers should say things such as "I don't really care about your brother's wedding," etc.

  Extremely laissez fare: These managers should constantly remind workers that the decision is of no interest to management. In other words, workers should be told, "do whatever you want," etc.

  Democratic: These managers should clearly frame the problem for workers, listen to their concerns, and actively lead them to a solution that has the widest acceptance while meeting the needs of the organization.
- Send managers back into the classroom with instructions to begin the role play. Managers should be clear that they are to model the behavior of their type of leader, e.g., autocratic, but not name it or describe it.

3. *Exercise (small groups: 30 minutes)*

- Give students a 5-minute warning after 25 minutes.
- Remind students to select a spokesperson.

4. *Scoring (first individually, and then as a group: 10 minutes)*

- Ask students to read the scoring instructions, and rate their managers accordingly.

5. *Report-out and discussion (full class: 30 minutes)*

- Ask students to report their scores, and record these in a visible place.
- Ask the managers to explain to the class what their instructions were.
- Discuss the implications for motivation and productivity.

Autocratic Manager

You are an autocratic manager in a division of Turnem, Inc. Currently, your team is working to complete the prototype for a valve that has a highly specialized use in the aerospace industry. A presentation is to be made on Monday to the industry's highest officials.

To get the project done, you and one member of your team will have to work this Saturday from about 5 p.m. to at least midnight. *Everyone will have to work at least twelve hours on Sunday.* To successfully complete the work, your team will have to function at its highest and most cooperative level on Sunday.

The work that must be completed Saturday night will take a high degree of technical knowledge and competence.

It is your job to decide who will work Saturday night. Your choices are the following:

- Employees 1 and 2, each of whom has the technical knowledge and ability necessary for the tasks that must be completed. Both have other commitments.
- Employee 3, who has the necessary technical knowledge and skills, but who is completely unwilling to work.
- Employee 4 has little of the necessary technical knowledge, needs the money, and very much wants to work.

Your budget will cover *only one* employee to work with you on Saturday night.

You don't really care what the conflicts and concerns of your subordinates may be. That isn't your problem! Your problem is to get the right person to do the job, and you intend to get the person you want, no matter what.

Listen to the concerns of your subordinates—but, make clear from the outset that you'll decide and they'll just have to live with your decision. Keep reinforcing that point whenever possible.

Tell your group only that you are their manager; do not tell them that you have been instructed to be autocratic.

Laissez-Faire Manager

You are a laissez-faire manager in a division of Turnem, Inc. Currently, your team is working to complete the prototype for a valve that has a highly specialized use in the aerospace industry. A presentation is to be made on Monday to the industry's highest officials.

To get the project done, you and one member of your team will have to work this Saturday from about 5 p.m. to at least midnight. *Everyone will have to work at least twelve hours on Sunday.* To successfully complete the work, your team will have to function at its highest and most cooperative level on Sunday.

The work that must be completed Saturday night will take a high degree of technical knowledge and competence.

It is your job to decide who will work Saturday night. Your choices are the following:

- Employees 1 and 2, each of whom has the technical knowledge and ability necessary for the tasks that must be completed. Both have other commitments.
- Employee 3, who has the necessary technical knowledge and skills, but who is completely unwilling to work.
- Employee 4 has little of the necessary technical knowledge, needs the money, and very much wants to work.

Your budget will cover *only one* employee to work with you on Saturday night.

You don't really care what the conflicts and concerns of your subordinates might be. That isn't your problem—it's theirs!

Listen to the concerns of your subordinates—but, make clear from the beginning that you're not going to interfere. While they're struggling with the problem, doodle, walk around, read the newspaper, or do anything other than pay attention to their struggles. Of course, you will want to let them know from time to time that they're probably not making the right decision.

Tell your group only that you are their manager; do not tell them that you have been instructed to be laissez-faire.

Democratic Manager

You are a democratic-style manager in a division of Turnem, Inc. Currently, your team is working to complete the prototype for a valve that has a highly specialized use in the aerospace industry. A presentation is to be made on Monday to the industry's highest officials.

To get the project done, you and one member of your team will have to work this Saturday from about 5 p.m. to at least midnight. *Everyone will have to work at least twelve hours on Sunday.* To successfully complete the work, your team will have to function at its highest and most cooperative level on Sunday.

The work that must be completed Saturday night will take a high degree of technical knowledge and competence.

It is your job to decide who will work Saturday night. Your choices are the following:

- Employees 1 and 2, each of whom has the technical knowledge and ability necessary for the tasks that must be completed. Both have other commitments.
- Employee 3, who has the necessary technical knowledge and skills, but who is completely unwilling to work.
- Employee 4 has little of the necessary technical knowledge, needs the money, and very much wants to work.

Your budget will cover *only one* employee to work with you on Saturday night.

Since the beginning of this project, you have been working closely with the members of your team, articulating the goals, guiding the process, serving as a clearing house, and involving the employees in decision-making processes that directly affect them.

Begin by setting out the goals and purposes of having the best person work on Saturday night. Put this in terms of their best interests and the best interests of the organization. Listen to the concerns of your subordinates, and help them achieve an outcome that is mutually beneficial and acceptable.

Tell your group only that you are their manager; do not tell them that you have been instructed to be democratic.

Employee 1

You are a member of a team at Turnem, Inc. The project on which you are working, development of a prototype valve having a highly specialized use in the aerospace industry, is due to be demonstrated to the highest officials of the aerospace program on Monday.

To be ready on time, it is necessary for you and your teammates to work all day this Sunday and possibly for you to work on Saturday night from about 5 p.m. until midnight. You are one of the key experts for this project on which you have worked seven days a week for more than a month.

You consider that you have a special reason for not wanting to work on Saturday night. It's your brother's wedding, you are part of the wedding party, and your whole family will be outraged if you fail to attend. Convince your manager that you should not be required to work on Saturday night.

Employee 2

You are a member of a team at Turnem, Inc. The project on which you are working, development of a prototype valve having a highly specialized use in the aerospace industry, is due to be demonstrated to the highest officials of the aerospace program on Monday.

To be ready on time, it is necessary for you and your teammates to work all day this Sunday and possibly for you to work Saturday night from about 5 p.m. until midnight.

You have been working on the project since its inception, including many nights and weekends. At this point you're feeling pretty burned out. Worse, however, is your family's reaction. Your spouse and children are angry at what they see as your rejection of them in favor of your job.

Sunday is your spouse's birthday, and a number of friends and relatives have been invited to help celebrate the day at your home. Unfortunately, you don't have any choice about missing that event, but Saturday evening is your youngest child's debut as star in the third grade play. Your family has made it quite clear that your presence is not an option.

Convince your manager that you should not be required to work on Saturday night.

Employee 3

You are a member of a team at Turnem, Inc. The project on which you are working, development of a prototype valve having a highly specialized use in the aerospace industry, is due to be demonstrated to the highest officials of the aerospace program on Monday.

To be ready on time, it is necessary for you and your teammates to work all day this Sunday and possibly for you to work Saturday night from about 5 p.m. until midnight.

You joined the project about two months ago, and while you're no expert, you certainly have the abilities and skills to do the work that must be done on Saturday night. However, you definitely do not want to work. As far as you're concerned, you're entitled to a life outside the workplace. You're not much of a team player, and you had originally asked not to be put on this job anyway.

There was a time in your life when you would have been at the head of the line to volunteer for this job—a time when your sole purpose in life was to get ahead, make more money, and gain power, prestige, and status.

About eighteen months ago, your best friend died in a car accident. It was a shock to you to be faced suddenly with the uncertainty and fragility of life. You have decided that you had better "live life while you have it"—and that doesn't mean spending it at work.

You're angry enough that you have to work on Sunday. As far as you're concerned, someone else can work on Saturday night, because you're not going to!

Employee 4

You are a member of a team at Turnem, Inc. The project on which you are working, development of a prototype valve having a highly specialized use in the aerospace industry, is due to be demonstrated to the highest officials of the aerospace program on Monday.

To be ready on time, it is necessary for you and your teammates to work all day this Sunday and possibly for you to work Saturday night from about 5 p.m. until midnight.

You joined the team about five weeks ago and have some minimal knowledge of the project.

You have been holding off taking a moonlighting job because this project, so far, has been keeping you busy seven days a week and evenings. While you're tired, you desperately need the money.

Convince your manager to let you work on Saturday night.

41

TROUBLE WITH THE TEAM PROJECT*

Group Size: Any number of groups of four to six.

Recommended Time: 90 to 120 minutes (5 minutes to set up; 5 minutes for individual preparation; 20–25 minutes for group decision; 20 minutes for small group discussion; 5 minutes per group for report out; open-ended discussion).

Provided: All instructions, descriptions, and observer form. Roles for role play are included in this instructor's manual and should be photocopied for distribution in class.

Also Required: No additional materials required.

Facilities: A large room with moveable chairs or several small break-out rooms.

Objectives

- To develop skills in team problem solving
- To explore methods and styles of conflict resolution
- To examine the ways in which leaders influence group processes

Background

This exercise was developed to help students examine, on a personal level, issues related to team dynamics, problem solving, conflict resolution, negotiation, and/or leadership influence. It is possible to focus on only one or two of these issues.

Suggested Outline and Timing

1. Set-up (full class: 5 minutes)

- Go over the background, instructions, and learning objectives.
- Remind students that they will have 20–25 minutes to reach a decision.
- Divide students into groups, and distribute roles to all but the managers. It is a good idea to have decided who will play the managers in advance of the class.
- If your groups are larger than six, assign some students the role of observer. For teams of four, omit Roles 5 and 6. Inform the team that their "uninvolved student" (Role 5) failed to make it to this team meeting.

Be sure that the teams have enough physical space so as not to interfere with one another's discussions.

* These case notes were written by Sandi Deacon Carr. Used with permission.

2. Exercise preparation (small groups: 5 minutes)

- Ask students who have been handed their roles to read them carefully and think about how they will justify their positions.
- Ask all students to carefully read the questions on the "Observer Sheet" and the "Questions for Discussion."
- Ask those who have been selected as managers to leave the room and wait for you outside the classroom door.
- Meet briefly with the managers. Distribute their roles to them, having approximately equal numbers of autocratic, laissez-faire, and democratic managers. Give them clear instructions on how they are to play their roles. (See the role descriptions in the instructors' notes for "Who Works Saturday Night?"—the exercise that immediately precedes this exercise.)
- Send managers back into the classroom with instructions to begin the role play immediately.

3. Exercise (small groups: 20–25 minutes)

- Give students a 5 minute warning after 20 minutes.
- At 25 minutes, instruct students to stop the role play and begin the small group discussion.

4. Small group discussion (small groups: 20 minutes)

- Ask students to discuss the "Questions for Discussion" and make careful notes on their responses.
- Ask each group to select a spokesperson.

5. Report out and discussion (report out, 5 minutes per group; discussion, open-ended)

- Ask the observers, if any, and the spokespersons to report on their findings.
- Ask one of each of the three types of managers to explain to the class what his or her instructions were.

Questions for Discussion

Problem Solving

1. How did the teams go about solving this problem?
2. By what processes will the papers be completed? How did the teams arrive at these decisions?
3. What grades do the teams feel their papers are likely to get given their plan? Why?
4. Did the teams focus on their common goals in trying to resolve the problem?

Conflict

5. How are the relationships among the team members? Does anyone feel angry, insulted, or upset with the team and/or the decision? Why? (Here you may want to address some specific questions to the "international student," who generally feels very insulted and condescended to by the leader and the team.)

6. Did the teams arrive at win/win decisions? Win/lose? Lose/lose? Why?

7. What impact is this likely to have on future team performance, e.g., preparing and delivering the final presentations?

Leadership Style

8. What style of leadership did each team leader demonstrate?

9. How did this style influence each team's decision-making process?

10. Did anyone else on any of the teams emerge as a leader? When? What impact did this have on the team's ability to solve the problem?

Do not tell the other role players that your role requires you to be autocratic. Instead, convey this leadership style through the portrayal of your role.

Role 1A
The Autocratic Team Leader

You were elected leader of this team during the team's second meeting. You are an "A" student, and you are finding this team experience very frustrating because you see that many of your team members are willing to settle for less than "A" work.

As the team leader you feel that you have done a vast majority of the work, both on the project and for the team itself. You are the one who has set the meeting times, meeting agendas, and deadlines. In addition, you have tried to deal with the following issues:

- Motivating an extremely lazy team member—to no avail.
- Scheduling team meetings around members' practice schedules.
- Keeping an international student from pushing a lot of what you consider to be not-very-good ideas onto the team.
- Getting everyone else to work up to your high standards and accept your ideas for the project.

Now, the day before the project is due, you are desperate and frustrated. You feel that you have done more than enough for the team, so much so that you feel your grades in other classes have suffered. You have a major accounting exam tomorrow and had planned to study for it all night tonight.

Since you are the only team member who has consistently met every deadline, you do not feel that you should have to work on the project tonight. You are no longer willing to sacrifice your grades in other classes. Besides, your word processing skills are nowhere near as good as those of others on your team.

You approach interactions with your team in a highly autocratic manner. You may listen to what your teammates have to say, but you certainly do not have to follow their suggestions. It is your job to decide how the paper will get done, and you will tell your team members how to do it.

You basically do not care what other plans your teammates have for the evening—this paper must be their priority.

Personally, you do not intend to help write the paper yourself. You are fed up with the team—they never should have let it come down to the last night. If they had listened to you earlier, the paper would have been completed last week.

Do not tell the other role players that your role requires you to be participative. Instead, convey this leadership style through the portrayal of your role.

Role 1B
The Participative Team Leader

You were elected leader of this team during the team's second meeting. You are an "A" student, and you are finding this team experience very frustrating because you see that many of your team members are willing to settle for less than "A" work.

As the team leader you feel that you have done a vast majority of the work, both on the project and for the team itself. You are the one who has set the meeting times, meeting agendas, and deadlines. In addition, you have tried to deal with the following issues:

- Motivating an extremely lazy team member—to no avail.
- Scheduling team meetings around members' practice schedules.
- Keeping an international student from pushing a lot of what you consider to be not-very-good ideas onto the team.
- Getting everyone else to work up to your high standards and accept your ideas for the project.

Now, the day before the project is due, you are desperate and frustrated. You feel that you have done more than enough for the team, so much so that you feel your grades in other classes have suffered. You have a major accounting exam tomorrow and had planned to study for it all night tonight.

Since you are the only team member who has consistently met every deadline, you do not feel that you should have to work on the project tonight. You are no longer willing to sacrifice your grades in other classes. Besides, your word processing skills are nowhere near as good as those of others on your team.

You approach interactions with your team in a fairly open and participative manner. You are willing to listen to each team member's concerns, and you attempt to solve the problem together. You try to get a handle on each member's constraints and then construct a solution that tries to make everyone satisfied. You believe this will result in a quality paper.

Do not tell the other role players that your role requires you to be laissez-faire. Instead, convey this leadership style through the portrayal of your role.

Role 1C
The Laissez-Faire Team Leader

You were elected leader of this team during the team's second meeting. You are an "A" student, and you are finding this team experience very frustrating because you see that many of your team members are willing to settle for less than "A" work.

As the team leader you feel that you have done a vast majority of the work, both on the project and for the team itself. You are the one who has set the meeting times, meeting agendas, and deadlines. In addition, you have tried to deal with the following issues:

- Motivating an extremely lazy team member—to no avail.
- Scheduling team meetings around members' practice schedules.
- Keeping an international student from pushing a lot of what you consider to be not-very-good ideas onto the team.
- Getting everyone else to work up to your high standards and accept your ideas for the project.

Now, the day before the project is due, you are desperate and frustrated. You feel that you have done more than enough for the team, so much so that you feel your grades in other classes have suffered. You have a major accounting exam tomorrow and had planned to study for it all night tonight.

Since you are the only team member who has consistently met every deadline, you do not feet that you should have to work on the project tonight. You are no longer willing to sacrifice your grades in other classes. Besides, your word processing skills are nowhere near as good as those of others on your team.

You approach interactions with your team with an "I don't care" attitude. You listen to everyone's concerns but feel no obligation to say or decide anything. In fact, you could care less at this point how or if the paper gets done.

It is up to the members of the team to decide what happens with the project—you have done enough. Feel free to opt out of the discussion; you can even begin to study for your accounting exams or write a letter to a friend if you wish.

You should also feel free to periodically interject when you hear a bad idea, e.g., let the international student write the paper, but you refrain from helping make any decisions.

Role 2
The Varsity Athlete

You are a varsity athlete and, because you have a major game coming up on Saturday, you have practice today from 4 p.m. until at least midnight.

Your coach has made it clear that anyone who misses a practice this week will not play on Saturday. You have been working extremely hard in practice, and the coach has told you that you will get your first start on Saturday—so long as you don't miss practice.

All semester long your management class project team has been willing to rearrange, cancel, or postpone team meetings to accommodate your practice schedule. You really appreciate their understanding, and now it has paid off for you.

Now you have to tell them that you can't be there, again, to help write the paper. However, you will offer to let the team use your quiet, spacious apartment, your computer, and your laser printer all night.

Role 3
The International Student

You are an international student who has some strong ideas about how the team project for your management class should be organized and written.

You speak English fairly well but are less skilled and less confident when it comes to writing.

You have no plans for tonight and are eager to share your ideas with the team and begin writing the paper. However, you do *not* want to work with the leader of your team. The leader has been especially condescending to you all semester and never thinks that your ideas are any good. The leader also constantly complains that s/he has been doing most of the work on this project.

While you're anxious and willing to put together a good project, you draw the line at spending the night working hard, only to be criticized and put down by the team leader.

Role 4
The Sorority or Fraternity President

You are the president of your sorority or fraternity, and you have your annual Greek ball tonight. Even though you're a great typist—and of everyone in your group, you have gotten the best grades on your papers all semester—there is no way you are going to miss this ball to write the paper. You have planned for this event since the beginning of the year. A lot of your really close friends who graduated last year have come back for the ball, and your date is arriving in one hour, all the way from the University of Tennessee—at your expense.

Knowing that you would not be available tonight, you did everything you could think of to help the team. For your section of the paper, you wrote a very thoughtful and detailed analysis. You even typed it, made hard copies for everyone, and provided the team with a copy on disk so that it would be easier for them to integrate it.

Role 5
The Uninvolved Student

You just completed your interview write-up, which was supposed to have been done a week ago. You arrived at the meeting, late as usual, because you had been using the time to scribble down a few ideas about your section of the paper.

You realize that the team had agreed that each member would come to the meeting with a two-page analysis, but you had neither the time nor the desire to do it. Besides, you hate this team stuff, anyway.

As is your usual experience with team projects, you feel that no one values your opinion, least of all the team leader, who has to have everything done his/her way. You have given up trying to be a productive member, and just want to get the whole thing over with.

You have made plans to go home for the weekend. Since your team presentation is not due until next week, and there is no quiz, you feel that there is really no reason to go to class. Your plane leaves at 4:30 this afternoon, you have nonrefundable tickets, and you have told all of your friends that you are coming.

You really do not care who writes the paper, as long as it gets done. You're willing to let the team use your laptop computer.

Role 6
The Actor

You arrive at this team meeting feeling angry and frustrated with the team because so many deadlines have been missed, and you know that they are going to want you to write the paper tonight.

At this point, the project is no longer a priority for you: You have the lead part in a musical, and your dress rehearsal is tonight. You have no idea how long rehearsal will take. It starts at 6:30 p.m. With opening night tomorrow, it is likely to go all night.

You have brought a handwritten, rough draft of your two-page analysis, but you know it is not that good since you have been preoccupied with the performance.

At this point, you are willing to settle for a decent paper—not great, but decent. You feel confident that with your skills in performing, and your ideas for the presentation, your team can make up the grade with an exceptional presentation.

42

MEADOWBROOK GARDEN CENTER*

Overview

Meadowbrook Garden Center provides an excellent opportunity for discussion about leadership, satisfaction and turnover, and job design. Key theories cited in the following discussion include Hersey and Blanchard's Situational Leadership Theory and Herzberg's Two-Factor Theory.

Brief Description

Located in Raleigh, North Carolina, Meadowbrook Garden Center competes as a greenhouse/nursery in the floriculture industry. The company was started in the 1960s by Bill Ward. In 1992, Bill retired and turned over the business to his son, Jack, and Jack's wife, Rebekah. Jack works as both general manager and greenhouse supervisor, and Rebekah as retail manager.

Jack prides himself on running a high-quality business with outstanding materials. However, Jack has also begun to recognize his limitations in improving his operations. Understaffing and low performance, complicated by extensive turnover, has directed Jack's attention away from management of the Garden Center despite the 70 plus hours a week he devotes to the operation. Problems continue to surface.

A key concern is that Meadowbrook Garden Center has operated under capacity for quite some time. Despite competition from other small operations, and garden centers in Lowe's, Wal-Mart, and other large retailers, demand for Meadowbrook's plants is sufficient to increase production by as much as 25 percent without acquiring surplus stock.

The case describes Jack as a micromanager of all activities in the organization. His authoritarian style prevents employees from developing professionally, creates dissatisfaction, and prevents employees from experiencing job satisfaction and fulfillment. In addition, employees are not trained, do not have written guidelines, and are given no formal evaluation or feedback. Recruiting for new employees classifies as eligible all applicants who are not weeded out by vague hiring criteria. Employees are not matched to specific job demands.

Jack indicates he does not have enough responsible employees, yet he requires that all employees receive specific instructions for each and every task directly from him. He states that employees are incapable of accepting responsibility and that he would like to have employees who are both willing and able to perform efficiently and effectively. He fails to recognize his role in diminishing any inclination or ability in his employees to develop

* These case notes were prepared by Tracy Tuten, Randolph-Macon College. Used with permission.

expertise or to assume positions of higher responsibility. The overall result for Meadowbrook Garden Center is a high rate of turnover, an overwhelming workload for Jack, and the slow degradation of the business itself.

Answers to Questions for Discussion and Extended Discussion

1. What are the key problems facing Jack and the Meadowbrook Garden Center?
   a. There is a lack of strategic direction for the organization.
   b. Jack spends time acting as the greenhouse supervisor.
   c. Employees lack clear direction, focus, responsibility, and challenge in their jobs.
   d. No formal policy or procedures exist.
   e. Jack demands complete control over all activities, thereby undermining employee growth and accomplishment.
   f. Conflict with Jack, combined with the nature of job, creates job dissatisfaction and, eventually, turnover.
   g. Lack of competent personnel results in inefficient operations and tasks left uncompleted.

2. How would you classify Jack's leadership style? Which leadership theory might be useful for Jack as he works towards solving Meadowbrook's problems? Explain why.
   a. Jack uses an authoritarian leadership style.
   b. Hersey and Blanchard's Situational Leadership Theory is useful for characterizing Jack's desires and perceived problems in leading his employees. The theory states that there is no one best way to lead, but rather employees have a level of readiness, or ability and willingness, in handling tasks. Appropriate leadership behavior is contingent upon this level of follower readiness. Jack currently assumes low employee readiness and responds appropriately according to the theory.

3. Using job design characteristics and Herzberg's Two-Factor Theory, explain the possible causes of dissatisfaction and turnover, how turnover could be reduced, and how employees can be prepared to handle more responsibility.
   a. Employees at Meadowbrook Garden Center fit classically into Herzberg's theory. The organization has provided no policies to guide employees; supervision is domineering in nature; working conditions are poor, as evidenced by the condition of the employee breakroom; peer relationships are difficult to develop due to frequent turnover; due to frequent terminations, security is low. Motivator factors appear to be entirely absent: Employees cannot find enjoyment in the work itself or from responsibility because Jack micromanages each and every task. Advancement is not available in the organization.

b. Dissatisfaction can be minimized and turnover reduced by improving hygiene factors and motivator factors. Some suggestions:

   i. Develop a formal evaluation system for employees and formal job descriptions (hygiene factor—organizational policies).

   ii. Improve training such that employees can have more autonomy and responsibility (hygiene factor—supervision quality and motivator factor—responsibility).

   iii. Design jobs to provide challenge, perhaps by allowing employees to specialize in different plant species (motivator factors—challenge and achievement and growth).

   iv. Improve employee breakroom conditions and other environmental hazards to improve employee perceptions of working conditions (hygiene factor—working conditions).

   v. Redesign organizational structure to include another layer of management. This would allow Jack to focus on planning for the organization and other "general manager" duties while the Greenhouse receives appropriate supervision as well. This will also provide employees with opportunities for advancement (motivator factors—advancement and growth).

4. How can Jack eliminate the problem of "unable" employees in future hiring practices?

   a. Develop formal applications that request data on past experience and knowledge of industry.

   b. Develop job descriptions with specific skills and demands.

   c. Use industry trade associations such as the local Nurserymen's Association and local colleges for sources of good candidates.

   d. Develop appropriate training programs.

References and Additional Readings

Hersey, Paul, and Blanchard, Kenneth (1988). *Management of Organizational Behavior.* Englewood Cliffs: Prentice-Hall, pg. 171.

Herzberg, Frederick (1968). "One More Time: How Do You Motivate Employees?" *Harvard Business Review*, 46 (Jan/Feb), 53–62.

Herzberg, Frederick, Mausner, Bernard, and Snyderman, Barbara Bloch (1967). *The Motivation to Work*, 2nd ed. New York: John Wiley.

43

LEADERSHIP AT PRODIGY ELECTRONICS*

This case is virtually full of smoke and mirrors, and if students aren't careful, they will be easily pulled into nonfruitful areas of analysis. Concentrating on the leadership successes and failures of Cafasso—and of Jackson—should yield the most meaningful results. Concentrating on racism, as Dennis Jackson ultimately seems to realize, may go nowhere.

Dennis Jackson is baffled by Tony Cafasso's performance as a manager. He tries to pin it on racism, but as he goes through his interviews with the workers, this appears increasingly unlikely. The trend that does emerge is that Cafasso does better with seasoned workers who know their jobs and need little guidance. His democratic/participative style probably is what allowed him to be successful at his previous job in which he was charged with the leadership of a cohesive group of seasoned workers. At Prodigy, however, the younger, inexperienced workers are frustrated by Cafasso's lack of willingness to give guidance, and they wish for more direction. This aspect of the case is a clear illustration of the Hersey-Blanchard Life Cycle Model of leadership.

The case can also be analyzed using other theories. In Fiedler's terms, Cafasso is a relationship-oriented leader operating under unfavorable circumstances for that style. Accordingly, performance is not what it could and should be. Using Leader-Member Exchange Theory, the older workers are the "in" group and benefit from being in that position, while the younger workers are left out and suffer. This also undermines mutual support among the workers and fails to develop the team atmosphere called for by the nature of the work.

The fact that Cafasso "treats everyone the same" is worth worry. His treatment of SooAe Kim, for example, is problematic, as he appears insensitive to individual differences, in her case, culturally based discomfort with public praise. Surprisingly, when he invites her to criticize her manager, Jackson also appears to be insensitive to what are likely to be SooAe's cultural values that require respect for one's superiors.

Jackson's overall behavior raises some concerns as well. It appears that he not only has some of the same cultural naiveté as Cafasso, but that he also sets a highly questionable precedent by going around Cafasso in his attempt to gather information about the division and Cafasso's management of it. Nowhere is there a suggestion that he has begun where he should—with Cafasso. Both the wisdom and the ethics of this kind of management of a subordinate are worth considerable exploration.

* These notes were prepared by Scott Weighart. Used with permission.

44

TWO SUPERVISORS—A STUDY IN STYLE*

This case helps students identify some of the benefits and drawbacks of participative management and explore the ways that varying management styles can meet different needs, often determined by the required tasks and the personalities and experience of employees.

Floors One and Two at this pacemaker manufacturer are charged with performing the same task, i.e., building defect-free pacemakers. In using this case, we have found it necessary to briefly explain the function of the pacemaker, that is, a miniaturized and surgically implanted electronic device that regulates the rhythm of the heartbeat.

Make clear to students that a defect in a pacemaker may result in severe physical crisis and even death for the user.

On both floors there are older workers, younger workers, and trainees, all with different needs. Statements from members of each group on each floor make clear what their concerns and interests are. It is useful for students to compare and contrast these statements for each workgroup on each floor, e.g., older workers on Floor One with older workers on Floor Two.

In addition to the different employee needs, supervisors on each floor have different management styles. On Floor One, Mr. Martin uses an autocratic style to ensure worker productivity and quality. He neither invites nor accepts worker input. It is clear that Mr. Martin needs to exert pressure continually on many of his employees, particularly the younger ones, to ensure their continuing to work at optimum levels. This becomes most obvious when he leaves the floor.

Mr. Franklin, the supervisor on Floor Two, uses a more participative style of management. This leads some of his employees to feel insecure about who might be overseeing quality and who will take the blame should a mistake be made. Other employees, however, feel they have a personal stake in seeing that mistakes are not made.

Students analyzing this case should consider the following:

- How does involving employees in decision making benefit them?
- How does involving employees in decision making benefit managers?
- How does involving employees in decision making benefit an organization?

Students should be encouraged to consider for which of the two bosses they would prefer to work and why.

Among the conclusions of students analyzing this case should be the recognition that involving employees generally improves morale, quality, and productivity, develops problem-solving skills, and captures experience and expertise. Employees can be involved through meetings, quality improvement teams, job design, and goal setting. Employee involvement may be limited due to work pace and in times of crisis. When commitment to a policy, practice, or idea is needed, especially when change is introduced or contemplated, employee involvement may be critical.

This case becomes the most interesting when students begin to examine which floor's pacemakers they would most trust. Students appear to relate to this questions best when posed as, "One of your parents needs a pacemaker. From which floor would you buy one?"

Be sure students are required to justify their answers.

45

THE FIRST FEDERAL BANK

This case requires students to consider not only what constitutes appropriate leadership, but the ways in which leadership style and the use and/or misuse of power can impact motivation and performance.

Sources of Power[1]

Each individual in the case has and uses various sources of power. There is no evidence that anyone other than Karina abuses power in any way.

Susan's main sources of power are expert and referent. Expert power is demonstrated by the fact that Susan has received several promotions during her time at the bank, is described as being competent, and is given many additional responsibilities by Stefan. Her referent power is evident in that she is well-liked by both superiors and colleagues.

Liz has all five sources of power and uses all but coercive power. She uses legitimate power in her role as Susan's supervisor. Along with legitimate power go reward and coercive power; Liz uses only reward power. She uses it in positive and negative ways; in a negative way when she gives Susan a warning about missing deadlines, and in a positive way when she gives Susan a "rave review" in the annual report. Liz also has and uses referent power, evidenced by the fact that Susan considered her "God's gift to marketing," and expert power, demonstrated by Susan often turning to her for help and advice on projects.

Jay possesses legitimate power in that he is Susan's and Liz's supervisor. He also has and uses expert power; both Liz and Susan seek out his professional advice and opinions. He has both reward and coercive power, but there is no evidence that he uses either. There is also no evidence that he has or uses referent power.

Stefan has legitimate power as the vice president of marketing, and has reward and coercive power as well, though he appears to use neither. Referent power is also not evident. He has and uses expert power, which is shown when Susan turns to him for assistance and directions on projects.

Karina has legitimate power as Liz's and Susan's supervisor. She also has reward and coercive power. Although she does not use reward power, she does use coercive power, which is evident in the memo she sent to the marketing employees. There is no evidence that Karina has expert power; although one could assume that twenty years of work experience would probably result in some degree of expertise, this is not the same as expert power. In addition, Karina does not possess referent power.

1. For a discussion of French and Raven's analysis of the bases of power, see Moorhead and Griffin, *Organizational Behavior*, 6th ed. (Boston: Houghton Mifflin, 2001) Chapter 14.

Leadership Styles

The leadership styles of Liz and Karina can be analyzed using several different theories. Behavioral theories, such as the University of Michigan Studies, would define Liz as an employee-centered leader and Karina as a job-centered leader. Liz is concerned with Susan as an individual and does all she can to assist Susan's professional growth and advancement. Karina demonstrates a detachment from her employees and makes clear that her main concern is getting quality work done on time rather than the needs of her employees. The Ohio State Studies, also a behavioral theory, would define Liz as a leader who displays consideration. This is evidenced by her concern that her relationships with colleagues and subordinates are positive ones, that her subordinates are encouraged to grow, and that subordinates are treated with respect. It can also be seen in her friendship with Susan. Karina, on the other hand, would be considered an "initiating structure" leader. She clearly does this in her interaction with Susan in which she redefines the reporting relationships and lines of communication which Susan must now follow.

Hersey and Blanchard's Life Cycle Model can also be used to analyze Liz's and Karina's leadership styles. Liz appears to operate in a participating mode (low task, high relationship), appropriate for Susan's level of job maturity. Karina operates in a telling mode (high task, low relationship). As Susan has been in her position for quite some time and is looking for support and the opportunity to take on increased responsibility rather than for someone to tell her what to do and when to do it, this leadership style is clearly inappropriate.

Motivation

It should be evident that Karina's leadership style and misuse of power will only serve to lower Susan's motivation and productivity. Susan is an experienced worker who has developed positive and productive relationships with her supervisors. This has resulted in professional growth and added responsibilities, all of which have been motivating factors for her.

Karina's style of leadership, no matter what theory is used, is inappropriate for Susan. Susan has shown that she is most productive with a leadership style that allows her to participate, to experience professional growth, and to build informal channels of communication. Karina's leadership style is the exact opposite of what Susan is used to, and the quality of her work is already showing a decline.

It is important for students to recognize that in her single-minded focus on productivity, Karina has neglected such basic employee needs as being able to use the new computer equipment. Although Karina's expectations of her employees are extremely high, by ignoring employee needs and neglecting to obtain input on such a major change as installing a new computer system, she essentially ensures that Susan will fail to meet her expectations.

Liz's Role

As Susan's supervisor, Liz needs to arrange for some type of training on the new computer system. It is unlikely that Susan will be able to meet deadlines and turn in the type of work she has shown herself to be capable of until this is done. Liz also needs to provide Susan with support and with the opportunity to participate in whatever decision making happens within their department, as it seems fairly clear that Karina will not be soliciting Susan's input on anything major. Liz might also want to provide Susan with opportunities to attend conferences or other forms of professional development. Ideally, Liz should discuss the situation with Karina; however, there is nothing in the case to suggest that this would have a positive outcome.

46

THE ELEVENTH HOUR: A FISH BOWL ROLE PLAY

Group Size: Done as a class with a group of four performing the role play in a fishbowl.

Recommended Time: One or two 80–90 minute class periods.

Provided: Background in student edition. Role descriptions for photocopying and distributing are at the end of these instructor's notes.

Also Required: No additional materials required.

Facilities: One large room with movable chairs.

Objectives

- To help students understand group dynamics
- To build skills in working in groups
- To sensitize students how they impact a group's efficacy
- To demonstrate how well-meaning individuals can create a degenerative group climate
- To explore sources and resolutions of conflict

Overview

This exercise was developed to help students understand how a group of well-intentioned individuals may degenerate into dysfunction. It is based on composites of actual and regularly recurring personalities and situations observed in student groups over a five-year period. Many students will likely see themselves in the personalities of the characters. As a result, this exercise helps sensitize students to some of the way in which they contribute to group dynamics.

The exercise consists of a series of role plays done by a group in a fishbowl format. Class members watching the first role play help analyze effective and ineffective behaviors and make suggestions for improvement. A second group then performs the same role play with the benefit of the learning from the first role play. This process continues until time runs out. Each successive role play provides a clearer model of what makes an effective group.

Although it may be tempting to compare groups as the exercise evolves, it is critical to point out that each successive group benefits from the aggregated learning. Those groups that go first serve an extremely important learning function and must be greatly appreciated for getting things started.

Background

The members of a group are usually well intentioned in their actions. This is the case with all of the actors in this role play.

Each role consists of a person who believes she or he is looking out for the best interests of the group. However, incidents occur that may lead group members to make unwarranted inferences about group mates. These inferences are usually not positive. Once inferences are made, the dynamic typically begins to deteriorate. Group members who feel they have sacrificed for the group begin to feel unappreciated. Students then begin focusing on specific acts and start to blame each other, which leads to defensiveness, attempts to justify actions, and retaliation with further blame. At this point, the dynamic deteriorates quickly.

The role play is intended to be conducted at least twice. This helps students realize that the way they deal with a situation, and the inferences they make about a situation, are important factors in how group dynamics progress.

The second role play takes place after the first has been discussed and debriefed. Students then attempt to improve the dynamic based on a new understanding of the situation. This helps them realize that they have a choice in how they react to a situation, how they interpret certain actions, and how the energy contained in their feelings is directed. Students need to understand that not only is addressing a situation important, but the manner in which it is addressed is also important. Many problems that arise in this role play stem from either not addressing an issue or handling it in an unsupportive and uncaring manner. Although it is often important to express one's displeasure, it must be done in a helpful way.

Many students assume that handling a situation in a supportive and caring manner means that the group is focused on making people happy at the expense of completing its task. It is important to help them realize that a group needs to address both tasks and relationships. Sometimes, the most helpful and supportive thing that can be done is to refuse to tolerate unproductive behavior. Addressing unproductive behavior in a nonjudgmental way respects the individual and makes clear that certain behaviors will not be tolerated.

Students should be encouraged to think of issues as problems to be explored and resolved. There are always multiple perspectives to any given situation, and students should try to understand these. They should also be aware that there is mutual responsibility for a given dynamic. It is not only the responsibility of the person exhibiting a behavior—but also the responsibility of the group—to understand how each contributes to the behavior and what can be done to support a change. Students should be aware that if they do nothing about a problem, they are contributing to that problem.

Conflict

Many unproductive conflicts are likely to arise during the role play. The exercise illustrates how people often jump to erroneous conclusions and that differing perspectives lead to conflict unless a group is able to listen to and understand each of its members. Some of the possible topics around conflict that can be addressed within the context of the role play include:

1. Conflict handling styles.

2. The role of perceptions in conflict.
3. The importance of sharing information to avoid misperceptions.
4. The role of communication skills.
5. Conflict management. There are many things the role play group could do to reduce its problems, e.g., discuss expectations, address problems when they arise, have a period for reflection placed on the agendas, and be more methodical in assignment of tasks.
6. The importance of acting in a supportive, respectful, and caring manner.

The Characters

The following explanations of the dynamics are based on actual experiences with groups and are representative of—but not exhaustive of—what often happens when group members are not skilled at addressing issues. The way group members perceive the situation and decide to address it will have considerable impact.

Pat

Pat is modeled after the classic A student who is reluctant to allow his/her grade to be put in the hands of others. Pat feels that s/he is helping the group by taking the lead and doing a lot of the tasks. What Pat fails to realize is that this may cause others to become demotivated. Pat is setting up a self-fulfilling prophecy. S/he believes that others cannot be trusted to do the work as well as s/he can and acts accordingly. Pat is likely to be critical of mistakes made by Lee and Billy without recognizing their efforts. This makes Lee and Billy feel that their work is not appreciated. For example, Lee hates math but feels s/he was making a sacrifice doing the financials for the group because nobody else wants to do the job. Although Lee puts in a tremendous effort, mistakes are made. Pat is likely to bring this up as an example of Lee's incompetence without seeing the efforts that Lee has made. The same is true for Billy's efforts to produce the required graphic. Although Billy also puts in a valiant effort, Pat only recognizes Billy's failures.

Chris

Having a busy schedule, Chris wants the group to be efficient. Chris does not want to burden the group with his/her scheduling problems and has gone to great lengths to juggle schedules to make group meetings. The group does not recognize this and has often rescheduled meetings at the last minute, causing problems for Chris. The group norm seems to be to ignore the fact that meetings do not start on time. This bothers Chris, who makes efforts to make the meetings at the scheduled times but is not always successful. Chris's tight schedule also means that s/he has to leave to go to other meetings when the group runs over its allotted time.

Chris writes down the wrong day for the last meeting, and the group becomes focused on the meeting that Chris accidentally misses. Although there is no data to show that Chris is late any more than others, they accuse Chris of being chronically late to meetings. There is little recognition of the attempts Chris makes to accommodate the group's changing meeting times. Chris becomes annoyed at the group's lack of recognition for his/her situation and the inability of the group to remain efficiently focused on the task. Chris, however, neither expresses these feelings to the group, nor explains his/her scheduling difficulties.

Lee

Lee tries to be very accommodating and often agrees to do things without thinking about potential difficulties. Lee perceives this as making a sacrifice. As an example, Lee accepts the job of doing the group's finances even though s/he hates math and would prefer to be involved in the creative aspects of the project. The group does not think to include Lee in other aspects of the project, and the finances turn out to be more difficult and time consuming than originally thought.

The group's being fined tends to overshadow the hard work that Lee has put in and makes it more difficult for the group to include Lee in other areas of the project. Lee perceives this as being excluded and psychologically withdraws from the group, often being seen doodling and distracted. The group perceives this as disinterest and a confirmation that Lee is not interested in the work. Since Lee feels excluded from the group, s/he is often distracted by friends.

This is justified in Lee's mind because the group is wasting time and not interested in involving Lee. The group often sees the distractions as further confirmation that Lee is not motivated. This is a useful situation for considering the topic of job design. Lee would likely be more motivated if the group redesigned his/her job to distribute some of the financial tasks and include Lee in more creative aspects of the project.

Billy

Billy has a learning disability and does not like to use it as an excuse. It usually takes Billy a bit longer to process a conversation, and s/he sometimes has difficulty expressing ideas clearly on the spur of the moment. The group's reaction, conscious or unconscious, is to leave Billy out of the conversations, which Billy perceives as being excluded.

The group also may view Billy's behavior as a sign of incompetence. This causes them to misinterpret his/her inability to produce exactly what the group wants in the graphic. Pat is especially likely to use this incident as confirmation that Billy is not trustworthy. Billy will feel this and is likely to withdraw further.

Billy is often a scapegoat. The group focuses on his/her failure to produce what the group wants and not communicate with the group that s/he is going to make changes. Billy's explanation that s/he attempted to do what the group wanted but couldn't because the software was not capable, gets ignored. The group finds it easy to use Billy as a scapegoat because there is a tangible product on which it can focus. Billy's efforts are of no consequence.

Suggested Outline and Timing

Timing may be flexible: Large group discussions may be brief or detailed; the role play may be done two or more times; role plays may be done in one or more class periods, depending upon your needs and time frame. The suggestions below are for one 80 to 90 minute class. If you choose to do one role play per class, the role play can easily last up to 20 minutes with the subsequent discussion filling the remainder of a class period.

1. Set-up (full class: 5 minutes)

- Explain that the purpose of the exercise is to learn what effective and ineffective behaviors are in groups. Students should be told that the class will observe a group role play during which they are to focus on observing helpful and unhelpful behaviors.
- Stress that those who go first provide a critical opportunity for observers to learn from their experience. Stress the service that the first group will be providing.

2. Hand out roles/student preparation (15 minutes)

- Decide ahead of time how you will hand out the roles, e.g., selecting role players whose personalities are consistent or inconsistent with their personalities. Students playing opposite personality roles must deal with "themselves" as they work with the person playing the role closest to their own personality. The drawback is that they may have a harder time playing the role of someone who is so unlike themselves. The drawback to having students essentially play themselves is that it may not be as personally effective, although this is likely to be addressed in the large group discussion. You may also elect to assign roles randomly.
- Have students read the background information or assign this before class to save time.
- Hand out the roles in roughly equal proportions, e.g., in a class of twenty-four, there will be six of each character. Give students time to prepare. Give everyone in the class only one role, as this helps them relate to a given character without being exposed to all of the hidden information. Explain that the more seriously they take their roles, the greater the learning. They should think about how they are feeling, what they want to say, how they will say it, etc.
- When the role play is ready to start, ask for a volunteer to play each of the four roles. Again, explain that the first volunteers will be providing an important service to the class. Be prepared to choose people if you do not get enough volunteers.

3. First role play (10–15 minutes)

- Have the four volunteers sit in the middle of the fishbowl or at the front of the room with the rest of the class positioned to observe. Tell them to begin, but do not provide any other instructions.
- In deciding when to stop the role play, keep in mind that students need enough time for issues to surface and group dynamics to become visible. At some point the pattern becomes clear, and there is little new to be gained by letting the role play continue.

4. Large group discussion (20 minutes or longer)

- There is a vast amount of material that can be covered during the large group discussion, e.g., ask students whether they feel that any of the characters were intending to harm the group. This is an essentially rhetorical question because the answer should be an obvious "no." Ask how they would characterize the dynamics of the group. The direction of the discussion will depend upon what happened in the group.

- It is likely that the class will say the group was dysfunctional. If this is the case, you might say something like, “If no one in the group intended to harm the group, then why did it so quickly become dysfunctional?” Students often start to blame a particular individual.
- At this point it is critical to stress that there is mutual responsibility. Ask how the rest of the group contributed to the problem, i.e., through inaction, failure to disclose important information, or more active involvement such as being judgmental, not listening, focusing on the negative without recognizing the positive, etc. If the dynamics were handled functionally, then ask the students to explore why. Ask if they could see the situation going in the opposite direction and what the difference would be.
- It is possible to end the discussion by asking for suggestions for each of the characters in the next role play.

5. *Second role play (10–15 minutes)*
   - Point out that it would be natural to expect this group to have learned from watching the first group and that it is not valid to be making judgments about the individuals in one group or the other based on a comparison of the outcomes.
   - Repeat Step 3.

6. *Large group discussion (20 minutes or longer)*

   There are many possible areas to discuss. Some points that can be covered:
   - Many conflicts arise because we make invalid judgments about others.
   - When group members withhold information, it is easier to reach false conclusions.
   - Self-fulfilling prophecies have a strong impact on group dynamics.
   - It is important to treat group members in a supportive, helpful, respectful, and caring manner.
   - People are usually not malicious and are typically not intending to harm a group.
   - It is important to increase self-awareness and understand one’s role in a situation.
   - All group members are mutually responsible for a situation. If you are not part of the solution, you are part of the problem.
   - Compare the dynamics in the first group with the second group. The second group will usually do better because it has benefited from the first group. Ask students to discuss the differences. What makes one group more effective than the other?
   - One issue that arises if the second group has been more respectful and supportive of each other is that the situation is characterized as not being “real.” Students often believe that because someone may feel angry or frustrated, it will be expressed in a negative manner. If the second group was able to channel the expression of its feelings in a more productive way, students feel that this is not the way people would really act. A discussion about feelings and the choices made about to express them is useful here. It is important that students realize that the opposite of expressing feelings in a negative way is expressing them productively, not withholding expression. It is also important

they realize that their choices of how to handle their feelings will impact the group dynamics.

7. *Wrap up*

Hand out a full set of roles to each student, or have four students who have played different roles describe what they were asked to do. This will help students further understand the issues involved in the role play.

Role 1
Pat

You are a solid student with a 3.8 grade point average. In this class, your course grade will depend on the success or failure of your group. In previous group projects, you have always gotten stuck doing most of the work.

You have made a number of observations of your group members: Lee seems to doodle all the time; Billy is very quiet and doesn't contribute very many ideas. When you ask Billy questions, the responses always seem shallow.

Chris never showed up at the last group meeting and didn't let anyone know. At the meeting, you, Lee, and Billy discussed Chris's chronic lateness and the fact that Chris also sometimes leaves meetings early. You agreed that missing a meeting without telling anyone was not acceptable.

You scheduled a meeting for Saturday morning at 9 a.m. and agreed that you would confront Chris at that time.

You called Chris Friday morning, said that a meeting had been scheduled for the next day, and said that it had better not be missed. Since the group was going to confront Chris, you figured it would also be a good time to resolve the problems with Lee and Billy. You plan to do so.

You are also hoping to get some work done and are anxiously awaiting the graphic that Billy is supposed to have created. You are praying it will be what you asked for. You don't really have much confidence in Billy.

You are now beginning the Saturday meeting and, as usual, you have to take the lead.

Role 2
Chris

In addition to going to school full-time, you work 40 hours a week. Your work schedule is erratic, often making group meeting times difficult. You never mentioned this to your teammates, because you didn't want to cause problems. You have tried to get off work in time to make group meetings, but sometimes you have been unavoidably delayed. Your teammates seem totally insensitive to your busy schedule, and they've even made some negative comments about your involvement in the Chess Club.

To make group meetings, you called your boss, who, although not very happy about it, allowed you to rearrange your work schedule. When Billy had to change the meeting time to pick up a relative, you had to once again call your boss and change your schedule. Again your boss was not pleased. Then Billy had to cancel the meeting because of emotional distress over the accident. The others accepted this even though it showed a total lack of regard for your situation.

The group's meetings are inefficient. Lee is constantly interrupted by friends, people show up late, and the group labors over decisions that seem obvious to you. You have been constantly late for other commitments because your group meetings always take longer than expected.

At the last meeting you wrote down that the next meeting was scheduled for Friday evening. On Friday morning, however, you got a call from Pat asking you where you were last night. You had no idea to what Pat was referring and, in fact, you had been working. Pat told you that there would be a group meeting tomorrow (Saturday) at 9 a.m. and that you had better show up. You immediately called your boss who said, "Okay, but one more time and your fired!" He said he doesn't care how good a worker you are, he needs someone who can be counted on to be there when scheduled.

You regret having taken the job of marketing director. This was a big job, but you knew you would be working with Pat as campaign manager, and the two of you had always gotten along well. After the phone call, you're not sure that will last. Lee's job as financial manager seems to be a lot less time-consuming. Oh well, you thought, what is done is done.

You are now beginning the Saturday meeting. Pat seems to be taking the lead as usual.

Role 3
Lee

You are not a financial expert, but you took the job of financial manager for your group because nobody else wanted it. Now you've caused the group to be fined, and while no one said so, you are pretty sure that they all blame you. This seems unfair since they don't seem to understand the sacrifice you made by taking the job. You hate math, but you decided that this couldn't be too difficult. After all, it's only a class project, and you were sure that you could figure it out.

You had really wanted to be working in a more creative area, but Pat and Chris seemed much more qualified.

Neither Pat nor Chris seems to value your ability to contribute to the team, and when they talk about anything other than the financial part of the project, they totally ignore you. There have been times when you have felt so excluded from the project that you have even started doodling. Fortunately, as soon as financial issues have arisen, you have been right back into the conversations.

While you've been concerned that the meetings never seem to get started on time, you haven't minded very much since you so often run into friends to talk to while the others are getting their acts together. If the group can't stick to starting times, at least you get to be with people who value you.

Chris never showed up at Thursday evening's meeting and didn't let anyone know. Pat, Billy, and you spent much of the time discussing Chris's chronic lateness and the fact that Chris has also left meetings early. You scheduled a meeting for Saturday at 9 a.m. and agreed to confront Chris at that time. You wonder whether this might also be a good time for you to bring up your feelings of being undervalued and excluded—although you really don't want to make any waves.

You are now beginning the Saturday meeting. Pat seems to be taking the lead as usual.

Role 4
Billy

Because of a fairly serious learning disability, you have always had to struggle in order to succeed. Through hard work, you have even been able to excel in several areas. Still, you prefer not to talk about your L.D. problem because you're aware that others often characterize people with learning disabilities as stupid or slow.

At the first meeting of your group, you suggested that the group didn't need a leader and that everyone should share responsibility and control equally. You were happy when the group finally agreed. Since then, however, Pat has been taking over, and Chris has gone along because they are friends. Lee seems disinterested at times. You are often totally left out of decision making. When you initially tried to make suggestions, Pat was impatient, gave you disapproving looks, and made nasty comments in front of the others. Now you mainly just sit back, watch, and do whatever work is assigned to you.

You tried to create a graphic that Pat wanted, but your software just couldn't do it. To save time, you decided to make some minor changes that you had suggested earlier but that the group had rejected. You changed a few colors and the shape of a few lines. By doing this, you got the job done on time so the group could move on. You hope the group will understand that you tried to do the job in the way it requested, but it wasn't possible, particularly in such a short time.

You missed one meeting because of a car accident. A child in the car that hit you had been thrown through the window and had been badly hurt. You were feeling too emotionally exhausted to make the meeting.

Chris never showed up at Thursday night's meeting and didn't let anyone know. At the meeting you, Pat, and Lee discussed Chris' chronic lateness and the fact that Chris sometimes left meetings early. You decided you could no longer accept this behavior and agreed to confront Chris at the meeting scheduled for 9 a.m. on Saturday. You think this might be a good time to bring up your feelings of being undervalued. One thing you know for sure is that you are going to have to tell the group that you modified the graphic they had agreed on.

You are now beginning the Saturday meeting. Pat seems to be taking the lead as usual.

47

THE TROUBLEMAKER

This case may appear to suggest that "nice guys finish last," but the real message is that misguided "niceness" can backfire when it takes the place of clear and meaningful communication. Unfortunately, Derek Hornfeldt's constant attempts to keep everyone happy fall into this category.

Hornfeldt, engineering manager for Belle Technologies, lost credibility among his workers. He became overly involved in meaningless details, such as the grammar and structure of internal documents, intruded himself into the personal lives of his workers, and seemed to be unaware of his failure to give input where needed and his tendency to give too much input when the need wasn't there. Students should be able to pick up any number of inappropriate behaviors on Hornfeldt's part: showing everyone his vacation photographs; buying doughnuts for everyone as a way to make conflict go away; demanding a justification for a 48-cent expenditure, and so forth. In trying to be both responsible and "nice," Hornfeldt lost perspective of what it means to be a manager.

Leadership Style

When it comes to leadership, Hornfeldt definitely had it backwards. The Hersey-Blanchard leadership model suggests that skilled and seasoned workers who are able and willing to do their jobs need little close supervision. With this kind of worker, a leader need only tell the workers what needs to be done and then let them do it. On the other hand, new workers who are unclear about how to do their jobs need supervision and support.

Hornfeldt held the hands of his experienced engineers, claiming, "I checked in with them as much as six times a day, asking if all the basic specs were right...." In addition, he failed to recognize the resentment of this skilled group of workers at his constant involvement. Their apparently sarcastic comments were experienced by Hornfeldt as temporary anger caused by stress, and Ted Olin's attempts to give him feedback about the causes of high turnover were seen as troublemaking. He never makes the connection between his overinvolvement and his workers' unhappiness.

While Hornfeldt acknowledges that the new engineers, most just out of college, "have no practical experience, so the learning curve is long," he says he left them alone to learn by making mistakes. He failed to recognize their anxiety and give them the support and help they needed to grow and succeed. In addition, he assigns them to routine work, separated from the more senior people who might have been able to serve as mentors, with apparently little chance for growth. Once again, he misses the signals and misinterprets the frequent departures of the young engineers as their impatience and giving in to the "smooth talk" of other companies. It's also interesting that, despite his professed interest in being a "people person," Hornfeldt tosses off these young engineers as "just college kids" who are "not hard to replace."

Sources of Power

As a manager, Hornfeldt should have had and been able to use all five sources of power described by French and Raven, i.e., legitimate, reward, coercive, expert, and referent. In fact, the only powers he seemed actually to have had and used were legitimate and reward, and these he failed to use effectively.

Hornfeldt had legitimate power due to his title of engineering manager. However, as he lost credibility because of his ineffectiveness, his legitimate power grew increasingly weak. In time, his subordinates seemed to only humor him in following his orders.

The opportunity to exercise reward power by apportioning a five percent increase in his department's payroll to his workers was another failure for Hornfeldt. His decision to treat everyone the same, despite likely differences in performance, along with telling each engineer that she or he did "outstanding work" became as empty a gesture as buying everyone doughnuts. His top workers were apparently resentful at having their efforts rewarded at the same rate and with the same words as those whose work was not at the same standard.

There is certainly no indication that Hornfeldt ever threatened to punish or punished a worker, and he is proud that he has never yelled and has stayed away from giving negative feedback. Thus, while he may have had coercive power, there is certainly no indication that he used it even with Olin, whom he considered to be a problem.

In addition, Hornfeldt appears to have lacked expert power. The case states that he had not kept up with his technical skills, and he displayed no specialized skill or understanding of even the skills of management. Finally, while Hornfeldt's workers agreed that he is a nice guy, he appears to have lacked totally any kind of charisma or personal magnetism. Rather, the workers seem to have perceived him as some sort of annoying flea that hopped around and wouldn't go away. Thus, he did not appear to have referent power.

Recommendations

With all the above, it is little wonder that Hornfeldt was unceremoniously demoted. The new managers will essentially have to do all the things that Hornfeldt failed to do, that is, supervise and mentor the new workers, delegate to and not look over the shoulders of the experienced engineers, give meaningful feedback, be open to feedback themselves, and use the sources of power effectively.

48

THE OUTSPOKEN EMPLOYEE*

Overview

This case asks students to examine the intentions and goals of management to invite employee participation and involvement. The issues of ethical behavior and confidentiality, as well as standards of normative behavior, are parts of the substance of the case.

This short case presents a provocative situation that clearly challenges management's intentions to open communication and illustrates the attendant risks open communication may evoke. Company leaders have available to them many response options, all of which help to send messages to the employee community regarding such issues as integrity, ethics, and control.

Questions for Discussion

1. What would you advise Jayne to do next? Why?

   Whatever Jayne and senior management do following the meeting sends a message to all employees. Given the volatile nature of the remarks of the "outspoken employee," many other employees will be waiting to see what will happen.

   Jayne could recommend that there be no more meetings of this type. She could recommend that meetings continue and that certain ground rules be established that, among other things, would prohibit personal attacks, reference to confidential information, and so on. Such boundary setting may be written in such a way as to help make the objectives of the meetings clearer and provide a safer environment for all concerned.

   Students should examine whether employee involvement, participation, and shared information are important company objectives. If so, then they must ask how such meetings be structured so that they are constructive events that stimulate employee involvement and learning.

2. What do you think the company should do about what took place? Now? In the future? Why?

   Company leaders may react to the "outspoken employee" matter in a number of ways. They could, among other things, do away with having the meetings; give future meetings more structure with pre-determined, employee-generated agenda items, and some meeting ground rules; or, they could ask employees for suggestions about having future meetings. Involving employees in developing meeting guidelines may help many work through whatever discomfort they may have felt during the disruptive meeting.

Students should consider what behavior company leaders might want to reinforce. If company leaders do away with the meetings or radically change the format and content of the meetings, students should consider what the messages are that are being sent to the employees.

- Company leaders may want to consider such questions as:
- Are the meetings of value? To whom?
- What has been learned from meetings in the past?
- Have employees expressed interest in the meetings?
- Do the meetings have any influence on employee performance, attitudes, or behavior?
- How do we know?

3. What do you think about the advisability of this kind of meeting? Why?

The content of open meetings where virtually any topic can be placed on the table may run a broad gamut. Meeting content may range from highly valuable information sharing sessions to enable performance improvement or reinforce company culture, or enhance shared understandings, to ugly and potentially destructive gripe sessions with "venting value" but not much else. Sometimes, of course, venting is a good thing.

Meeting purpose is paramount. Company leaders have to clearly understand their own motives and expectations. They are using valuable company assets, i.e., time and people, to have the meetings.

It might be a good idea to survey the employees, formally or informally, to determine what they think about the meetings in terms of value, content, frequency, and so forth.

49

THE X-Y SCALE*

Group Size: Any number.

Recommended Time: If used alone, 45 minutes (10 minutes for students to complete and score the scale; 35 minutes for discussion). If used as the first step to an in-class case analysis, 120 minutes (10 minutes to complete and score the scale; 45 minutes to analyze the case; 65 minutes for report out to the class; and open-ended discussion).

Provided: All forms, instructions, and descriptions.

Also Required: No additional materials required.

Facilities: A large room, preferably with moveable chairs.

Objectives

- To help students to identify their own beliefs relative to Theory X-Theory Y
- To examine beliefs relative to motivation and ways in which those beliefs can become self-fulfilling prophecies
- To identify instances in which each theory would be more appropriate than the other

Background

This exercise may be used alone, as a springboard to a discussion of Theory X and Theory Y, and/or as a first step to an in-class analysis of a motivation case.

One highly recommended use of this exercise is to have students complete and score the scale, then either divide the class into two separate groups (one of Theory X students and one of Theory Y students) or into small groups of four to six students (each group should contain only Theory X or Theory Y students), and have the groups analyze a motivation case followed by a report out and class discussion.

As would be expected, students with Theory Y beliefs look at the case from a very different perspective than students with Theory X beliefs. It's almost always a revelation to students when they are able to see the degree to which these beliefs influence both their analysis of the case and the solutions that they propose.

* This exercise was written by Gail E. Gilmore.

Discussion

In the case of the exercise being used alone, discussion is generally most productive when centered on the ramifications of each leadership style for employee motivation and productivity, as well as the relationship between each style and the concept of self-fulfilling prophecy.

If the exercise is used as a first step to an in-class case analysis, discussion focusing on the ways in which the students' beliefs influence both the way in which a work problem is perceived and the solutions developed for that problem, as well as a discussion of the likely ramifications of the solutions proposed by both the Theory X group(s) and the Theory Y group(s) will tend to generate the most interesting observations.

50

DANGER: RADIO ACTIVITY HITS COUNTRY IN LONG ISLAND*

This case may be used to demonstrate issues of leadership, uses of the sources of social power, motivation, organizational culture, and management of change. The following discussion focuses on leadership and the uses of the sources of social power.

Applications of Leadership Theories

Virtually any situational leadership theory can be employed effectively in analyzing this case. First, consider the state of radio station WPOP when Craig Sugerman was leader. He was a laissez-faire task and achievement-oriented leader who used a highly delegating style, a style, when looked at within the context of Hersey-Blanchard life cycle model, works best with highly mature workers who are willing and able to do their jobs. In the days of the Top 40 WPOP, Max was clearly a mature (M4) employee, while Barb was somewhat less so (perhaps M3). As such, Max loved Craig's style, while Barb basically tolerated it, preferring instead more participative leadership.

In Fiedler's terms, Craig was task-oriented. Max was likely in Category 1, which would also have been a good match, his job being fairly structured. Barb was likely in Category 7, which is also a pretty good match in terms of performance since her job was far less structured.

Using the Path-Goal Theory, Barb has an internal locus of control, adequate experience, and high perceived ability. Subordinates with an internal locus of control prefer a participative style, which explains her initial dissatisfaction with Craig. Max is more external and thus liked Craig's style.

When Rex arrives, Max regresses to being an immature (M1) employee with low experience—country and western music is not within his purview—and low perceived ability. When Rex makes Max's job structured by spelling out the play list, Max is in Fiedler's Category 5, a good match for a relationship-oriented leader. When Rex removes the structure the following week, Max is in Category 7 and, as Fiedler probably would predict, his performance suffers accordingly. Likewise with the Hersey-Blanchard life cycle model, i.e., when Rex stops using a "telling" style (S1), Max's performance slips. Seen within the framework of the Path-Goal Theory, and given the new job demands, Max now needs a directive style.

As for Barb, her previous experience in selling ads for country and western radio stations keeps her in the same categories in which she had been previously. However, her performance still slips, because she is managed by a different type of leader: a relationship-oriented one whose use of a directive style (S1) with her is not successful.

* These case notes were prepared by Scott Weighart. Used with permission.

Uses and Abuses of Social Power

Many areas of the uses and abuses of social power need to be explored. From the outset, Rex virtually fails to develop referent power, although he makes attempts to do so. He has legitimate, reward, and coercive powers, certainly, which appear to work against him. Perhaps due to the nature of their previous boss, or perhaps due to something in their own personalities, Max and Barb are not candid with Rex and seem to fear the potential use of his reward or coercive powers.

Barb's expert power in some areas, and loss of expert power in others, and Max's loss of expert and referent powers, are relevant issues. For Max, his fall from popularity in the community and his lack of familiarity with the music he is being asked to play have great impact. Barb loses her ability to use her referent power fully, based on her relationships with the advertisers who she has taken great pains to cultivate, as she is forced to turn to other sources of potential revenue, sources in which she has no existing relationships and for whom she has little respect. It is with these new and somewhat alien sources that she likely forgoes at least some of her expertise, despite the fact that she earlier has demonstrated meaningful expertise in her skill as a salesperson.

Solutions

Rex should keep using an S1 style with Max for the time being, while using an S3 participative style with Barb. It should be noted that it may take time to undo Barb's negative first impressions of Rex, who she believes misjudged her abilities and experience. That, combined with her previous experience with Craig, indicates that it may take time to get her to open up to the participative style she appears to need.

Rex has the correct mindset in terms of an "open barn door" philosophy, but he will have to be persistent and build referent power while acknowledging the expert power of Barb. He will also have to be sympathetic regarding Max's loss of expert power and likely loss of referent power in the community, both of which leave him feeling pretty powerless for a guy with a twenty-year history in the business.

Altogether, Rex needs to be more cautious about his leadership style and more sensitive to the needs and abilities of his subordinates. He will also need to recognize that he brings a foreign culture to the New Yorkers who apparently consider themselves at least different if not more sophisticated than what is needed for a country and western format. Changing the organizational culture, both in terms of the leadership style and the style of music, requires both time and patience if it is to be accepted.

51

THE CODFISH COMPANY*

Group Size: Any number of project groups.

Recommended Time: Up to 3 hours in and out of class. This exercise may be used as an out-of-class assignment prior to commencing as a group project. Groups should report their progress on the assignment to the full class.

Provided: All instructions and descriptions.

Also Required: No additional materials required.

Facilities: A large room or several small breakout rooms.

Objectives

- To examine the components of a group project
- To examine the setting and maintenance of group norms and expectations
- To explore the impact of norms and expectations on the process and outcome of a group project
- To consider ethics and responsibility

Background

This exercise was designed to accompany a group project assignment. Completing the exercise helps students understand the steps of structuring and planning a project by breaking it into its components. Please refer to the student text for details of the timing of each step.

Have students complete Part 1 of the exercise in their project groups.

More than one class period may be necessary to get the maximum amount of discussion time—particularly in Part 2 which raises ethical issues.

Ask each group to designate a recorder to report to the full class at the end of each part of the exercise.

* These notes were prepared by Bruce Leblang and Janet W. Wohlberg. Used with permission.

Part 1

Ask each group recorder to report on his or her group's goals. Record these on the blackboard, and discuss the similarities and differences of each group's goals. Do the same with each step of the exercise.

Explore the different ways in which students selected their leaders, defined the component parts of the project, and so forth.

Part 2

Use Part 2 as a jumping off point for a discussion about the responsibilities of group members to a group and the effects of firing a group member.

Issues of leadership, particularly in a situation in which all group members are effectively peers, should be a topic for discussion in this part as well.

Students should consider issues of how to motivate peers, personal responsibility, and the ways in which planning and structure afford solutions to problems as well as ways to prevent their occurrence.

Part 2e asks students to look at the issues of group responsibility and accountability:

- Was the group process really successful if two of the group members failed to become motivated to do the work to support their group mates?
- Was the process successful if two of the members apparently felt no responsibility to the group?
- Was the rest of the group successful if its members failed to build the necessary group cohesion and did not structure in checks and balances on accountability?
- How might strengthening the structure and planning for such contingencies that presented themselves have helped?

This part of the exercise gives students a chance to air their feelings about ethics, a discussion that can be fairly open-ended. In addition to ethics, however, the key word, "successful," should force the students to go back over their stated norms and goals to determine whether with two fake interviews they met their goals and stayed within the boundaries of their stated norms.

52

ASSIGNING THE TEAM PROJECT TASKS

Group Size: Any number of groups of four to six.

Recommended Time: 90–95 minutes.

Provided: All forms, instructions, and descriptions.

Also Required: No additional materials required.

Facilities: A large room, preferably with moveable chairs, or several breakout rooms.

Objectives

- To help students identify their strengths and weaknesses, and to communicate these to their team members
- To assist students with the process of examining the collective talents of the team and how to capitalize on them
- To enable students to assign team project tasks in a way that best utilizes each member's individual strengths and talents

Background

Assigning tasks to those team members who are best suited to perform them seems to be one of the most difficult issues with which members of a student team have to deal. We often see team projects fall apart because the student with the weakest writing skills was assigned to write the paper, or the team's international student was assigned to proofread it. Team members often fail to recognize the various strengths and talents within the team and so fail to capitalize on all that team members could contribute. Finally, tasks are often assigned without regard to skills and talents, thereby compounding weaknesses instead of utilizing strengths. By working through this exercise, students should be able to articulate to their teammates what it is that they do best, and team members should be able to recognize the skills, talents, and weaknesses within the team and assign team project tasks accordingly.

Discussion

Discussion should focus on how this process of task assignment differs from those with which students have had prior experience. What are the advantages and disadvantages of this method? How did the team deal with situations in which there were either too many people qualified for a particular task—or no one qualified?

Students should be encouraged to think about the benefits and/or drawbacks of applying this methodology in the workplace and to consider ways in which it could be successfully implemented.

53

MANAGING GROUP PERFORMANCE*

Psychological contract, performance plan, peer review, and feedback exercises

Author's Note

The content of this series of exercises is mostly the same as in the 5th edition, however, the introductory material for each exercise has been placed in one section at the beginning of the series. The intent is to provide the student's with a complete overview and, at the same time, shorten the actual exercises. You should instruct students to read the entire background once and then have them reread the background for each exercise as you assign it. There are a few changes to the content of the exercises: 1) students are asked to do a self evaluation; 2) formal observers were eliminated from the in-class peer feedback session; 3) students are now asked to discuss how the group helps bring about the behaviors being discussed and to develop a mutual plan for addressing them; and 4) if time permits, students are asked to discuss the team as a whole during the in-class feedback session.

You can find research on the outcomes of this series of exercises in:

Druskat, Vanessa Urch and Wolff, Steven B. (1999). The Effects and Timing of Developmental Peer Appraisals in Self-Managing Work Groups. *Journal of Applied Psychology,* 84(1): 58-74.

Objectives

- To provide a structured means for project groups to manage performance and address problems
- To provide experience in developing explicit psychological contracts
- To provide experience in developing performance plans that include clear policies and procedures
- To provide experience giving and receiving performance feedback, including observing and evaluating performance

Background

Project groups in management classes, as well as in the business world, are generally most effective when they use structured methods for managing performance. As an inherent part of this, members of project or workgroups must be open to giving and receiving feedback in a meaningful and helpful way.

The five exercises in this module were developed for use in courses in which students have been assigned a group project or will work in the same groups throughout the semester and, therefore, must manage their group processes. The exercises use a building-blocks approach, with each exercise highly dependent on information generated by the previous exercise. Thus, while it may be possible to use one or two of the earlier exercises alone, the last three must be used in sequence with the first two.

While the exercises may be started in the classroom, all but the final "Performance Review/ Feedback" exercise are meant to be completed outside of class time. For this reason, the instructions are given without recommended time limits.

The first exercise, "Forming a Psychological Contract," asks students to get to know one another and, as a group, develop an explicitly shared psychological contract. Therefore, this exercise should be assigned shortly after group formation. The second exercise, "Developing a Performance Plan," asks students to set performance norms and to develop a performance plan. It should be assigned after the groups have had at least a week or two to work together. A preferable situation is to assign two group projects with the exercise to be completed shortly after the first project is due. The third exercise, "Observing Peer Performance," should be an ongoing process beginning once the Performance Plan has been completed.

Finally, the "Peer Evaluation" and the actual "Performance Review/Feedback" exercises function as a single unit with the first part to be completed out of class and the second an in-class exercise. If possible, this last piece should be done near the due date of the final project. We have found that most students do not work earnestly on term projects until the last week or two. Using this exercise just before "crunch time" seems to spur activity. Many students find this exercise a safe way to convey their feelings and frustrations toward their fellow students and a safe venue within which to be reminded that they must do their fair share. They also find it an excellent opportunity to validate and acknowledge the positive accomplishments of their teammates.

We strongly recommend that students be required to hand in copies of their performance plans, i.e., their expectations, policies and procedures, and Performance Appraisal Forms. If you require this or other actions, ask students to add your requirements to the appropriate checklists.

Samples of the required pieces of written work have been supplied at the end of these teaching notes. While they may be removed from the book, they are not intended to be copied for distribution to a class. Instead, to avoid their use as templates, we recommend having them available for casual inspection only. You may want to leave them temporarily on a desk, have them available in your office, or make overhead transparencies of each to show when you explain the assignment. We advise encouraging students to create their own format.

Developing a Psychological Contract

A psychological contract is an important tool for effective group performance. This exercise asks group members to get to know one another and develop a set of shared expectations for the group, the course, the assigned project, and each other. Instructions for what should be included in the psychological contract are intentionally vague. Each group should include whatever is relevant for its members.

Prepare students for this exercise by explaining psychological contracts. This may be done in the very first class as part of explaining the semester's syllabus, since this explanation, which includes asking for and answering questions, constitutes the making of an explicit psychological contract between teacher and students. Sherwood and Glidewell's model for managing psychological contracts [see "Planned Renegotiation: A Norm Setting O.D. Intervention," in *Contemporary Organization and Development: Orientations and Interventions*, W.W. Burke, ed. (Washington, D.C.: NPL Institute, 1972) pp. 35–46] is a useful basis for the discussion.

In discussing psychological contracts, it is important to note that information should be shared and expectations made explicit; that when something begins to feel wrong, i.e., a "pinch point," there needs to be an explicit conversation that renegotiates the contract; and that students have a responsibility for their learning and should not let a pinch point degenerate into a "crunch point" in which they would psychologically withdraw from the class and limit their learning.

Developing a Performance Plan

Developing performance plans is an important piece of managing productivity and is practiced, in one form or another, in the vast majority of organizations. In this exercise, students should work as a group outside of class to define the following items, examples of which are attached to this teaching note:

- *Performance Norms* describe the expectations of team members in behavioral terms that make clear what constitutes satisfactory and unsatisfactory performance. Students may want to cover areas such as meeting attendance, timely performance of assigned tasks, quality of work, contribution of ideas, degree of cooperation, class attendance, maintenance of academic integrity, i.e., no plagiarizing, falsifying interviews, etc.
- *Procedures* define the actions that will be taken in the event that a team member's performance is outside the agreed upon norms. For example, students may want to include procedures for giving rewards, issuing a warning, putting someone on probation, and termination. We encourage instructors who allow groups to terminate a member to require students to include, at a minimum, a procedure that incorporates the following:
    - Written notification signed by all other members of the team
    - Provision of a copy of the termination notice to the instructor
    - A minimum 48-hour notice
    - Hand delivery or return-receipt postal or courier delivery

- An opportunity for the notified team member to correct the problem whenever possible

If termination of a group member is permitted, have students add to their checklists that they have included the required procedures.

Students should also be encouraged to develop procedures for rewarding positive behavior and contributions.

- *Policies* describe the conditions under which each procedure should be invoked. For example, students may wish to define unsatisfactory performance in the area of academic integrity as immediate grounds for beginning termination procedures. They may define a policy that states that one missed deadline is grounds for placing a person on probation and a second missed deadline is grounds for beginning termination procedures.
- *Performance Appraisal Forms* are based on the performance plan. They are a concise way of representing the expectations that have been defined. This form is to be used in the peer reviews as a way of summarizing the team's feedback since it is easier to look at one summary sheet than all the data from each teammate. Because the form is to be used as the basis for performance reviews, it should also contain an area to evaluate strengths and opportunities for improvement. Remind students that if they have used rating scales, e.g., 1 to 5 or excellent to poor, they should include room for comments. The scale rating does not contain enough information to be helpful.

This assignment encourages students to think about the performance of their group and what they must expect from each other if they are to be successful. It also encourages them to agree on what the consequences are for performance outside the agreed upon norms.

Defining performance norms is the first step in managing performance. If people are not aware of what is expected of them, performance may not be as effective as it could be, and any feedback is likely to elicit a defensive response. The more specific and behaviorally oriented the expectations, the easier it will be to measure performance against expectations and the less likely it is that there will be misunderstandings.

Performance appraisal is something that is often done poorly. This exercise will give students experience in the process. Stress the seriousness of this process and make it clear that performance appraisal not done properly can do more harm than good. When done properly, it may cause some anxiety, but individuals learn how to be more effective group members and the group generally performs more effectively.

Observing Peer Performance

Managers or team members observe employee performance and evaluate it against the agreed upon criteria laid out in a performance plan. This exercise gives students a hands-on opportunity to use a performance plan to document the performance of their teammates.

Included with this exercise is a "Performance Observation Sheet" for recording observations. Each group member should record his or her observations for each of his or her teammates on a separate form or facsimile. Some students react negatively to writing down their observations. Stress that performance reviews must be based on actual examples of behavior and that relying on memory is not adequate. The form ensures that accurate examples can be provided during the formal in-class review.

The form has sections in which group members should record both helpful and unhelpful behaviors and a section to record the effects of these behaviors on them as individuals and on the group as a whole. Focusing on behaviors helps avoid evaluating or attacking the person. Explaining the effects of the behaviors helps the person being evaluated understand the impact of his or her behaviors. Students should be encouraged to provide specific examples only in areas where it is possible for the person to modify his or her behavior.

Remind students that these forms will be shared, and encourage them to complete the forms as soon after team meetings as possible. If groups have been meeting before this assignment has begun, students can describe previous behaviors as long as they can be explicitly documented.

In the sixth edition, students are asked to fill out a "Performance Observation Sheet" on themselves. This helps the student reflect on his or her behavior but, more importantly, it allows the person who provides the performance review to know what the person already knows about his or her performance. Areas that may come as a surprise can be considered more thoroughly before feedback is provided.

Peer Evaluation

The peer evaluation process incorporates the observations and comments of each team member in developing a performance evaluation. This helps minimize any attempts to use the review process to settle personal vendettas. It also provides multiple perspectives that should result in a more accurate evaluation. The final evaluation is then used in a formal peer review in which the person being evaluated is provided with oral feedback on his or her performance.

Using the observations that have been documented in the earlier exercises, each student should complete a performance appraisal form, as developed by the group, for the person they are reviewing.

Preparation for the in-class review should take place outside of class. Since the group portion of this assignment takes only about five minutes, we suggest asking the students to bring their forms to class to exchange in a brief meeting either at the end of class or immediately after.

The first order of business will be for the group members to select who will give feedback to whom. Once this is decided, each person should collect the "Performance Observation Sheets (POS)" from their teammates for the person to whom they will be providing feedback, including the POS the person filled out on him or herself. The information from the POS's should be consolidated and one performance appraisal form filled out. Students should be instructed to combine the POS's and the performance appraisal forms into a packet to be handed to the person being reviewed after the in-class feedback session.

Stress that the composite evaluation should represent the perspectives of all teammates except the person being reviewed, not one individual's personal evaluation. Differences in perspectives should be clearly described in the comments.

We recommend that students be required to hand to the instructor one copy of the signed composite appraisal forms on the day of the in-class peer review along with the related POS's. If you require a hand-in copy, this should be added to the students' checklists. A copy of the entire review package should go to the person who has been reviewed.

Stress the importance of practicing the review before coming to class. Suggest that students review the "Guide for Giving and Receiving Effective Feedback." As they practice, they should anticipate reactions and try to maintain a helpful composure. You should stress to students that the intent of the performance review is to be helpful and caring. The purpose of the exercise is to help their teammates understand their strengths and improve on their weaknesses. If, as they practice, students find that they are not being helpful, then they should modify their message until it is supportive and delivered in a caring way. I always tell my students that if they find that something they are planning to say is not helpful, then they simply shouldn't say it.

In-Class Performance Review

Group Size: Any number of groups of five to seven.

Recommended Time: 90 minutes (total time may vary depending on the size of each group); 10 minutes for set up; 10 minutes per review, including observer reports; 20 minutes for debriefing.

Provided: Instructions.

Also Needed: Students will need to provide performance review packets as detailed in each exercise, including multiple copies of the observation forms or facsimiles.

Facilities: One or more large rooms with moveable chairs or enough small breakout rooms to provide one per group.

Objectives

- To provide experience using a performance plan to evaluate performance
- To provide experience giving constructive feedback
- To provide experience receiving feedback

Background

In culmination of the work done in the previous exercises, in this exercise each student is reviewed by a peer. This provides practice in conducting a performance review and helps students develop skills in giving and receiving feedback. Sometimes giving honest feedback can be an anxiety-provoking process. Proper preparation is critical, but the process should not be avoided because it raises anxiety. It is important to remind students of the importance of maintaining an atmosphere of helpfulness.

Suggested Outline and Timing

1. *Set-up (full class: 10 minutes)*

   Ask students to list what makes good and bad feedback and write these lists on a chalk board or flip chart. Students generally understand that feedback, good or bad, can be harmful if given improperly, but they often need to be reminded. As you discuss the lists that have been generated, stress that feedback must be intended to be helpful, and it must be something that the person can do something about. The group should also be willing to help the person correct the problem addressed by the feedback. Explain the importance of performance feedback for maintaining productivity.

   Do the following:

   - Have the students review the "Guide for Giving and Receiving Effective Feedback."

- Go over the meanings of good and bad feedback.
- Divide the class into groups.
- Refer students to the necessary forms in the student edition.
- Ask students to arrange their chairs so that the two people conducting the review are facing each other with the remainder of the team arranged on either side.

If you choose, you may ask the groups to assign observers. One person should observe the behaviors of the feedback giver and another should observe the behaviors of the feedback recipient. After each review, observers should provide feedback to their teammates who gave and received the review.

Stress that this is a two-way communication process. The person being reviewed should not necessarily sit quietly, but should ask for clarification, make sure the feedback is understood correctly, etc.

In the sixth edition, students are asked to discuss how the group contributes to the behaviors being discussed and to develop a mutual plan for addressing them. Remind students that behavior is often a function of the context. For example, a quiet member may feel overpowered by a dominant member. Simply asking the quiet member to speak up will not solve the problem.

2. *Performance review (small groups: 10 minutes per review)*

Have the teams conduct a performance review of no more than 10 minutes, including observer feedback, for each team member. If students finish a review in less than 10 minutes, encourage them to discuss the process. Have the observers discuss what they saw and have the participants discuss how they felt during the process. If students finish the entire process before time is up, encourage them to discuss the team as a whole. What is the team doing well, and what could use improvement?

As students are conducting the reviews, briefly observe each of the groups. While you should not interrupt the actual review, you may want to help students reflect on the process of giving and receiving feedback after the review is completed. This may include summarizing some of your own observations.

Some questions that may be helpful:

- Do you feel that the person giving feedback was trying to be helpful? What did she or he do to make you feel this way?
- Do you feel that the person receiving the feedback was listening effectively and understanding what was being said? What did she or he do to make you feel this way?
- What does it feel like to provide performance feedback? To receive feedback? You might want to point out that the group has a responsibility to offer support when someone needs to improve. Ask the students what responsibility the group members have in this situation and whether they asked their teammate how they could help. A typical case is the quiet foreign student. The group should not lay all the responsibility for participation on the quiet member.

3. *Debrief (full class: 20 minutes minimum)*

Consider using the following question to begin the debrief: Many organizations do not do a good job with performance reviews and providing feedback. Based on your experience, why do you think that is?

Other areas for consideration include:

- How did it feel to give feedback? How did it feel to receive feedback? What effect do you think this process had on your group?
- Discuss anxiety and how people behave when they are anxious, e.g., avoiding the situation or making light of it. Ask: Were any of you anxious about giving feedback? Receiving feedback? Which made you more anxious? How do people react when they are anxious? Did you see any of these behaviors in your group?
- What are the benefits of providing feedback? What negatives are there in providing feedback?
- What are the benefits of not providing feedback? What are the detriments of not providing feedback?
- In what ways were your performance plans helpful or not in this process?
- Given this experience, would you want to change anything in your performance plan?
- What is it like when you don't receive continuous open and honest feedback? Were there any surprises? What did it feel like to hear something for the first time during the peer review? Did anyone feel the group was avoiding saying something negative? What did it feel like when you thought your groupmates wanted to say something and wouldn't say directly?
- Were you told about any of your positive and helpful behaviors of which you were previously unaware? What do you see as the benefit of being given positive feed-back?
- How can you use what you learned to make your group more effective? How can you apply this in the real world?

Psychological Contract

We have discussed our expectations for each other, the group, and the course. The following documents these expectations.

Expectations of Each Other

We expect each team member to:

- Maintain a sense of humor.
- Be considerate of other team members.
- Be concerned with producing a quality group product.
- Carry their fair share of the workload.
- Be concerned with learning from the group experience.

Expectations for the Group

We expect that our group will:

- Provide an opportunity to learn about group dynamics.
- Maintain a supportive environment.
- Be fun.
- Work to get a good grade on group projects.
- Be able to meet at a time convenient to all members.

Expectations for the Course

Our expectations for the course are that:

- We will learn how to be better managers.
- The instructor will make the class interesting.
- We will understand how to make groups effective.
- We will be graded fairly.

Performance Norms/Expectations

The performance norms of our group fall into the following four categories: meeting attendance, integrity and trust, task performance, and teamwork.

Meeting Attendance

As a group member you should:

- Be present at all group meetings including those in class.
- Be prompt so meetings can start on time.
- Notify members, if due to an emergency, that you cannot attend.
- Notify members, if due to an emergency, that you are going to be late.

Integrity and Trust

As a group member you should:

- Always uphold a standard of honesty.
- Abide by group agreements.
- Not falsify any work, including interviews.

Task Performance

As a group member your work should be:

- Done on time.
- Grammatically correct and contain no spelling errors.
- Complete and thorough.
- Neat and professional-looking.

As a group member you are expected to:

- Rehearse your interview so you thoroughly understand its contents.
- Conduct your interview in a professional manner.
- Send a thank-you letter to the person you interview.

- Perform your responsibilities as agreed upon by the group.
- Rehearse your in-class presentation.
- Meet as needed for the group to complete its work.

Teamwork

As a member of the team you should:

- Listen to your teammates perspectives.
- Be cooperative.
- Take an active role in group discussions.
- Treat your teammates with respect.
- Be flexible so that consensus can be reached.
- Be open and honest.
- Address conflicts rather than avoid them.
- Work to help the team achieve its goals.
- Stay focused; don't divert the group discussion.

Policies and Procedures

Procedures

The group has defined the following procedures: oral feedback, warning, and termination.

Oral Feedback

1. Team members should generate specific examples and effects of poor performance.
2. A time should be set to provide oral feedback to the teammate.
3. The team should meet and discuss the performance problem.
4. The teammate should be told how his or her performance can be corrected.

Warning

1. A memo should be prepared that describes the poor performance.
2. The memo should include a plan to correct the problem.
3. The memo must be signed by all team members.
4. The memo should be given to the teammate with poor performance.
5. A copy should be given to the instructor.
6. A team meeting should be arranged to discuss the performance.
7. Progress in meeting the performance-improvement plan should be monitored.

Termination

1. The teammate must be given written notice signed by all members.
2. The notice must include what must be done to stop termination.
3. The notice must be hand delivered or return-receipt mail.
4. A copy of the notice must be given to the instructor.
5. Termination will not be effective for 48 hours from time of delivery.
6. If possible, the person must have, or have had, an opportunity to correct the performance.

Policies

The following policies have been agreed to for initiating each of the three procedures: oral feedback, warning, and termination.

Oral Feedback

1. At least three team members must agree that oral feedback is needed.
2. Oral feedback may be given for any unsatisfactory performance as defined by the performance plan.

Warning

At least three team members must agree that a warning is needed for one of the following reasons:

1. Two or more absences from group meetings.
2. Two or more times showing up to meetings more than 10 minutes late.
3. Any unsatisfactory task performance.
4. Second unsatisfactory performance in teamwork category.

Termination

All members other than the teammate to be terminated must agree that termination is needed for one of the following reasons:

1. Any repeated unsatisfactory performance for which a warning was issued.
2. Any unsatisfactory performance in the integrity and trust category because there is no opportunity for remediation.

Performance Appraisal Form

Person being reviewed:______________________ Reviewer:______________________

Rate team member's performance in meeting attendance category.

Excellent_______ Good_______ Fair_______ Needs Improvement_______ Unsatisfactory________

Comments (include examples of behaviors and their effects):

____

____

____

____

____

Rate team member's performance in integrity and trust category.

Excellent_______ Good_______ Fair_______ Needs Improvement_______ Unsatisfactory________

Comments (include examples of behaviors and their effects):

____

____

____

____

____

Rate team member's performance in task performance category.

Excellent_______ Good_______ Fair_______ Needs Improvement_______ Unsatisfactory________

Comments (include examples of behaviors and their effects):

____

____

____

____

____

Rate team member's performance in teamwork category.

Excellent_______ Good_______ Fair_______ Needs Improvement_______ Unsatisfactory________

Comments (include examples of behaviors and their effects):

____

____

____

____

____

Comments on team member's strengths:

____

____

____

____

____

Comments on opportunities for improvement:

____

____

____

____

____

54

CALENDARS AND CLIPS, PARTS 1 AND 2

Group Size: Any number of groups of three to six.

Recommended Time: 120 minutes (5 minutes to set-up; 10–15 minutes, individual preparation; 20–30 minutes, Part 1; 30 minutes for report out and discussion; 40–60 minutes, Part 2)

Provided: Background, instructions, and Observer Sheets in student edition. Roles for photocopying and distribution in class follow these notes.

Also Required: No additional materials required.

Facilities: A large room with moveable chairs or a number of small breakout rooms.

Objectives

- To examine the role of feedback in employer-employee relations
- To practice the skills of active listening and two-way communication
- To practice dealing with problems in stressful situations
- To practice giving feedback and setting goals

Background

Before using this role play, it is helpful if students are familiar with basic theories of communication, gatekeeping, encoding-sending-receiving-decoding models, one-way versus two-way communication, and the role of communication in performance appraisal. In discussing both parts of the exercise, students should consider whether the messages sent by each party were the same as the messages received and whether the parties were giving one another opportunities for clarification. If feelings and goals are not clear, or if each party has a different idea of what the other's feelings and goals are, then the likelihood of conflict is heightened, and feedback becomes ineffective. Given the situation presented in "Calendars and Clips," failure to arrive at mutual agreement on goals will likely result in frustration for both owner and salesperson as well as a breakdown in the work relationship.

Students often have personal experiences to share of their own frustrations in job or other organizational situations in which they were not given clear direction, were not allowed to give input into the realistic or nonrealistic nature of goals, or were unable to have goals defined clearly enough to be able to work towards them.

The Problems

In Part 1, the owner has a number of goals: defusing the salesperson's anger; getting the customer back; dealing with the embarrassment of having an employee throw a temper tantrum in front of customers; further developing the personal service areas of the business; getting the salesperson to make cold calls; and possibly dealing with what may be the very aggressive nature of the salesperson's selling behavior.

A mistake often made by managers is to attack the entire list of goals in a single session. This is counterproductive, but when done in anger with an angry employee, it is usually disastrous, serving only to make each party more hostile and defensive. The owner must therefore select which of the issues should be dealt with immediately and which can be dealt with at a later date and in a less-charged atmosphere. Observers will often pick up on the owner's inability to stay focused on the immediate occurrence—it may remind students of arguments they have had with family members.

One of the reasons for staying focused on the immediate issue is because the salesperson has goals, none of which seem to even overlap with those of the owner. The salesperson is concerned with keeping his or her job; not having enough time to do the extra work his or her boss seems to want done; being appreciated; getting feedback; and not being blamed for something that seems beyond control.

This vast difference in goals can make conversation difficult. It will be important for students to see this problem and to seek ways to arrive at a common point.

Many of these problems could occur in Part 2 where substantive differences exist between the goals of the owner and those of the salesperson. Students should explore ways for the owner and the salesperson to set mutual goals at the outset and then establish methods for achieving them.

Apparently of concern to both parties is cold calling. This may be a starting point. However, making this the only focus of the meeting will not suffice. Larger issues of the owner's goals and concerns and the concerns, time pressures, abilities, and needs of the salesperson must be addressed for there to be long-term gain.

Repeating the exercise after class discussion has taken place often gives students a chance to practice what they have learned from the experience.

This exercise is also useful when carried out by a dyad in front of the class with other class members serving as observers and the exercise repeated several times, each time followed by discussion. For Part 2, use different dyads.

Instructions

1. Set-up (full class: 5 minutes)

- Review the objectives, instructions, and background.
- Ask students to read the questions on the "Observer Sheet."
- Divide the students into groups of at least three with at least one member serving as observer.

2. *Student preparation (small groups: 10 minutes)*

   Distribute Part 1, Role 1, and Part 1, Role 2 to equal numbers of students. Assign all others to observer roles.

   Ask students to read their roles and prepare their parts.

3. *Role play (small groups: 20–30 minutes)*

4. *Report out and discussion (full class: 30 minutes)*

5. *Part 2 (60–90 minutes) Repeat Steps 1 to 4 with Part 2.*

Part 1: Role 1
The Owner

You are sole owner of Calendars and Clips, a store that sells stationery and office supplies. Three years ago, you hired an eager, just-out-of-college kid to handle the growing demand by local businesses for personalized service, i.e., regular sales calls, on-site ordering, fast delivery, etc.

So far, you've been happy. Most of the business has been generated by word-of-mouth, advertising, and contacts you have made socially. The business is growing. Occasionally, friends who are also customers have made joking comments to you about your salesperson's aggressive sales style, but so far this hasn't really been a problem. You know that the customers have been generally happy with the service.

You believe that the potential for developing the personal service aspect of the business is still wide open, but you haven't been particularly successful in getting your salesperson to make cold calls.

When your salesperson walks in part way through the day and makes the announcement that the store's biggest customer has gone elsewhere, you are astounded. In addition, you're feeling angry and embarrassed at the way the announcement by the salesperson was made.

You excuse yourself, ask someone else to wait on the customer with whom you have been working, and go to your office to face your salesperson. You're not sure what you're going to say, but you had better think of something to say fast that will turn things around and get your salesperson back on track. You also wonder if there's any way to get your big customer back.

Part 1: Role 2
The Salesperson

You have been working as the outside salesperson for Calendars and Clips, a store that sells stationery and supplies, for three years since graduating from college. You like your work—calling on customers, taking orders, demonstrating new product lines, and helping customers with inventory control. You know that the business has increased markedly since you began—a fact that shows in the commissions you are making.

While you like your boss, you're not sure that your hard work is really as appreciated as it should be, and you get very little feedback. Frankly, you don't know where you stand, and you find that to be frustrating.

While calling on the store's biggest customer today, an accounting office headed by the first cousin of your boss's spouse, you were told that they had decided to take their business elsewhere. When you asked why, the office manager told you that she wasn't sure, but that it was an order from above. She tells you that she's really sorry because she thought you were doing a really good job.

You're not sure what to tell your boss, but you're concerned that you'll be blamed and may lose your job. Your boss has been on your back lately to do cold calling on potential customers, which you would probably do if you had time, but at this point, you figure this is probably the end anyway. You feel fairly defensive and wonder how you can save your job.

Part 2: Role 1
The Owner

Two weeks ago, your outside salesperson returned to the shop frustrated and despondent over having lost the store's biggest account. You managed to temporarily put the pieces together and get the salesperson back to work. However, during the discussion, it became apparent that your salesperson wanted and needed more feedback and guidance from you.

You set up today's meeting for a formal performance appraisal at which you intend to set some long- and short-term objectives and help your salesperson define the job. Among your objectives is to expand the business by having your salesperson do cold calling on perspective customers.

Before meeting with your salesperson, briefly review the description of your role in Part 1. Then, using the steps and techniques of performance appraisal, conduct a performance appraisal meeting with your salesperson.

Part 2: Role 2
The Salesperson

You're fairly nervous about today's meeting, agreed to by you and your boss two weeks ago when you announced that you had lost a major customer. You want feedback, but you're not sure you can handle criticism. In addition, you are concerned that this is going to turn into another harangue about cold calling. The number of customers you are serving now takes up virtually all of your time, and you don't really think you can handle much more. Worse, taking time away from existing customers is likely to cut into your commissions.

You are going into this meeting feeling ambivalent—somewhat defensive and yet wanting feedback, direction, and support.

55

NO FOLLOWERS? NO LEADERS! THE LANGUAGE OF EMPOWERMENT*

Group Size: Any number of groups of eight.

Recommended Time: 30 minutes per role play (total role play time will depend on the number of people per group); 15 minutes for set up; at least 15 minutes for report outs. It is also possible to do fewer rounds or to do two or three rounds in front of the entire class with all those not playing roles serving as observers.

Provided: Instructions, role plays, and "Questions for Observers."

Also Required: No additional materials required. There is a short clip in the film *Five Easy Pieces* in which Jack Nicholson tries to order a sandwich that we have found useful in illustrating the underlying points of this exercise.

Facilities: One or more large rooms with moveable chairs. The rooms should be large enough or numerous enough to allow at least six feet between groups.

Objectives

- To help participants explore decision making and action options of followers
- To develop skills for fostering a knowledgeable and responsible followership
- To practice the skills for communicating empowerment as a leader and as a follower

Background

When people look to an individual for goals, inspiration, and coaching and don't find it, the individual looked to isn't a leader, and the people looking aren't, therefore, likely to follow. For those in leadership positions, therefore, it is important to understand and be able to perform the skills that create a knowledgeable, responsible, and empowered followership. These skills include knowing how to listen for what is important and meaningful and to convey to followers that they are being heard. The leader must also know how to establish an empowering environment with appropriate priorities and guidelines that set the boundaries within which the follower may act.

Followers also must develop skills. They must be able to convey their ideas and needs openly, they must be able to listen to and understand the priorities and guidelines that are being set, and they must be able to perform responsibly within the field of action.

Giving feedback and conveying empowerment is a responsibility shared by both followers and leaders. This requires active listening and sharing of thoughtful and helpful insights. For communication of feedback and empowerment to be effective, it must be:

- Honest
- Clear
- Respectful
- Genuinely Enthusiastic
- Open

This exercise, developed as a training tool for middle managers, gives students the opportunity to practice their leadership, followership, and shared skills. Though the roles are scripted, they are based on actual situations described by clients. Each of the roles involves circumstances in which cooperation between leader and follower, and empowerment of the follower to act, are by far the best paths. However, there are some obstacles: it's late in the day; energy is low; followers are anxious and fearful based on prior experiences; and so forth.

The exercise is offered as a role play to give participants the opportunity to practice what to say and how to say it. It is meant to be a self-driven exercise in which students are responsible not only for carrying out the role play but also for giving one another feedback. By allowing students to carry out this exercise with minimum outside facilitation, you are empowering them to think and act.

Suggested Outline and Timing

1. Set-up (full class: 15 minutes)

In setting up this exercise up, briefly review what it means to empower employees. Suggest that this includes:

- educating and training.
- providing a field of action.
- providing an atmosphere which encourages employee decision making and action taking.
- providing regular feedback.

Do the following:

- Briefly review the instructions for the exercise.
- Encourage followers to select different roles from the six offered.
- Remind students to read the instructions and roles carefully and to take the time to fully prepare their roles, whether as leader, follower, or observer. This means reflecting on what they believe they should do if placed in the positions described in the roles.

- Ask for and answer any questions about how to proceed.

2. *Role play and debrief (small groups: 30 minutes each)*

During the role play, be available to answer any questions that might arise.

Flag two time periods:

- After the first 15 minutes (the first 20 minutes in round one) remind groups that they should stop the role play and begin to debrief.
- After the next 15 minutes (the next 10 minutes in round one), remind students that it is time to move on to the next role play.

Do this for each round.

After a role play and debrief have been completed, group members should repeat the exercise until every group member has played a leader or a follower at least once.

3. *Discussion (full class debrief: 15 minutes minimum)*

During this time period, debrief the exercise in the larger group. Because the exercise is written to allow for debriefing of the individual role plays within the small groups, this should not be the focus of the large group debriefing. Instead, ask participants to discuss larger lessons learned and how they feel they might use the language of empowerment in the workplace.

The discussion might include or focus on such issues as:

- resistance of employees to taking responsibility.
- difficulties in breaking old leadership and followership patterns and behaviors.
- helpfulness of the feedback process.
- how participants might better make their needs understood.

Conclude the discussion by stressing the business benefits of empowering individuals.

56

EARTHQUAKE
A TEAM BUILDING SIMULATION*

About This Team-Building Exercise

"Earthquake" takes approximately 1–1½ hours to conduct. While developing this simulation, we asked ourselves, "How can we make this one different from other survival simulations?" We decided that instead of asking participants to rank order a strategy and/or salvageable item list, Earthquake participants would rank order a sequence of action steps critical for their survival and rescue.

The topic of surviving an earthquake was selected because it is a frequent occurrence throughout the world and is a media favorite. The California area was chosen for the site of the simulation because it experiences frequent tremblers that often reach 6–8 on the Richter Scale.

There are also many other parts of the world that are vulnerable to quakes. Beyond the borders of the United States, in places like Mexico, China, Armenia, the Philippines, and Iran, quakes have taken a devastating toll on human life and property and will continue to be a worldwide problem.

Since most people can relate to the feelings and emotions associated with being in a natural disaster, an earthquake simulation is a "real" topic to which "real" people can relate. It is a predicament in which any one of us could be involved at some point in our lives.

Earthquakes actually do occur with some frequency; thus, in addition to providing a perfect backdrop for a "true to life" simulation, participation in "Earthquake" can provide group members with a valuable lesson in survival.

The information in the scenario and *Facilitator's Guide* is designed to be educational. Every effort has been made to ensure that the information is as accurate as possible. Nonetheless, the contents are recommendations only. It is important to keep in mind that this simulation was designed for the purpose of building better communication skills and enhancing individual contributions in a team setting. Therefore, the authors, Aviat, Inc., and the experts assume no liability or responsibility for any consequences resulting from the use of the information contained in the simulation or the *Earthquake Facilitator's Guide*.

We have developed Facilitator Slides/Overheads to complement the exercise. Although their use is optional, they can greatly enhance the experience of participants. These 35 mm slides or overheads help the facilitator present the scoring rationale. Each set includes individual slides or overheads for each strategy step and ranking selection.

We hope you find this team-building simulation to be as earthshaking as the subject itself!

CHAPTER I
THE OBJECTIVES OF EARTHQUAKE

As the facilitator, think through your objectives for using this exercise as a team-building or training tool. Some common facilitator objectives are to:

- Examine a group's problem-solving and decision-making process.
- Increase individual and team effectiveness.
- Improve team communication.
- Build synergy in a work team.
- Help a team understand "task" and "maintenance" behaviors and their effect in a workgroup. (These terms are defined in Chapter IX.)
- Build a group's skills in the use of positive confrontation, leveling, and supporting behavior.
- Demonstrate how rational problem solving on a team is enhanced by good interpersonal relationships.
- Provide a "warm-up" activity for a team-building or training session.

All of these objectives fit nicely with the intent of "Earthquake." The simulation was created for the purposes described below.

To Examine a Group's Problem-Solving and Decision-Making Effectiveness

This simulation allows a team to study its problem-solving/decision-making methods both from an individual and a group point of view. The observation can be performed by a designated observer, the facilitator, or the group members themselves. After the exercise has been completed, it is valuable to conduct a discussion of the process and provide feedback on the participants' behavior during the exercise. The participants can then apply the insights they gain to everyday problem solving and decision making in the work setting.

To Allow Participants to Practice Effective Interpersonal Behavior in a Team Setting

Once participants learn the characteristics of effective groups, they can practice the required skills during the exercise. Through experience, participants can discover that an overemphasis on either task or maintenance behavior is dysfunctional in a team setting. After assessing their expertise in both areas, participants may continue to build their interpersonal skills back in the workplace.

To Demonstrate the Advantage of Team Decision Making Over Individual Decision Making

Team-building exercises use firsthand experience to demonstrate how teams can effectively utilize their resources to produce decisions that are superior to the individual decisions of the team members. In fact, research indicates that a team decision is superior to the average of individual team members' decisions in a majority of cases.

To Provide Feedback on Team Performance

The participants learn from timely and specific feedback how their team performed, especially in the areas of idea utilization, information handling, conflict management, decision making, and time management. The feedback, which can be provided by a designated process observer, a group facilitator, and/or the members themselves, should focus on strengths as well as weaknesses of the team's performance. The insight gained can be invaluable in improving the quality of future team experiences.

To Provide Feedback on Individual Performance

Since individuals comprise a team, it is also worthwhile for the participants to focus on their individual performance in the simulation. Examining individual skills of active listening, decision making, leveling, etc., allows group members to assess their level of expertise in these areas and to observe the effects of these skills on the behavior of the group.

To Examine the Dynamics of Group Behavior

In addition to interpersonal dynamics, other group phenomena can be examined via the simulation. Topics such as trust and openness, participation, leadership, and communication are examples of areas the simulation will highlight.

To Provide an Education in "Group Process"

"Group process" refers to the often-implicit methods and practices a group's members use to accomplish their goals and interact with one another. It is a group's unique style or way of operating and relating. Group processes occur with such regularity that they become unconscious to group members, even though they can exert significant influence on the group's effectiveness. The simulation heightens participants' awareness of the group process and provides an opportunity to examine and adjust it when appropriate.

To Provide a Warm-Up Exercise

This exercise is an excellent initial experience in a training session, in a project task assignment, or prior to the formation of a new team. When used before a training session, the simulation provides firsthand evidence of how the group communicates, solves problems, and makes decisions. It highlights areas that require training attention. When the simulation is used with a new team, members become aware of potential trouble spots for group interaction and can take proactive steps to avoid future problems.

This exercise can also be used as a warm-up experience in an intensive team-development program such as Aviat's *Building More Effective Teams Through Role Negotiation.*

HOW TO MAXIMIZE THE IMPACT OF THE SIMULATION

To enhance the learning experience of this exercise, Aviat offers the "Group Process Questionnaire." Taken immediately after the simulation, it helps the team analyze the simulation process rather than its content. Too often a group will focus on the wrong issues—such as when members argue over whether the utilities should be shut off before a water supply is secured. When this happens, valuable opportunities for learning are lost. What matters is the process the group used to reach its decision, not what answers were picked. The "Group Process Questionnaire" provides a structured method for discovering the underlying process that guided the group's interaction.

CHAPTER II
TEAM FORMATION, MATERIALS, AND SETTING

How to Form Simulation Teams

Teams for the simulation can be formed in any way the participants and/or the facilitator desire. They may consist of regular management teams, task forces, project groups, cross-functional and cross-departmental teams, or whatever corresponds with the objectives of the session. The teams may be appointed by the trainer, self-selected by the participants, self-selected by counting off, etc. Although these instructions assume you are conducting the simulation with multiple groups, it is also possible to run the simulation with only one team—the same logic applies.

If a participant indicates that she or he has gone through the exercise previously, (1) have the person join a team that is not aware of the participant's prior knowledge to see how the team handles the participant's input, or (2) have the person serve as a process observer.

You may wish to appoint a process observer to each team. A process observer does not participate in the exercise, but watches the group members' interaction as they work through the simulation and provides feedback that allows the team to enhance its effectiveness. A process observer can be a trainer, a human resources professional, or simply a member of the workgroup. If you are working with only one or two teams, you may wish to play this role. (See Chapter VIII for further discussion of the role of the process observer.)

Team Size

Optimal team size is five participants. Teams of fewer than four or more than seven are not recommended. If time is an issue, use small teams since smaller groups tend to finish the problem in less time. Extra people may be used as process observers.

Materials

Each participant should have the following:

- A copy of "Earthquake"
- A pen or a pencil with an eraser

The facilitator or consultant should have the following:

- A flip-chart with newsprint and marking pens or a blackboard and chalk
- A copy of the *Earthquake Facilitator's Guide*
- A calculator

Optional: A set of the Earthquake Facilitator Slides/Overheads, projector, and screen

Setting

Two options exist for providing the right setting for the simulation:

1. A meeting room large enough for the teams to move away from each other while working on the problem. (If the tables are too close to one another, participants will be distracted by noise and activities at other tables.)
2. A large conference room and individual break-out rooms. Participants can hear the instructions in the large room, break up into smaller groups to conduct the simulation in break-out rooms, and reassemble for the debriefing process in the large room. In either case, round tables should be used for small-group discussion.

CHAPTER III
INTRODUCTION/ADMINISTRATION OF THE EXERCISE

Facilitators differ in the way they introduce a simulation. Some begin with an explanation of group process, an overview of effective team behavior, and guidelines for how to reach a consensus decision. Other facilitators don't provide much background, preferring to educate participants after the simulation is complete.

There are pros and cons to each approach. Introducing the simulation with an explanation of effective group process helps the group be sensitive to these issues throughout the simulation and allows participants to practice new behaviors. However, equipped with these cues, the group is likely to be on its best behavior. Group members may not exhibit their normal patterns—the very patterns that may be interfering with the group's effectiveness. Hence, the opportunity to surface and examine real group problems is lost.

Beginning the simulation without such an introduction has the converse effect. Participants tend to display their natural behavior in the simulation and have an opportunity to evaluate it in a constructive way. However, they are not equipped with enough information to be able to practice new behavior during the exercise.

There is a way to have the best of both worlds: We often run a "pre-test" simulation without much introduction. We then debrief it, provide instruction on effective group process, and run another simulation that allows participants to use new skills and correct dysfunctional behavior patterns. This way, the group has the benefit of evaluating a natural group interaction, as well as learning and practicing new skills. Additional simulations are available from Aviat, 1-800-421-LEAD (5323).

Whatever method you choose, the simulation itself can be conducted by following the steps below. The instructions assume you are working with multiple groups. If you are working with only one team, the same basic guidelines apply.

STEP 1: The exercise can be introduced with the following statement:

"This simulation is based on extensive research of past earthquakes in the California area, as well as speculative studies from several California agencies (the Bay Area Regional Earthquake Preparedness Project, the Office of Emergency Services, and the Seismic Safety Commission). The events in this simulation are similar to real circumstances that occur during earthquakes."

STEP 2: Hand out the "Earthquake" exercise to the participants. Ask them to read the story, and give them the following instructions:

"There are seven action steps that you should take to ensure your survival and rescue and five action steps that you should not take because they are either unnecessary or may harm you. Decide which seven of the action steps listed you would take, assigning a "1" to what you would do first, a "2" to your second step, etc. (1-7). Then continue the ranking with the remaining five steps you would not take, numbering them 8–12, the twelfth being reserved for the most dangerous or least helpful step, the eleventh the next least dangerous step, etc.

Complete the individual ranking without discussing the situation with anyone else. Place your answers in Column A entitled "Your Rank." You'll have about 10 minutes to complete this step."

While the individuals are working, you as facilitator should draw the results grid (see Page 18) on a flip-chart or chalkboard that is visible to all participants.

STEP 3: (Optional) When the individuals are done with their ranking, discuss the need for active listening, differing, leveling, and supporting behavior. Tell the group that they are about to break into teams to decide by consensus which action steps to take and how to rank them. (See Chapter IX for an explanation of these terms.)

As discussed in the introduction to this section, you may wish to skip this step. If your training design, or your goal, involves seeing how well (or poorly) the participants do on this exercise without any new information or training (e.g., a pre-test at the beginning of a team-building program), you may want them to proceed to the group ranking immediately. Giving them information at this point will help them work more effectively in their teams.

STEP 4: Form the teams. How you form the various teams will depend on your objectives and the nature of the participants (see Chapter II). Once the teams have been formed, advise the group:

"Now that everyone has finished the individual ranking, it is time to do the team ranking. You will have 20 minutes* to complete the ranking as a team (Step D in the workbook). This step should be done by ______ o'clock."

If applicable, say to the group, "You will be assigned a process observer whose job is to assess the group's behavior and dynamics. S/he will also assist you in scoring the exercise and the "Group Process Questionnaire" (if used). In addition, s/he will give the group feedback concerning what s/he observed during the exercise."

* If participants are moving to break-out rooms, they should receive 20 minutes from the time they get to their location.

STEP 5: Circulate among the groups as they are working to see how they are doing. If any group is not managing their time well, remind them when they have 15, 10, and 5 minutes left.

STEP 6: (Optional) Once the rankings are finished, make a decision about whether you, as the facilitator, wish to "debrief" (see Chapter VIII) the group's simulation activity now or whether you will wait until the scores have been tabulated. The rationale for debriefing the simulation before scoring is that the participants are not yet biased by their knowledge of the results. They will carefully assess their group's interaction because they don't know yet whether they did well or poorly on the exercise.

A danger is that a team who learns that they did well on the simulation may not spend energy evaluating the method they used. However, it is not uncommon for teams to arrive at the right decision using the wrong method or process! This can happen, for example, when the team's manager takes control of the group's decision-making process because s/he believes that it is his/her position to do so. Although s/he may have picked the right answers, did s/he allow for participation from other group members? What expertise did s/he ignore? What effect did his/her control have on the motivation of the other group members? These are important process questions that still must be answered, whether or not the group came up with the correct answers.

If you choose to debrief at this stage (before the scores are tabulated), you have three options:

A. If you are using Aviat's "Group Process Questionnaire," pass it out for the participants to complete. Conduct the debriefing process as it is explained in detail in the *Group Process Questionnaire Facilitator's Guide*.

B. If you used process observers, ask them to provide feedback to the team they observed (or if you played the role yourself, provide your own input). Guidelines for giving effective feedback are offered in Chapter VIII.

C. If neither the "Group Process Questionnaire" nor process observers have been used, the group may debrief itself. Before they do so, however, provide participants with some guidelines so they will know what to discuss and analyze. (See Chapter VIII.)

STEP 7: Reassemble the large group. It helps if each team's members sit together for the debriefing and scoring.

STEP 8: Read, or present in your own words, "The Situation in Brief" section of Chapter IV. If you elect, use the Facilitator Slides/Overheads to assist in the debriefing.

STEP 9: (Optional) If you have a particularly skeptical group, you may want to give them some of the information from Chapter VI, "Background Of The Simulation-Development Process, The Experts And Authors," to add credibility to what follows.

STEP 10: Read or paraphrase the "Ranking and Rationale" sections of Chapter IV. Have the group members mark the expert ranking in Columns B and E of the exercise workbook. Chapter VII contains additional background earthquake-preparedness information. Use it to support the ranking and rationale if necessary. While most simulations are used to learn about effective group problem solving, this particular exercise also contains accurate information on earthquakes and earthquake preparedness, which gives the experience dual value.

STEP 11: Go through the scoring process as outlined in Chapter V, marking the various scores on a large results grid displayed on a flip-chart or blackboard that all participants can see. Pay particular attention to the process scores—Synergy Score (Step I in workbook) and Percent Change (Step J in workbook), and to the key indicators—Lowest Individual Score on the Team (Step K in workbook) and Number of Individual Scores Lower than the Team Score (Step L in workbook). The optional Facilitator Slides/Overheads can assist in the Ranking and Rationale.

STEP 12: (Optional) If you have elected to debrief the group process after scoring (instead of before), do so here. See Step 6, Sections A, B, and C for instructions.

STEP 13: When you are working with more than one group, have representatives from each team do brief reports to the large group on what they learned about effective teamwork. They do not need to get into all the details of who said or did what, or report the actual scores from the "Group Process Questionnaire" (if used). A summary of the highlights is sufficient.

STEP 14: (Optional) If used, ask the process observers to give a summary presentation of what they observed as the teams worked on the exercise (or provide this summary yourself if you are the observer). Each process observer's presentation should be no longer than five minutes.

Weave a discussion about group process into the feedback given by the process observers. Support their observations by offering comments about the importance of active listening, leveling, supporting behavior, and communication effectiveness (see Chapter IX). Tie in incidents that occurred in the team(s) to your discussion of these behaviors.

STEP 15: Offer your concluding remarks and make a transition to the next part of the training program, or close as appropriate.

CHAPTER IV
WHAT THE EXPERTS SAY

The Situation in Brief

On July 27 at 7:12 p.m. Pacific Standard Time, an earthquake hit in downtown San Francisco. The temperature was 59 degrees. It was still light out, but there were only about 1½ hours of daylight left. Most of the downtown business people had gone home.

The earthquake scenario described will most likely result in the following:

- thousands of people dead
- several thousand people hospitalized with serious injuries
- over one hundred thousand people significantly injured, but not requiring hospitalization
- tens of thousands of people homeless
- critical damage to all international airports and many major highways (enough to slow down or possibly halt transportation of emergency services and personnel)
- most, if not all, utilities (gas, electric, and water) nonfunctional for at least 72 hours
- communication systems (telephone, radio, etc.) severely damaged and others overloaded by the influx of calls
- significant ground failure and liquefaction, rendering most Bay Area marinas inoperable, causing highways and buildings to crumble, and damaging railroads beyond use for at least three days
- hundreds of large fires occurring simultaneously throughout the city, overwhelming the fire department
- hundreds of toxic chemical leaks, resulting in fires and explosions, making evacuation of many of these areas essential

There are several things that the group members have going for them:

- The building wasn't damaged enough to cause a cave-in.
- No one was seriously injured.
- They have enough water to last more than two weeks.
- They have supplies to purify their water sources if necessary.
- They can keep in touch with the outside world.

- They are able to signal for help.
- Even though it is mostly blocked, there is fresh air coming in through the elevator shaft and the crack in the foundation.
- The crack in the foundation wall gives the group a way to let rescuers know where they are and is possibly a way out.
- It is probable that a family member or friend will begin to look for someone in the group within the next 24 hours. However, since the earthquake was so devastating, it may be days before professional rescuers are able to extricate the group from the building. In either case, they will most likely be rescued.

The following factors are working against the group:

- There may be panic and fear on the part of some of the group members. (This could hamper timely and accurate decision making.)
- Being trapped in a building puts the group lower on the priority list for rescue. (Injured people, the fires, and more lethal situations will most likely be attended to first.)
- They are without utilities.
- The group is trapped in a structurally damaged building with no apparent way to escape.
- The aftershocks that occur will probably upset the group both physically and mentally.

Ranking and Rationale of the Action Steps

The ranking of the action steps is based on the premise that the safest way to survive the earthquake is to wait it out in the basement. The group has plenty of supplies to survive for several weeks. They also have appropriate materials for signaling rescuers who will inevitably search for trapped people within the next few days.

1. SHUT OFF ALL UTILITIES

Since the building sustained severe structural damage during the earthquake, it is extremely important to turn off all the utilities at their primary control points. Most of the cables and piping for the utilities are located underground. During a strong earthquake, building movement and the subsequent displacement can rupture the utilities at the point where they connect with the building. With this much movement, it is not uncommon for at least some of the utilities to rupture and become hazardous and/or be rendered inoperable. Aftershocks can also jolt utility systems into causing further destruction if they are not shut off. A water main break, a gas leak, or live electrical wires could put the group at serious risk since they are trapped in a confined area. Thus, securing the utilities is of utmost importance to the group's safety.

All utility shutoff points are located in the basement of the building and are therefore readily accessible to the group.

- Electricity—the electric switch at the fuse box

- Water—main valve at the water meter
- Gas—the main valve at the gas meter (this may require a wrench)

2. *CHECK FOR INJURIES AND ADMINISTER FIRST AID*

In earthquakes of this size, it is common for people to sustain some injuries. People and items are often thrown around enough to cause bruises, cuts, or possibly broken limbs. In this scenario, only a few people were injured and need medical attention. The group has a small first-aid kit to treat these injuries. This should be done as soon as possible, so that people do not suffer continued physical discomfort.

3. *ASSIGN SOMEONE TO MONITOR THE RADIO AND LISTEN FOR UPDATES*

It is critical that the group members stay well-informed. Listening to the radio will provide essential information. The radio stations will broadcast periodic updates on the conditions of the Bay Area. The group could get some clues on measures to ensure their survival and rescue. The radio may give them an idea of when to expect help to arrive. The type of signaling techniques they choose, as well as their long-term survival discussion, could be impacted by the information they hear on the radio. Finally, the radio can serve as a calming factor. If the group is well-informed, they may feel more in control of their surroundings.

4. *LOCATE AND SECURE A WATER SUPPLY*

Since it is probable that the group members will be stranded for at least 72 hours, they will need to locate a water supply in order to survive. To stay properly hydrated, each person should consume 1–2 quarts of water per day. The minimum amount of water needed for a three-day stay would be 18 quarts. It makes sense to locate and use the largest supply of water first. There are many water sources in the basement, the largest and most convenient of which is the water heater. Most office building hot-water heaters hold 50–100 gallons of clean water. Once the utilities are turned off and the faucet in the fill line to the water heater closed, the group can collect uncontaminated water from the faucet at the bottom of the water heater. This water supply will last a minimum of 17 days (2 quarts/person/day from a 50-gallon tank) to a maximum of 66 days (1 quart/person/day from a 100-gallon tank).

As stated in the scenario, there are six cans of cola and three full ice cube trays in the refrigerator. The cola isn't water, but it is a liquid and the sugar in the cola may get the group through a hungry moment or two. Therefore, it may be wise to save the soda for the second or third day.

There is also water located in the coffee machine. Most modern office coffee machines have a one-pot reservoir of water in them that can be extracted by tilting the unit forward or taking the top off the machine. There will be approximately one pot of clean water to drink.

In the event the group runs out of clean water sources, the water in the bathroom could be used. There will be some water left in the system. If the drain in the sink is stopped up and the water is turned on, the water in the system should come down by the force of gravity. Draining the pipes in this way should be done as soon as possible to avoid contamination of the water in the pipe system. If the toilet has a tank, it may be full of water and can be used. They should not use the bowl water for drinking purposes. If the tank on the toilet has disinfectants or a bluing agent in it, this water is unsafe to drink. If the tank is clear of disinfectants, it can be used for consumption, but it needs to be purified first.

The other dilemma the group faces is that a latrine area needs to be established. The group has to decide if they will need the water in the bathroom for drinking purposes before they begin to use the bathroom as a latrine. Since the utilities are turned off, the toilet will no longer flush automatically. Someone will have to put water in the toilet to flush it. In all likelihood, the group will have the luxury of using the bathroom water for bathroom purposes and using some of their primary water source for manually flushing the toilet every couple of days.

5. *DEVELOP DAY & NIGHT SIGNALING TECHNIQUES; BEGIN SIGNALING IMMEDIATELY*

Developing signaling techniques is the next logical step for the group to take. Once the group's basic needs have been met, the members should decide what signaling methods they are going to use, which individuals will be in charge of signaling, and a rotation schedule or shift. A rotation schedule will allow some members to sleep while others stay awake to watch and listen for rescuers and to continue signaling efforts. Having a day and night signaling plan in place could get the group rescued more quickly. Unless a relative or a friend of someone in the group knows that she or he was in the building at the time of the earthquake, it is unlikely that rescue personnel will be able to locate them immediately. This also assumes that the person or people who know where the group is are all right themselves and able to contact the proper help.

6. *DISCUSS LONG-TERM SURVIVAL STRATEGIES AS A GROUP*

After the group has decided on signaling techniques and watch times, long-term survival strategies should be discussed. A healthy exchange of ideas on what should be done in the following days will prove most useful. The group members should begin by paying particular attention to news reports they hear on the radio and using this information to guide their decision making.

The strategy session should serve several purposes. First of all, they need to decide how to best ration their supplies, taking into account that they may be stranded for days or possibly weeks. If the individuals in the group do not make good decisions now, they may put themselves at risk in a short period of time.

The strategy session could also be used to address group members' fears and concerns. The days following a natural disaster can be very trying for anyone, particularly a group of people trapped in a basement. There is already an indication that some members of the group are scared, panicky, and as a result, somewhat argumentative. People in crisis situations can manage their emotions by talking things out. They should rely on each other for idea testing, comfort, and emotional support. This crisis may also be compounded by the aftershocks following the quake, which will most likely take a toll on the mental well-being of the group. Comforting each other over the next few days will be very important.

As with many things the group does, the strategy session can result in a sense of control. Focusing on what needs to be done next will provide an effective diversion from the emotional stress of their dilemma. If a plan is in place and everybody knows what actions they must take individually and as a group, they may feel more at ease with the situation.

During the long-term survival discussion, the group members should discuss how they can provide entertainment for themselves. Word games, singing, charades, reading, or playing cards may release some of the tension they feel. Games can provide a pleasant distraction for the group, and a distraction for certain group members could be essential to their survival.

It may be necessary to have a strategy discussion every few days to see if the group is on track with its plan and to see how everyone is dealing with the crisis. Keeping on top of the radio reports will provide the additional information needed for these update discussions. Nonetheless, it is important for group members to avoid spending much time in conversations about problems. Sometimes, these discussions can become counterproductive. If group members begin to argue with each other and/or the discussion becomes unfocused, they should go on to something less stressful.

7. DIVIDE SANDWICHES & EAT THEM THIS EVENING

Group members will probably become hungry later in the evening or early the next morning. They should go ahead and eat the sandwiches at this time, before they spoil. According to registered dieticians, poultry should not be left out more than two to four hours at room temperature. The risk of food poisoning increases significantly after this time. Since the utilities are no longer working, the interior of the refrigerator will eventually warm up. If the door of the refrigerator is not opened, the sandwiches could be safe to eat for six to seven hours. It is not a certainty that anyone eating these chicken salad sandwiches after this time would get sick enough to require medical attention. (Some people's digestive systems are able to process slightly contaminated foods without suffering noticeable side effects.) But, because the group is trapped in the basement with no way to seek medical attention, it would be wise to eat the sandwiches in the next seven hours or so. Having full or semi-full stomachs the first night will also give the group one less thing to worry about at this critical time.

These first seven steps are the ones the group should take to assure its survival. The eighth step is optional. (It probably does not need to be done, but it won't hurt.) The final four steps present dangers to the group's survival (in order of increasing severity) and should be avoided.

8. PURIFY THE WATER SOURCE (optional)

Purifying the water source is in the eighth position because, if the group chooses to do this, it would be neither harmful nor helpful. Purifying the water source is only necessary if the group uses the water in the bathroom. The main water sources—the water heater, ice-cube trays, and the coffee machine—will all be safe to drink without purifying them.

If the group decides to use the bathroom water or someone in the group becomes ill from drinking contaminated water, it would be wise to purify the remaining water sources by adding 5–10 drops of the liquid chlorine bleach (which is with the cleaning supplies) to one gallon of water. If, after the water stands for approximately 30 minutes, the chlorine can be smelled or tasted slightly, then the water is safe to drink.

9. POUND ON THE PIPES WITH THE STEEL WRENCH

It would not be safe to "pound" on the pipes. Hitting a steel wrench against a metal pipe could cause a spark and possibly an explosion or fire if there is a high enough gas content in the air trapped in the basement. The scenario states that someone smelled gas and another person heard a hissing noise. If there is any chance that gas lines are damaged, pounding on the pipes with a steel wrench could threaten the group's safety. It is also remotely possible that someone could hit a gas or water pipe hard enough to damage the crumbling structure around them. Although these situations are unlikely, it is not a good idea to do anything that could put the group at risk.

10. DIVIDE THE SANDWICHES AND RATION THEM OVER THE NEXT FEW DAYS

The amount of food in this situation will not significantly extend the group's survival time, so there is no reason to ration it out. As indicated earlier in the ranking, the sandwiches should be eaten on the evening of the quake or early the next morning, before they spoil. As bad as their predicament is, they are not going to starve to death. Normal, healthy people can go approximately three weeks without food. This group will most likely be rescued before that length of time goes by.

While deciding to eat the sandwiches later may not prove to be life threatening, it could make the group members uncomfortable and possibly dehydrate them if the sandwiches have spoiled and people get food poisoning.

The worst case scenario would be that someone in the group would suffer from food poisoning (salmonella) and require medical attention. Since the group is trapped in the basement library, getting the proper medical help is impossible. It is a much wiser decision to eat the sandwiches while they are safe to eat, thus avoiding the complications of food poisoning.

11. ATTEMPT TO REMOVE THE RUBBLE FROM THE ENTRANCE TO THE FIRST FLOOR

Removing the rubble could cause a cave-in, injure someone, or kill the person or persons attempting to remove the debris. The group does not have the proper equipment to remove the rubble safely. Special tunneling equipment and techniques are often necessary when removing stone and concrete in order to prevent further destruction. It is safer to remove the debris from the top of the pile, working downward, rather than working from the bottom up. Much of the weight of the debris may be supported at the bottom of the pile. Also, the aftershocks that commonly occur after an earthquake could jar the rubble enough to cause further damage or trap someone.

It is best to wait for someone outside to rescue the group. When the group is found and emergency rescue personnel arrive on the scene, they will be able to decide the best way to extricate people from the basement. Rescuers may choose not to attempt to remove the rubble but instead to expand the hole in the foundation wall enough for the group to escape. On the other hand, they may decide that clearing the elevator shaft from the main floor down to the basement is the best alternative.

12. *LIGHT THE CANDLES SO THAT YOU CAN SEE AND RESCUERS WILL BE ABLE TO LOCATE YOU*

Since someone smelled gas and heard a hissing sound after the earthquake, lighting a candle could prove deadly. If the building suffered significant structural damage during the quake, gas could be leaking from damaged pipes. Residual gas can float along gas lines even after the gas company shuts off the gas to the area. Under these circumstances, it is not wise to light open flames. Although remote, there is a chance that lighting a candle could spark a gas explosion or ignite a spilled chemical solution, especially in a confined area such as a basement. Using the flashlight as a light source and for signaling purposes when necessary is a much safer option.

CHAPTER V
SCORING AND EXPLAINING THE SCORES

How to Score This Exercise

Several scores are calculated from this exercise. Each represents a specific aspect of the simulation and deals with one of two general kinds of measures.

Content Scores
Individual Score
Average Individual Score
Team Score

Process Scores
Synergy Score
Percent Change
Key Indicators
Lowest Individual Score on the Team
Number of Individual Scores Lower than the Team Score

Listed below are instructions on how to compute the scores, followed by an explanation of what each represents.

The Content Scores

The Content Scores are discrepancy scores—that is, they measure the difference between the decision made by an individual or team, and the experts' decision. By calculating the difference between Columns A and B, you derive the appropriate score for each Action Step made by the individual. Place this score, ignoring whether it's positive or negative, in Column C. Add down Column C to get the Individual Score. In this exercise, the lower the score the better, as low scores reflect only small differences with the experts. Repeat this process for D, E, and F to get the Team Score.

After the Individual Scores for each team member have been calculated, they need to be averaged to obtain the Average Individual Score for each team (Step G in the workbook). To do this, add the Individual Scores for each team member, and divide by the number of members in that team.

At this point, have the team members double-check their arithmetic. It is normal for Individual Scores to differ, but when the members of a team independently calculate the Team Score and the Average Individual Score, they should come up with the same results.

Once these scores have been calculated, start filling in the Results Grid that you have displayed on a flip-chart or blackboard. Ask each team for its Average Individual Score, and then its Team Score (Step G and Step H). Write these on the grid as they report them.

The Process Scores

Calculating the Synergy Score (Step I) is simple. Subtract the Team Score from the Average Individual Score. If the team did better (scored lower) than the individuals, this score will be positive and represent synergy. If the team did worse (scored higher), this number will be negative and will generally indicate that the team did not work together very effectively. To calculate the Percent Change (Step J), divide the Synergy Score by the Average Individual Score. This yields the percent change.

Key Indicators

Ask each team for its lowest (best) Individual Score (Step K) and how many people (if any) scored lower than the team (Step L). Write these numbers in the last two rows of the grid.

WHAT EACH SCORE MEANS

Explain the significance of each of these scores as you fill in each row of the grid, or complete the grid and then explain the whole thing, or create a compromise between the two.

Content Scores

Each participant's Individual Score represents how well s/he solved the earthquake problem working alone. It can reflect how much a person knew about earthquakes, how much s/he knew about survival techniques, or how good s/he was at figuring things out without much prior knowledge of the problem. It is a content score because it deals with the subject matter of the problem and not the group process.

The Average Individual Score is a conglomerate measure of the quality of the information all group members brought to the group. Since it is simply the average of how each member did alone on the problem, it does not represent how well the group worked together.

The Team Score is a measure of how well the group solved the problem—whether they came up with a solution that would enable them to survive in the basement, as well as a strategy for prompting their rescue. It is content-based in that it measures only the quality of their decision, not how they arrived at it.

Process Scores

By comparing results obtained by members working alone (Average Individual Score) with those obtained working together (Team Score), we get our first indication of group effectiveness—the Synergy Score. For a team to do better than its individual members, the members have to use their collective information well. The larger the Synergy Score, the better they functioned as a team. Groups that post negative Synergy Scores had better information and ideas within their group than they were able to utilize. When the groups debrief the process through (1) discussion, (2) the use of the "Group Process Questionnaire," and/or (3) feedback from the process observers, they will be able to identify the factors that contributed to their Synergy Score.

Percent Change is a finer and often more accurate look at how each group functioned. The Average Individual Score may be described as the amount of improvement possible in any group. If a group averaged 31.2 points working separately, and a perfect Team Score would be O, then they could conceivably gain 31.2 points. If they gained 15.2 points, for instance (Team Score = 16, Synergy Score = 15.2), they would have improved by 49 percent. On the other hand, a group with an Average Individual Score of 20.8 and a Team Score of 9 would have a Synergy Score of 11.8, quite a bit less than the first team, but a Percent Change of 57 percent, indicating they made more progress than the first team. Groups that start with low Average Individual Scores should not be penalized for knowing a lot about the problem or being good at figuring out the answers; hence the additional calculation of the Percent Change. In either case—large Synergy Scores or large Percent Change—the groups should be commended for functioning as synergistic teams.

Key Indicators

The Lowest Individual Score on the Team can say a lot about how well the team worked. If any member did better alone than the team did together, then it is obvious that there was some sound information available to them that they did not utilize. What role did the owner of the lowest score play? If his/her score was lower than the Team Score, did that person fail to contribute, or did other members shut him/her out?

Number of Individual Scores Lower than the Team Score is an extension of the Lowest Score on the Team Concept. Teams that function effectively seldom have more than one person who did better alone than the members did collectively. (They often have none.) Groups that work poorly together usually have a number of members who work better alone. Again, in the debriefing, it is useful to discuss what happened with information the group did not or could not use effectively.

Results Grid

	Team 1	Team 2	Team 3
Average individual score			
Team score			
Synergy score			
Percent change			
Lowest individual score on team			
# individual scores lower than team score			

CHAPTER VI
BACKGROUND OF THE SIMULATION-DEVELOPMENT PROCESS, THE EXPERTS, AND AUTHORS

The Simulation-Development Process

The development process of this simulation was quite interesting.

Dr. Fisher came up with the idea of using a natural disaster as a setting for a team-building simulation because he felt people could easily relate to the idea and that it was important to have a greater understanding of the topic.

Dawn Peters began to research the topic through information she received from the Bay Area Regional Earthquake Preparedness Project. She supplemented that information with general research on earthquakes.

An actual simulation was created and written. The Aviat team brainstormed ideas for this scenario.

After the simulation was completed, it was field tested with the Aviat staff and several other groups to refine the clarity of the language and make sure the scoring worked properly. Several revisions were made.

Dawn traveled to San Francisco to meet with the experts. (Aviat collaborates with experts to make our simulations as accurate and realistic as possible.)

The experts were asked to review the simulation in great detail to make sure we had covered all the bases. During the process, the team of experts and the author dealt with many of the same issues that the team-building simulation is designed to help people work on. Different perspectives and opinions had to be synthesized, conflicts arose about what and how things should be said, and the Ranking and Rationale were debated. This group went through a process very similar to that of participants so as to arrive at the best possible outcome.

After the team meeting, the experts' contributions and changes were added. As a result, "Earthquake" is a very sound team-building tool.

The Experts

Thanks go to the members of the Bay Area Regional Earthquake Preparedness Project members who reviewed and commented on "Earthquake." With their help and support, we have created a fun, exciting, and educational team-building tool. Special thanks and appreciation go to the experts listed below who participated in the team meeting to develop the Ranking and Rationale.

RICHARD K. EISNER is the director of the Bay Area Regional Earthquake Preparedness Project (BAREPP) of the Governor's Office of Emergency Services. As director, he developed and now oversees a planning and technical-assistance program that provides support to local governments and businesses throughout the ten-county San Francisco Bay Region. His primary focus is on issues of seismic design and urban earthquake hazard reduction. Richard has gained extensive experience with earthquakes and earthquake preparedness in the past 15 years. He has served as program manager on a National Science Foundation project to develop model hazard reduction and preparedness techniques based on Japanese practice. Mr. Eisner has also participated in several post earthquake investigations, including those in El Centro (1979), Coalinga (1983), Morgan Hill (1984), Palm Springs (1986), and Whittier (1987), and served on the State of California's investigating team that visited Mexico City in September of 1985. He received his undergraduate degree with Honors in Architecture and a Master's Degree in City and Regional Planning from the University of California, Berkeley. Most recently, Mr. Eisner presented papers on California's comprehensive approach to earthquake preparedness to the US/Japan Workshop on Urban Earthquake Hazard Mitigation and the 9th World Conference on Earthquake Engineering in Tokyo and Kyoto. On top of these professional accomplishments, Mr. Eisner is a Member of the American Institute of Architects, the American Institute of Certified Planners, and serves as Chairman of the Committee on Urban Earthquake Hazard Mitigation of the Earthquake Engineering Research Institute.

LYNN MURPHY is a Project Planner for the Bay Area Regional Earthquake Preparedness Project of the Governor's Office of Emergency Services. In her current position, she assists local governments and community organizations in the planning and implementation of earthquake-preparedness programs in the areas of hazard mitigation, emergency response, and post-earthquake recovery. Prior to joining BAREPP, Lynn served as assistant director of the Center for Community Development and Design at the University of Colorado, Denver campus. While with CCDD, she worked with local governments and community groups to develop and carry out economic-development projects in urban neighborhoods and rural towns throughout Colorado. Ms. Murphy's professional experience also includes planning, management, and program development with agencies of the federal government, community-based social-service programs, and institutions of higher education. She also belongs to the American Planning Association and the California Emergency Services Association. Lynn received her Master's Degree in Planning and Community Development from the University of Colorado in 1974.

The Authors

D. DAWN PETERS is the research and development specialist at ORION International, Ltd. Dawn received a Bachelor's Degree in Psychology, with a specialization in Organizational Communication, from the University of Colorado, Boulder. Upon graduation, she gained valuable business experience working for a large international service organization located in Troy, Michigan. Ms. Peters' primary responsibilities include the research and development of training programs for Aviat, a subsidiary of ORION International, Ltd. She has co-authored several management-development products, including ENVISIONing, a guided process for exploring and planning the future of organizations and *The Entrepreneurial Edge*, a system designed to maximize entrepreneurial activity and innovation within organizations.

D. JOSEPH FISHER, Ph.D., is a consultant who has worked with a wide range of organizations in both the public and private sectors for the past twenty years. He consults with key executive teams and facilitates programs in which managers gain better understanding of themselves and their roles in their organizations. He has designed and delivered state-of-the-art stress-management programs and organization culture-change projects. His organization, Aviat, based in Ann Arbor, Michigan, offers "cutting-edge" learning technologies that help individuals, teams, and organizations compete effectively in the market while achieving high levels of personal satisfaction and fulfillment. His experience has prepared him to assist organization leaders and their companies in coping with change and transformation. Dr. Fisher has a Ph.D. in Education and Psychology from the University of Michigan and is a licensed psychologist. He is an active member of the American Psychological Association, the American Society of Training and Development, and a lifetime member of the National Rehabilitation Association.

CHAPTER VII
EARTHQUAKE PREPAREDNESS

Earthquakes and Their Impact on the World

As mentioned in the introduction, an earthquake was chosen as the topic for this team-building exercise because earthquakes are a frequent occurrence throughout the world. A large portion of the United States population lives along major faults. It is probable that many individuals will experience an earthquake at some time in their lives. As a president of the United States once stated, "...We must learn more about the earthquake threat so that we can take appropriate actions to reduce losses when an earthquake occurs....An informed and educated citizenry is essential to reducing the earthquake risk."

The best way to survive an earthquake is to be prepared and to have a good understanding of the proper procedures for earthquake survival. Loss of life and injury can occur when individuals make bad decisions before, during, and after earthquakes. Many people are injured or killed each year because they do not have the supplies stored to survive an earthquake or because they react inappropriately during or after a quake.

What should you do in order to survive an earthquake?

The following information provides suggestions on what to do before, during, and after an earthquake. This information was obtained from several organizations that research earthquakes and are knowledgeable about emergency procedures.

Before an Earthquake

It is important for both families and organizations to have an "Earthquake Action Plan." This plan could save lives. In addition to the safety factor, being prepared gives people a sense of control. They will act more appropriately during the crisis if they have the information and knowledge they need to survive.

Action Steps: These are the steps you should take with your family and/or employees to ensure that you are ready for an earthquake.

- **Map out a floor plan of your home or office building**. This diagram should display the following things:
    - primary and secondary escape routes from each room
    - the safest place to take cover in each room
    - location of the utility shutoff points for the gas, water, and electricity
    - hazardous areas in the house or office during an earthquake (windows, large unsecured furniture, brick or unreinforced masonry, kitchen, etc.)
    - location of the earthquake emergency supplies
    - location of fire extinguishers
    - a designated area where family members or employees can reassemble after the quake
- **Know where the nearest hospitals and emergency shelters are located and several routes to reach them.**
- **Place a 12-inch, adjustable, or appropriate wrench near the gas valve**, in case you have to turn off the gas.
- **Purchase at least one multi-purpose dry chemical fire extinguisher.** An office building needs a minimum of one extinguisher per floor. Check with your local fire department for requirements.
- **Put together an emergency kit.** It should include the following items:
    - battery-operated radio with fresh batteries
    - flashlight with extra batteries
    - first-aid kit, including specific medicines needed for employees or family members
    - first-aid book
    - bottled water (one-week supply for each member in the family or organization)
    - canned and dried foods (one-week supply for each person)
    - non-electric can opener
    - pet food
    - portable stove (butane or charcoal) and stove fuel
    - waterproof matches

***Note**: You should not light matches or stoves until it has been determined by professionals that there are no gas leaks in the area.*

- fire extinguisher
- blankets, clothing, and comfortable walking shoes
- tools (especially a wrench to turn off the gas)
- cooking and eating utensils
- water purification tablets
- utility knife
- sanitation supplies—toilet chemicals, toilet bags, and toilet paper
- 50’ utility rope/cord
- 8’ x 10’ heavy plastic tarp

- Place a mini-survival pack in your car and office. **Be responsible for your own survival.** don’t assume this has already been done for you.
- **Check with your school or day-care facility** to see if they have an “Earthquake Action Plan” in place.
- **Establish an out-of-state contact person to call.** After an earthquake, call to let him or her know you are O.K.
- **Secure all heavy objects** in your home or office (computers, stereos, microwaves, file cabinets, and bookcases), and place heavy items on lower shelves.
- **Secure** hanging plants, light fixtures, pictures and other items **on the wall or ceiling** with Quake-Grip™, braided wire, hooks, cabinet latches, or brackets.
- Strap the water heater and make sure it is fitted with a flexible gas-supply line.
- Make sure all primary and secondary **exits are clear**.
- **Protect large windows** with a 2–4 mil window coating or security film to prevent glass from flying.
- Move beds and large furniture away from windows.
- **Make sure your home or office is bolted to its foundation and cripple walls are braced** to prevent your house from falling off its foundation.

Be prepared to be self-sufficient for at least three days. Most emergency services/ communication systems will be significantly delayed or unavailable for three or more days.

What to Expect During an Earthquake

Panic causes people to “react” instead of “act.” Many injuries and deaths are a result of people reacting improperly during and after an earthquake. If you are aware of some of the situations that are likely to occur during an earthquake, you may be calmer and, as a result, act more appropriately. Be prepared for any or all of these situations to occur:

- Utilities may be knocked out.

- The building may shake violently.
- Glass may shatter and fly around the room.
- Door frames and elevators could possibly bend and jam.
- Large pieces of furniture, bookshelves, computers, etc. may overturn or fall.
- Items suspended from the ceiling may come loose (chandeliers, plants, etc.).
- Smoke alarms and sprinkling systems could be activated.
- The noise level will be heightened. The quake itself will sound like thunder. Glass will shatter and loose items may crash to the ground.
- Doors often swing back and forth.
- If you are in a car, it will feel like you have flat tires.

During an Earthquake

- **STAY CALM!**
- **Follow the earthquake plan** you and your family or organization have developed.
- **If inside a building** during an earthquake, **take cover** under a desk, table, or against an inside wall.
- **If in a car, pull over** to the side of the road. Stay away from trees, power lines, overpasses, and light poles. Stay in the car until the quake is over and you are sure glass and other harmful objects will not fall on you.
- **If outdoors, get away from** high buildings, power wires, glass windows, or **objects that could fall**.

After an Earthquake

- Check for injuries. Apply first aid if necessary.
- Take time to gather yourself together. Being in an earthquake is very frightening. Acknowledge this and give yourself time to settle down.
- Wear shoes at all times. The glass and debris that scattered during the quake could injure you.
- Use a flashlight to inspect for damage. **DO NOT** use a candle.
- Turn on your battery-operated radio and listen for emergency information and updates.
- If your home or office has sustained structural damage, or if someone smells gas or locates damaged pipes, wires, etc., turn off the utilities.

Note: It is only necessary to turn off the utilities if damage occurred as a result of the earthquake. Once shut off, a utilities service person may have to come to the building to reinstate services. It can take several weeks for the city to become fully operational after a major earthquake. Therefore, it is important to determine if it is absolutely necessary to turn off the utilities. Turn them off if:

- the building/home suffered significant structural damage.
- someone smells gas (shut off the gas).
- a major appliance (such as the water heater) was broken as a result of the quake.
- wires or pipes were damaged (shut off electricity and/or water).

- **Assess building damage.** It is important to determine whether it is safe to stay in your home or office. Aftershocks can cause further destruction to a building that has sustained structural damage.
- Mark and block off hazardous areas if necessary.
- **Unplug appliances** to avoid damage caused by power surges. Surges can occur when the power company is trying to reinstate service.
- **Locate the emergency kit.** Make sure the food, water, and other materials are accessible and in a safe place.
- **Call out-of-state contact person(s)** to let them know your whereabouts.
- **Confine wandering pets.**
- **Do not turn the utilities back on** until you are completely sure that it is safe to do so. It may be best to have this done by a professional.
- **Do not drive unless it is an emergency.** Keep roads clear for emergency personnel and rescue crews.
- If you have to vacate your home or office, **leave a note to let others know where you can be reached**.
- **Take care of yourself.** Make sure you drink enough fluids, eat properly, and get as much rest as possible. The best way to survive an earthquake is to be mentally and physically alert at all times.

CHAPTER VIII
Role of the Process Observer

The role of the process observer is to observe the group's interpersonal behavior during the simulation; i.e., to watch "group process." Group process refers to the implicit methods group members use to accomplish their goals and interact with one another. Simply stated, a process observer does not analyze what a group does, but rather how it does it. Some of the most critical areas for the process observer to be alert to are listed in Section 1 of this chapter.

When a process observer is assigned to a group that works together on a regular basis, she or he can play a critical role in helping the team analyze its long-standing behavior patterns and determine whether they help or hurt the group's ability to reach its goals. With new or temporary groups, the process observer can highlight potential team trouble spots, identify emerging norms, and help individuals understand the roles they play in group interaction.

The person who serves as process observer does not do the problem-solving exercise but instead watches the group as the members work so that she or he can identify and evaluate the behaviors that led to effective or ineffective team decisions. The process of feeding back observations and analyzing the group's process is called "debriefing."

If the level of trust and openness in a group is high, the group may be able to debrief itself without the assistance of a process observer. However, since self-debriefing can be sensitive, an observer is recommended under most circumstances. If you are working with only one or two teams, you as the facilitator may be able to provide the debriefing.

When the simulation is complete, the process observer has several options for introducing the debriefing session. She or he can begin by asking participants for their own observations of the interaction. The advantage to this approach is that the participants have the first opportunity to "own" their behavior before the process observer calls attention to it. The process observer then needs only encourage the participant to ask other members how the behavior affected them. The disadvantage to this approach is that there's a chance the process observer will lose control of the discussion because participants frequently begin arguing about the content of the exercise (such as whether it was really necessary to turn off the utilities) rather than group process. In this case, the process observer must refocus participants on the intent of the debriefing exercise, which is to analyze how the group worked, not the answers it selected.

Another option is for the process observer simply to begin offering his or her observations about the group process and to engage participants in an interactive analysis. The following is a suggested way to begin:

"Let's talk about how the group interacted during the simulation. As you know, my role was to watch the team and take note of any behaviors that seemed to help or hurt the team's ability to problem solve and communicate. One significant thing I noticed was that Dorothy did not say a word throughout the exercise. Dorothy, what was going on in your head? How did the group feel about the fact that she wasn't participating?"

A final question before moving to the next process observation would be:

Is this a behavior that is common for this group? If so, do you wish it to continue or change? In either case, how will you make sure it does?

The people chosen for the process observation should have a positive, supportive attitude toward the training event and an understanding of group process. (See Chapter IX for more information on this topic.)

It also may be necessary to be sensitive to organizational circumstances when selecting people for the process observer role. Remember that the process observer's responsibility is to provide feedback to a team, some of which may be critical or negative. Be careful not to put someone in an awkward position, as can be the case, for example, when a process observer must provide negative feedback to his or her manager or other people who are at upper ranks in the organization. Although providing upward feedback is the essence of healthy organizational communication, some organizations are not ready for this type of exchange. In this case, the process observers should come from outside the organization.

One way to mitigate this problem is to state clearly the role of the process observer before the simulation begins. If the teams' expectations are that the process observer will be providing evaluative feedback, they will be more receptive to it when it occurs.

Responsibilities of the Process Observer

1. Analyzing Group Process

During the simulation, the process observer should silently observe the behavior of the team. She or he should pay close attention to the following areas:

A. The Decision-Making Process of the Group: Did the team use an autocratic (control by one person), democratic (voting), or consensus method of decision making? (See definition in Chapter 1.) What effect did the choice have on the quality of the group's decision? Did the group expressly decide on the method together, or did it simply evolve? What effect did this have?

B. Leadership: Who took the leadership role, and when and how did the person(s) do so? Was the leader(s) resisted, and if so, why? What type of leadership style did the leader(s) practice, and was it effective?

C. Task and Maintenance Behaviors (See Chapter IX): Did the group over-emphasize either task or maintenance behavior? If so, what impact did this have? Which members seemed to have task or maintenance preferences, and how did this affect their acceptance and interaction in the group?

D. Organization: How did the team get organized? Did they discuss a method of working together? If so, how long did their decision hold? What happened, if anything, to change their method?

E. Participation: Did one person dominate the group's air time, or was participation balanced? What was the effect of under or over-participation on the discussion? Did anyone try to encourage those who weren't participating fully to provide their input?

F. Communication: To what extent did people listen actively to one another? How often did interruptions occur? Were ideas left suspended in mid-air? Was communication hampered by status differences, if any, in the group? Did people "level" with one another in a constructive way?

G. Conflict: Were people willing to express differing opinions? When conflict arose, was it ignored or confronted? What was the result, and what effect did it have on the group's behavior and decisions?

H. Time Management: Did the group use its time well? If not, in what ways was it wasted or under-utilized? Was anyone keeping track of the team's progress vis-à-vis the time allotted for the task?

I. Creativity: What conditions seemed to help and hurt the group's ability to be creative? How willing were group members to offer new and innovative ideas? When new ideas were offered, what reactions did they produce? How much risk taking occurred?

While these are not the only areas that the process observer can be alert to while observing a group work, they are some of the more important ones. See Chapter IX for additional information on group process and what to look for during process observation.

Since the process observer must feed back his/her observations to the team in the debriefing session, s/he may wish to take notes during the simulation. This will make it easier to provide examples and other supporting data to substantiate observations.

2. Managing Time

The process observer should keep track of the time and warn participants when they have 10 minutes left, and again when they have 5 minutes left. (If the group is having a particularly difficult time, a 15-minute warning might also be needed.)

3. Scoring

The team will need assistance in computing individual and team scores (Steps C and F in the workbook) and the "Group Process Questionnaire" scores, if used.

4. Providing Feedback

It is very important that the process observer provide constructive feedback to the team about how it interacted. When applicable and appropriate, the observer should share his or her observations with respect to the questions shown in Section 1 of this chapter, and provide feedback about any other areas that helped or hampered the group's effectiveness.

It is also extremely important that the process observer be candid with the group! When critical feedback is withheld, the group loses a rich opportunity to correct problems that may be interfering with its effectiveness. An effort should be made to balance positive and negative feedback; a team can benefit from knowing its strengths as well as its weaknesses. Guidelines for giving effective feedback are set forth in the next section.

Guidelines for Giving Effective Feedback

Feedback is the process of giving individuals or groups information about their behavior and actions. Its purpose is to allow the recipient to assess the consequences of those behaviors or actions and make adjustments, if appropriate.

Feedback is constructive when it:

1. Focuses on a person's or group's behavior rather than the person or group itself. Consider the difference between these two statements:

   Statement 1: "Bob, when you told Susan that her idea was naive, I noticed she stopped participating in the simulation."

   Statement 2: "Bob, you were quite insensitive to Susan when you told her that her idea was naive. She was so angry that she stopped participating."

   Notice that in Statement 1, the feedback relates to Bob's behavior—a simple description of what he said or did. In Statement 2, the feedback relates to Bob as a person because it implies that he is insensitive. Bob will be much better able to handle and respond constructively to Statement 1 because it is not a personal attack.

2. Offers observations rather than inferences. In Statement 1 of the last example, the process observer related only observations, without trying to interpret their meaning. In Statement 2, the process observer inferred that (a) Bob was insensitive, and (b) that Susan was angry

as a result. These interpretations can not only be inaccurate, they can bias the perceptions of the recipients. It is far more valuable to simply offer observations and then to ask participants how they experienced the interaction. The ideal process-observer response in this situation would have been: "Susan, when Bob told you that your idea was naive, I noticed that you stopped participating. What were your thoughts at the time, and why did you respond as you did?"

3. Provides descriptions rather than judgments. It would not be productive to say to Bob: "Bob, telling Susan her idea was naive was another example of your pulling rank. It was wrong, and you should avoid this in the future." Rather, the process observer should prompt the group to discuss the behavior and the impact it had. When the process observer is judgmental, his or her input will be rejected by the group.

4. Focuses on specific rather than general behavior. General feedback is usually not useful because the recipient is left to guess about what she or he should change or continue to do. Consider the impact of the following two feedback statements:

   Statement 1: "Diane, I think you played a key role in getting the group to agree on the overall strategy for the exercise. You handled that very well."

   Statement 2: "Diane, I think you played a key role in getting the group to agree on the overall strategy for the exercise. When you asked everyone around the table for his or her opinion, the group realized that they were all really saying the same thing. Then when you summarized what you thought the strategy was and asked the group for confirmation, it pushed the team over the hump."

   Notice that in Statement 1, Diane receives a compliment that undoubtedly makes her feel good but does not tell her exactly what she did right so she can repeat the effective behavior in the future. Statement 2 is specific enough that Diane can use the feedback to guide her future actions. The more specific the feedback, the more of an impact it has on the recipient.

   Following these guidelines will help to ensure that feedback provided by process observers will be received non-defensively by group members and provide enough information to help them be more effective in the future.

BRIEFING THE PROCESS OBSERVER

The process observer must be fully informed about his or her role prior to the exercise. The facilitator should include the following points in a pre-exercise discussion:

- An explanation of the responsibilities set forth in Sections 1–4 of this chapter
- An overview of the simulation and explanation of the scoring process and experts' ranking of the Action Alternatives and Salvageable Items
- If used, an explanation of the "Group Process Questionnaire" and the scoring method that accompanies it
- A copy of the "Guidelines for Giving Effective Feedback" (For this purpose only, the Guidelines section may be copied from this chapter .)

CHAPTER IX

Guidelines for Effective Group Functioning

The purpose of this chapter is to provide you as the facilitator with background information about how effective groups function. You can use this information in several ways. One option is to use it as lecture material that you present to the participants before or after the simulation. When presented prior to the simulation, the information will allow participants to practice new behaviors and skills during the exercise. When presented after the simulation, participants gain a clearer understanding of what may have gone wrong in the simulation activity and learn how they can have more productive interactions in the future. (See Chapter III for a discussion of the pros and cons of both approaches.)

Another option for using this chapter is simply to use the material as background information that you draw upon throughout the session as needed. If, for example, a team has trouble reaching a decision, a spontaneous discussion of consensus decision making might be just what the group needs.

Another possibility is to use the information as the basis for training process observers. Process observers, especially those drawn from the organization, often do not have a broad background in group dynamics. This material can help fill that void.

However you choose to use it, the chapter is offered to provide an overview of the kinds of skills and behaviors a group must master if they are to become a fully functioning "team."

Characteristics of an Effective Group

A group that is functioning at an optimum level is indeed a marvel. We occasionally have an opportunity to observe such a group, or better yet, be a fully functioning member. But these experiences are rare. More often, we are members of a group that performs reasonably well or one that gets by, and occasionally one that simply falls apart. Unfortunately, most organizations do not place much emphasis on enhancing group dynamics, even though the majority of work takes place within a group.

Over the years, we have had the opportunity to work with and observe hundreds of groups in action. We have asked them what characteristics they would use to describe the functioning of a highly effective group. Here are their responses:

- Clearly defined, measurable objectives
- The ability to resolve issues rather than avoid them
- Idea and thought contributions from every member
- Members who feel empowered to do the best that they can
- Members who actively listen to one another
- Members who support and trust one another
- Enthusiasm, boldness, and willingness to take risks
- Willingness to hear and accept others' ideas

- The ability to accept conflict as a reality and work it through to a successful outcome
- The ability to build on each other's ideas
- A sense of humor
- The ability and willingness to communicate openly and frankly
- A strong commitment to goals and the group's mission
- An emotional investment in each other
- Decision making by consensus
- Effective leadership that can move around
- Total participation by all members of the group
- Willingness to differ in a way that brings out other perspectives
- The ability to evaluate its own effectiveness
- The ability to adapt to change

Our respondents also mentioned characteristics that inhibit group performance. Some of these were:

- Excessively aggressive behavior
- Group members who compete for "air time"
- Domination by special interests
- Members who argue for argument's sake
- Autocratic decision-making methods
- Lack of respect for others' opinions and needs

It is often worthwhile before a simulation to ask the group(s) you are working with to identify the characteristics of effective and ineffective groups. You can then put their responses in two lists on a flip chart or blackboard and refer to the lists later when you debrief the simulation. An effective debriefing technique is to ask participants which of the effective and ineffective characteristics they observed as their team worked on the exercise. It's not uncommon for a team to acknowledge that it did everything on the wrong list! This can be a powerful learning experience for participants.

Task and Maintenance Behaviors in a Team Setting

Both "task" and "maintenance" behavior are essential to the success of a workgroup. Task behavior is action directed toward reaching the objectives of the group or accomplishing the task at hand. Maintenance behavior is action directed toward creating or preserving the cohesiveness and health of group relationships. Simply stated, task behaviors focus on task/goal concerns, and maintenance behaviors focus on people concerns.

Teams that are good at "task behavior" stay focused on the subject at hand, approach problems in a logical, systematic manner, and see projects through to their completion. An over-emphasis on task, however, can create problems for a group. Creativity and individual differences may be downplayed in an attempt to "get the job done." Feelings and "people" issues may be devalued.

Groups that are good at "maintenance behavior" listen well to one another, support one another, encourage each other to participate fully, and deal with differences in a productive way. However, when maintenance behaviors are over-emphasized, necessary decisions may not be made and task accomplishment may suffer because the group places a higher value on meeting group members' social needs.

In order to be fully effective, a group must strike a balance between task and maintenance activities. The following lists contain descriptions of specific actions group members can take in order to strengthen performance in either category. Aviat's "Group Process Questionnaire" provides an overall measure of team effectiveness and then looks at its component parts in greater detail.

Task Behaviors

Initiating: proposing tasks or goals; defining a group problem; suggesting a procedure or ideas for solving a problem.

Seeking information or opinions: requesting facts; seeking relevant information about a group concern; asking for expressions of feeling; seeking suggestions and ideas.

Giving information or opinions: offering facts; providing relevant information about a group concern; stating one's beliefs; giving suggestions and ideas.

Clarifying and elaborating: interpreting ideas or suggestions; clearing up confusion; deferring terms; indicating alternatives and issues before the group.

Summarizing: pulling together related ideas; restating suggestions after discussion; offering a decision or conclusion for group reaction.

Consensus-Testing: probing to see if the group can agree on a decision; sending up a "trial balloon" to test a possible conclusion.

Maintenance Behaviors

Listening: paying attention to other members' ideas, opinions, and suggestions; not interrupting others; focusing on others when they speak.

Harmonizing: attempting to reconcile disagreements; reducing tension; getting people to explore differences.

Gatekeeping: helping to keep communication channels open; facilitating the participation of others.

Encouraging: being friendly, warm, and responsive to others; openly accepting others' contributions.

Compromising: settling differences through mutual concessions; admitting error; seeking workable alternatives.

Standard setting and testing: checking to see whether the group is satisfied with its procedures; suggesting alternative procedures; testing whether group norms contribute to group cohesion and productivity.

Critical Skills for Optimum Group Performance

The balance of this chapter will deal with attributes that are significant for optimum group performance: consensus decision making, active listening, creative thinking, supporting behavior, and leveling. These areas are particularly important to pay attention to as you watch a group interact during the simulation. Either before or after the exercise, you may wish to talk about these topics in depth.

Consensus Decision Making

Decisions can be made in a variety of ways—unilaterally, by majority vote, by minority vote, or by consensus. Often the best decisions are those reached by consensus because they demand the participation and expertise of all members of a group. Our observation is that groups who use consensus decision making in simulations often arrive at superior solutions and strengthen their interpersonal relationships in the process.

Consensus does not mean that everyone must think alike. Rather, it requires that everyone provide input and participate in a give-and-take exchange of thoughts and opinions. Differences are debated and compromise takes place. The decision is "massaged" until every member of the group can say: "I can support and implement this decision, even though it is not exactly what I would have done or wanted. It is sound enough that I am satisfied."

One of the biggest advantages of consensus decision making is that it does not create winners and losers. The issues surrounding the decision are worked until everyone feels solid about the decision, even if it's not each person's first choice. Although it takes time to arrive at this level of acceptance, the reward in the long term is superior decision quality and implementation.

Active Listening

There is a significant difference between mere hearing and active listening. Active listening is the psychological activity that involves "listening" to all the messages a person is sending. This means paying attention to three sources of meaning: words, tone, and nonverbal signals such as eye movement, facial expression, and posture.

Active listening is poorly performed in most group settings. Usually, while one person is speaking, another person is half listening and half thinking about what she or he is going to say in response. Symptoms of inactive listening are splinter conversations, interruptions, and jumping from one subject to another. Lack of active listening in a team often results in the loss of vital information, lack of idea utilization, and a tendency to make decisions without adequate exploration of alternatives.

Suggested Remedies: The following are offered as tips for individuals who wish to work on their active listening skills:

- Do not dismiss an idea because of its source. Instead, objectively absorb the information being presented and evaluate it on its own merits. Periodically review and summarize what is being said to the satisfaction of the person speaking.
- Pay attention to nonverbal behavior for congruency or incongruency with the words being spoken.
- Try to empathize with the speaker's point of view, even if you do not agree.

Creative Thinking

Edward DeBono differentiates "lateral thinking" from "vertical thinking" in his books *PO* and *New Think*. Vertical thinking is the rational, logical type that uses ideas and information. Lateral thinking is thc non-rational, non-logical type that discovers and creates ideas.

Lateral thinking requires suspending judgment, accepting ambiguity, and questioning tradition. Most ideas generated from lateral thinking are not implemented, but each idea stimulates another idea until eventually an idea that can be implemented emerges. Unconventional ideas can sometimes be developed and refined into new means of creatively solving a problem.

Blocks to Creative Thinking: When a group of people get together with the purpose of finding innovative ways to solve problems, their creativity is likely to be suppressed by:

- Spending too much time talking about the problem and too little time thinking of innovative actions.
- Having identified a pretty good idea, spending too much time discussing it without searching for more good ideas. One good idea usually triggers more good ideas.
- Being trapped by conventional thinking. A wild idea frequently can be engineered to fit the practical requirements.
- Being too quick to reject ideas.
- Being impatient with the creative process. The right idea may take a long time to surface.

Suggested Remedies: The following rules help stimulate creative thinking in small groups:

- When you run out of ideas, change your focus. Rephrase the question or the problem. Switch to another question, problem, or goal.
- State your ideas positively as suggested actions, not as questions.
- Make no negative comments. Defer judgment. Evaluate later.
- Be positive and receptive to all ideas. Reinforce others' ideas.
- Don't over-talk an idea. Once it's understood, move on to another.
- Be a good listener. Build on others' ideas. Think of as many ideas as possible.

- Forget constraints and normal limits. Later look for ways to overcome barriers.
- Think of wild, radically different ideas. They can be engineered to reality later.
- Be informal. Have fun!

Supporting Behavior

A supportive climate tends to make people more creative, which contributes to more effective problem solving. In many groups, there is a strong tendency to shoot first and ask questions later.

Additionally, many groups tend to focus on negative rather than positive aspects of their team. This negative focus creates a frustration resulting in a "what's the use" attitude.

Supporting behavior requires a particular "mind set" that another person's idea(s) has merit even if initially it may not appear to be useful. It also requires encouraging others in their learning, participation, and recognizing the successes of others. Self-centered, cynical, or aggressive people often see support as weakness. However, support is human nourishment that we all need!

Suggested Remedies: The following actions are suggested means of giving support:

- Listen actively.
- If you can't support someone's idea, look for and acknowledge some aspect of it that you find useful.
- Verbally express your appreciation for others' contributions.
- Encourage others to participate.
- Display empathy (not necessarily agreement) with the other person's perspective.

Leveling

Much attention is devoted to "sending" skills in communication, i.e., the art of speaking or writing clear, concise messages, and to "receiving" skills, i.e., the art of listening and interpretation. However, very little attention is given to "leveling", i.e., the art of being honest with oneself and others.

By accident or by design, some of the messages we receive cause us to feel a threat and may trigger negative emotional reactions. Types of threats and examples of messages that cause them are as follows:

Self-Image Threat

"Ted, you've been taken in."

"You know better than that."

"My six-year-old knows more than you do."

Security Threat

"There's just one problem with your report, Pete."

"Unfortunately, the brass discovered the discrepancies."

"I couldn't avoid pinning the blame on you."

"Sorry, Pete, but one more mistake, and you're through."

Intellectual Threat

"You know how I feel about placing a woman in that role."

"I'm not sure your report was very well thought out."

"What were you using for brains?"

Suggested Remedies: To improve openness and candor in communications, and thus enhance group effectiveness, leveling is required. Leveling is giving an honest report of the emotional reaction experienced from a disturbing message or action. Leveling responses are:

"Bill, I'd like to be able to finish my thoughts on this topic. Can you monitor your interruptions?"

"I feel like I'm under attack. Can we backtrack so that I can understand where you're coming from?"

"Although I respect your opinion, I can't agree with it. Let me explain."

Conclusion

Working with groups can be both a fascinating and frustrating experience! The task is fascinating because of the rich dynamics that occur when unique personalities interact to perform a task in a group setting. The task is frustrating for the same reason—these dynamics can be so subtle and complex that they may appear at first to defy understanding.

The value of a simulation such as "Earthquake" is that it allows you to cut through that complexity by creating a group interaction and providing a rare opportunity to analyze it. During analysis, group members can ask (1) What implicit methods and practices did we use to accomplish the task? (2) Did those methods and practices contribute to our effectiveness?

The learning that results from the "Earthquake" experience can give a group and its members the insights they need to become a fully functioning *team*. Repeated administrations of a simulation can help a group gauge its progress toward this goal. For additional simulations and other team-building products, contact Aviat at 1800-421-5323.

CHAPTER X

References

Calhoun, Fryar. *EARTHQUAKE Survival Guide*. Berkeley, CA. Magnet Press, 1990.

Earthquake Preparedness Society. *Earthquakes and Preparedness, Before, During, After*. Downey, CA. 1990.

EQE Incorporated. *Home Earthquake Preparedness Guide*. San Francisco, CA. 1987.

Governor's Office of Emergency Services. *Beat the Quake*. Sacramento, CA.

Gould, Stanhope (Producer), Chase, Sylvia and Gould, Stanhope (Writers). 1990. *The Quake That's Coming* (Film). San Francisco, CA: KRON Channel 4 TV.

For more detailed information on Earthquake Preparedness, contact the following organizations:

Bay Area Regional Earthquake Preparedness Project (BAREPP), MetroCenter, 101 - 8th Street, Suite 152, Oakland, CA 94607, (415) 893-0818, (415) 540-27 13

The Governor's Office of Emergency Services, 2800 Meadowview Road, Sacramento, CA 95832, (916) 427-6659

Southern California Earthquake Preparedness Project (SCEPP), 1110 East Green Street, Suite 300, Pasadena, CA 91106, (818) 795-9055

Southern California Earthquake Preparedness Project (SCEPP), 1350 Front Street, Suite 4015, San Diego, CA 92101, (619) 238-3321

Central U.S. Earthquake Consortium, 263 East Holmes Road, Memphis, TN 38118, (901) 345-0932

Center for Earthquake Research and Information, Memphis State University, 3890 Central Avenue, Memphis, TN 38152, (901) 678-2007

57

THREE BRAINSTORMING EXERCISES

Group Size: Ideally not more than 50, or any number of small groups.

Recommended Time: 60 minutes per exercise.

Provided: Instructions and background information.

Also Required: Flip chart, chalk boards, or white boards.

Facilities. A large room with clear view or several small breakout rooms.

Objectives

- To practice the technique of brainstorming
- To examine the impact of discounting on the creative process
- To practice using brainstorming for problem solving

Background

These exercises were developed to give students a chance to practice brainstorming as a problem-solving technique. (For additional information on brainstorming, see "Techniques for Problem Solving and Heightening Creativity" on Page 14 of the student text.)

Use the first exercise as an open forum with a running commentary on how to appropriately participate in and lead a brainstorming session. With the entire class, as opposed to small groups, and facilitated by the instructor, students can see firsthand just how this technique works. For example, ideas generated are often humorous, yet laughing at someone's idea—particularly if the idea generator didn't mean to be funny—can close that person off from further contribution because s/he has been made to feel foolish. Therefore, we remind students often of the impact of their behavior on the success or failure of the outcome.

Using the first exercise with the entire class allows the instructor to demonstrate the role of the facilitator. One important approach for the facilitator, for example, is to request of an idea generator, "tell me more," when the idea presented is unclear or ambiguous, thus encouraging additional participation. Another is for the facilitator to demonstrate his/her own neutrality. When a facilitator commends an idea, that idea gains additional credibility which may diminish the value of other equally good ideas. (See "Methodologies and Skills" in the student text for more on the role of the facilitator.)

We have used the first exercise, "Flying Down to Rio," in various forms, fairly extensively and with good results. Proposed solutions have included: sell my stereo; rent my car to someone; return the unused portion of my meal plan for a refund; ask my employer for an advance; get a cash advance on my credit card. Illicit proposals have also been made: sell drugs; sell my body; run an illegal raffle; pretend I'm collecting for a charity. As facilitators, we have included these on the original lists without comment. Students are quick to recognize the practical and realistic, the illegal and immoral, etc., and have been able to use these categories during idea structuring, ultimately striking down those which are socially inappropriate. However, some of the illegal and/or immoral suggestions have led to realistic and acceptable ideas. The most common has been to note that many of the illicit ideas require spreading the effort out to reach more than one possible source. My personal favorite resulting response has been "ask 40 friends for $10 each."

Students recognize the power of the group in generating responses and in stimulating their own creative thinking. We have been fascinated to see that the technique is subsequently widely adopted by students in their own group work.

Try using the second exercise with the whole class and a student facilitator. Then, move to the third exercise in small groups. It is far more complex—and is based on an actual situation that was ultimately resolved by cross-training the police and firefighters.

Suggested Outline and Timing for "Flying Down to Rio"

1. Set-up (full class: 15 minutes)

Go over the six steps of brainstorming as detailed in the methodologies section of this text.

Read the problem aloud to the students, highlighting the issues and limitations.

2. Exercise (full class: 40 minutes)

Use the six steps in brainstorming. As you go through each step, explain what you are doing and why.

Either the instructor or a class member should serve as facilitator. If you serve as facilitator, explain what you are doing and why. For example, explain that you're making a point to neither laugh at nor praise a suggestion so as not to weight it differently than any other suggestion, etc.

Record ideas in a visible place.

58

WHAT DO YOU MAKE OUT OF THIS JUNK?

Group Size: Any number of groups of four to seven.

Recommended Time: 90 minutes (5 minutes for set up; 40–60 minutes for exercise; 10–15 minutes for report out; open-ended discussion).

Provided: Instructions, background.

Also Required: Zip-top plastic bags filled with shredded paper, approximately one for every two groups.

Facilities: A large room with moveable chairs.

Objectives

- To practice the technique of brainstorming
- To give participants a chance to examine and practice the facilitator's role in brainstorming
- To practice problem solving

Background

This exercise was developed to give students practice in group decision making using the brainstorming method. Students should be familiar with the steps of brainstorming prior to participating in "What Do You Make Out of This Junk?" "Three Brainstorming Exercises" provide useful models. It also helps to have the brainstorming steps listed in a visible place or on a handout.

Closely monitor the progress of the groups, as many students want to take short cuts or find ways to short circuit the process. Particularly, monitor reactions to ideas, pointing out when they are commenting verbally or nonverbally on ideas as they come up and thus inhibiting participation. It is not until students have used brainstorming in its structured and intended form that they begin to really appreciate the wisdom and effectiveness of the method.

Suggested Outline and Timing

1. *Set-up (full class: 10 minutes)*
   - Review the brainstorming process and its rationale.
   - Divide the students into groups.

- Ask students to select a facilitator from their group.
- Ask the students to read the background information.

2. *Exercise (small groups: 40–60 minutes)*

Distribute the lock-top style plastic bags stuffed with shredded newspaper. (A standard office shredder works well for this otherwise messy preparation.) I usually do this by tossing them to group members. Tossing them adds an air of fun. Some students like to hold the bags while they are thinking—a sort of inspirational tool—and students often get ideas from batting the bags around.

- Monitor the groups to be sure they are following the process.
- Remind students that they must brainstorm a name for their product after they have found its use.
- Ask students to select two reporters, one to report on their product, the other to report on the process.

3. *Report-out and discussion (full class: 15 minutes minimum)*

- Ask first the product reporter and then the process reporter to describe their group and its solutions to the class.
- Examine the role of the facilitator in controlling the process.

59

DOING THE IMPOSSIBLE*

Group Size: Any number of groups of five to seven.

Recommended Time: 50 minutes: (5 minutes to set up; 30 minutes for exercise; 3–5 minutes per group for report out; debriefing discussion is open-ended).

Provided: Instructions and background information.

Also Required: 1–2 pieces of 2X3 poster board and 3–5 color markers per group.

Facilities: One or more large rooms to allow for at least six feet between groups. Moveable chairs. Table space (optional).

Objectives

- To help participants explore ways to challenge and move beyond their personal assumptions
- To help participants better understand individual and organizational barriers and resistances to thinking about and doing things differently
- To help participants explore the ways that individuals and groups can be powerful forces for creativity in the change process from old ways of thinking and doing to new
- To help participants explore the role of a leader in facilitating change

Background

Doing things in new ways requires individuals to change from their old approaches to their work to approaches that lack familiarity and comfort. Yet, if an organization is to move ahead, thinking that goes beyond traditional models is a must. Individuals and organizations tend to resist or create barriers to new paradigms because they feel economically or psychologically threatened.

Resistance to change is not just a phenomenon among an organization's followership. Individuals in leadership positions are also likely to resist change when they do not fully understand and embrace the need for it. Therefore, it is critical to educate people at all levels. One approach to doing this is to begin by formulating a clear statement of the message at the top and then broadcast the message downward until all employees have been reached.

In this exercise, resistance to thinking differently is likely to be mainly psychological—"It can't be done," "We're sure to fail," or "If we don't come up with something good, we might look bad."

In the workplace, economic threats might include: "If I can't do this, I won't get ahead," "If my thinking is wrong, I might lose my job," "If our idea doesn't sell, the company will lose money," etc.

To help break down economic and psychological resistance to change, it is important to educate people around whatever new goals have been set and the roles they will play in meeting them. It is also important to involve individuals and groups in finding ways to develop the necessary skills to meet the new goals. This means sending the messages, "this is what to expect," "we will train you," and "you will be a part of it." Doing so allows an organization to move ahead.

Of paramount importance in allowing people to move beyond their personal assumptions is the establishment of an atmosphere that accepts mistakes as a normal part of trying something new. Employees who fear punishment for honest errors will be unlikely to take risks, no matter how great the possible benefits.

Educating and involving organizational members to be ready for change requires a knowledgeable and committed leadership that is able to pass their understanding of and enthusiasm for the new goals on to their subordinates.

This exercise asks students to come up with a concept and graphic depiction of a safe way to read while jogging. The parameters for this, i.e., whether this means jogging on a treadmill, open road, etc., have been left purposely vague. Do not share this with the participants until the debriefing session. The vagaries are meant to allow the leaders to establish the vision as they see it. Being vague may produce anxiety and limit risk taking among leaders and followers, an outcome that will need to be carefully explored during the debriefing.

Suggested Outline and Timing

1. Set-up (5 minutes)

Go over the instructions and the learning objectives of the exercise.

Remind participants that they are to come up with a graphic depiction that illustrates their invention or design and that they will have an opportunity to explain what they have come up with, why, and how, during the debriefing.

Remind participants to read the "Questions for Consideration" before beginning. It is the answers to these questions that should form the basis for the debriefing discussion.

Do not answer any additional questions concerning the task. Instructions for the participants are self-explanatory, and it is important for the group leaders to define and convey the vision. Interpretation of the instructions should be part of that role. Tell the groups only how much time they have to complete the task.

2. Exercise (30 minutes)

During this time, resist the temptation to become involved in problem solving for the groups. If you are asked questions, limit your response to, e.g., "I'm sure you'll be able to figure that out," or "That's a really good question. How would you go about solving it?"

After 20 minutes, let the groups know they have 10 minutes remaining.

3. *Report out (large group, 15 minutes or more, depending on number of groups and availability of time)*

Ask the spokesperson for each group to briefly describe their solution and the rationale for it. Use the "Questions for Consideration" as a guide for the debriefing, exploring what barriers or resistances were encountered. Stress particularly the ways the groups overcame these barriers and the leaders' roles in facilitating innovative thinking.

60

CYRIL AND EDNA: THE MANAGER AS MEDIATOR

Group Size: Any number of groups of three to six.

Recommended Time: 90 minutes recommended minimum (5 minutes to set up; 10 minutes for student preparation; 30–40 minutes for role play; 15 minutes for Worksheet 1 and small group discussion; 10 minutes for Worksheet 2 and small group discussion; 20 minutes or more for report out and large group discussion).

Provided: Instructions, manager's role, worksheets, and Observation Sheet in the student edition. Roles for Cyril and Edna are in the *Instructor's Resource Manual.*

Also Required: Enough photocopies of Cyril's and Edna's roles to provide one of each for each group. No other materials required.

Facilities: Moveable chairs. Enough room for approximately six feet between groups.

Objectives

- To help students develop skills for managing and mediating conflict in the workplace
- To help students practice the skills of active listening
- To help students practice the skills of making one's needs understood
- To help students recognize the superordinate goals common to both parties to a conflict

Background

"Cyril and Edna" is a classic case of unaddressed interpersonal conflict in the workplace. Lack of communication around small differences continues until a larger issue, possible racism by one party, brings both parties into the arena armed not only with the present issue but with a slew of unresolved historical ones, real and/or imagined, as well. Since both parties have approached the manager for help, it provides a wonderful opportunity for the manager to use mediation techniques to help the parties resolve their differences and build a better relationship.

Students should be familiar with the philosophy and steps of the mediation process before trying this exercise. It will also be useful for them to review the process of active listening, described on Page 9 in the "Methodologies and Skills" section of the student text.

Two things are likely to be especially difficult for students to manage in this role play: the issue of racism and the tendency of angry people to repeat themselves. In the first, it is going to be important for the manager to allow Cyril to talk about how he feels when he hears racist jokes or remarks. The manager will probably have to reframe Cyril's comments more than once to focus the issue on the feelings raised in Cyril rather than Edna's blame. Not doing this will likely push Edna into a defensive stance rather than into a position of being able to listen to and understand Cyril's feelings.

With regard to the tendency of angry people to repeat themselves, many managers find it difficult to interrupt and refocus a disputant who is ranting and raving without a break and generally monopolizing the floor. In addition, that kind of behavior may elicit anger in the manager who may then try to control the situation by belittling the disputant and/or his or her concerns. Those managers who are successful at redirecting the angry disputant should be encouraged to share how they did it and what their feelings were.

While observers are not critical in this exercise, they tend to be extremely useful.

Suggested Outline and Timing

1. *Set-up (full class: 5 minutes)*

   In setting up this exercise, briefly review the steps in the mediation process. Suggest that this includes:

   - Setting out the reasons for the meeting and the role of the manager.
   - Clarifying the process and the guidelines.
   - Getting agreement from the disputants to keep open minds.
   - Helping the disputants to find their common interests.
   - Focusing on the future relationship.
   - Reaching a specific agreement on resolving the problem.

   Do the following:

   - Briefly review the instructions for the exercise.
   - Ask for and answer any questions on how to proceed.
   - Divide students into their groups.
   - Distribute the roles of Cyril and Edna to those who have been assigned to play them.

2. *Student preparation, role play, and small group debrief (small groups: approximately 65 minutes)*

   During the role play, be available to answer any questions that might arise. Flag four time periods:

   - After the first 10 minutes, remind students to stop preparation and begin the role play.
   - After the next 30–40 minutes, ask students to stop role play, and complete Worksheet 1.
   - After the next 15 minutes, ask students to complete Worksheet 2.
   - After the next 10 minutes, ask for small-group report outs.

3. Report out and discussion (20–minute minimum recommended)

During this time, debrief the exercise in the larger group. Ask a spokesperson for each of the groups to first describe the process, its successes, and areas for improvement.

Next, ask each spokesperson to describe one or more of the elements of his or her solution. Handling the report out in two steps, rather than having each group report on both process and solution at the same time, helps keep the groups not reporting from losing focus. Ask the students to discuss what they see as the usefulness of the mediation process.

The discussion might include or focus on such issues as:

- The difficulties in handling issues around racism.
- The difficulties in handling angry disputants.
- The importance of the resolution coming from the disputants rather than the manager.
- In what ways the mediation process helps build better future communication.
- How students might use mediation techniques in their own lives.

Conclude the discussion by stressing the business benefits of helping individuals deal with their workplace disputes directly rather than allowing them to undermine productivity and morale.

Cyril

You have been employed in the technical support division of a medium-sized software development firm for slightly more than two years, having joined right after you got your undergraduate engineering degree. Despite the stresses of spending all day on the telephone talking to frustrated and sometimes abusive customers, you really like your job, your boss, and the people with whom you work. You sit in a cubicle that is separated from the adjoining cubicles by partitions that are approximately five feet high. Edna's cubicle is next to yours.

Edna, a white woman who is about twenty years older than you, has been in the division about two and a half years. She has a high, squeaky voice that is often shrill and loud when she's on the phone, and her conversations with customers seem to go on forever, sometimes making it difficult for you to concentrate.

Edna has the annoying habit of borrowing your things without asking. When you're missing a stapler, a reference book, or any of your office or personal supplies, chances are Edna has it. On more than one occasion, you have gone to her cubicle while she has been away from her desk to "borrow back" what she has taken. On the one or two occasions when you have asked Edna to stop borrowing your things, she has gotten angry and told you that they all belong to the company anyway.

Edna is really good at her job, and more than once she has been an immense help to you with a customer problem. Unfortunately, something happened yesterday that made you angry and upset with her. You had just finished a customer call when you overheard Edna talking to a coworker on the other side of her cubicle. As you wrote up your customer notes, you realized that Edna was telling a not very funny joke about two black men who stole a car. The joke was filled with racial stereotypes and bigotry. As a black man, you were offended and furious at their lack of sensitivity.

When you went to complain, your manager suggested that the three of you—you, Edna, and your manager—get together to talk things over.

Edna

You have been employed in the technical support division of a medium-sized software development firm for about two and a half years, having joined right after you got your undergraduate degree in computer science. Before going back to school for your degree, you stayed home to raise your children who are now sixteen and nineteen.

Despite the stresses of spending all day on the telephone talking to frustrated and sometimes abusive customers, you really like your job, your boss, and the people with whom you work. You sit in a cubicle that is separated from the adjoining cubicles by partitions that are approximately five feet high, and you often talk over the partitions to your neighbors.

Cyril, a black man who is about twenty years younger than you, has been in the division a little over two years. His cubicle is next to yours. It annoys you that he regularly hangs his coat over your common partition, but you haven't said anything because you haven't wanted to make trouble. You also know that Cyril has often gone into your cubicle when you haven't been there and taken things from your desk and from your desk drawers. When you've tried to borrow office items from Cyril, he has told you to "get your own," but in other ways he has generally been cooperative.

Occasionally you have been irked to overhear Cyril imitate you when talking to your coworkers. As a result of a botched tonsillectomy when you were nine, you have a high and squeaky voice.

You have ignored most of Cyril's behavior as simply petty annoyances and have attributed most of it to his youth. After all, he isn't much older than your own son, and you're impressed by his competence on the job.

Your manager has suggested that the three of you—you, Cyril, and your manager—get together today to talk over some problems that have arisen. You're not exactly sure what this is all about, but you do see this as an opportunity to deal with some of the things that have been bothering you.

61

CONFRONTATION AT CAPTAIN COOK'S: PARTS 1 AND 2*

Group Size: Any number of groups of three to seven participants.

Recommended Time: 110 minutes (60 minutes for Part 1; 50 minutes for Part 2, which is optional).

Provided: All instructions, roles, and Observer Sheets are in the student edition. An optional "Curve Ball" is provided below.

Also Required: No additional materials required.

Facilities: One or more rooms, large enough to allow for approximately six feet between groups, with moveable chairs.

Objectives

- To examine the origins of conflict
- To examine personal styles in reacting to conflict
- To practice the skills of managing conflict through confrontation

Background

This exercise is based on the actual experiences of the author and has been extensively classroom tested. Captain Cook's is described as a seasonal restaurant on the southern coast of Maine, but the conflict that arises could happen anywhere in a wide range of settings.

"Confrontation at Captain Cook's" gives participants an opportunity to examine their usual ways of responding to conflict and, for those who play the role of Mickey (the wait person), how they respond to authority. The central focus, however, is to help participants understand how to structure and carry out conflict management through confrontation.

Be sure to ask students to read about "Active Listening" on Page 9 and "Twelve Tips for Managing Confrontation Effectively" on Page 13 in the student text prior to coming to class.

As in many situations involving conflict, in "Confrontation at Captain Cook's," the behavior of each of the disputants drives the behavior of the other. In classroom use of this exercise, the students who play Mickey almost immediately contend that they should not have been leaving the host-cashier desk to wait tables since they had agreed to taking the host-

* These notes were prepared by Sandra L. Deacon and Janet W. Wohlberg. Used with permission.

cashier position. However, those students who were improperly confronted by the manager became extremely defensive and refused to admit that they had been wrong. Managers who attacked Mickey, instead of Mickey's behavior ("You idiot, I thought I could trust you....") found that their employees were angry, resistant, and equally confrontational. The confrontation was much less successful and much less satisfying than those in which the manager focused on the behavior and listened to the employee's side of the story. Had all the managers listened first, they might well have heard statements such as, "I know I was wrong," "I need the money, but that's no excuse," and even "I'm sorry." Instead, the managers' failure to listen almost inevitably ensured a battle.

Suggested Outline and Timing

1. Set-up (5 minutes)

In setting up this exercise:

- Briefly review the key points in active listening and managing conflict by confrontation.
- Remind students that role plays work best when they project themselves into the roles.
- Stress the importance of the observers' roles.
- Divide students into groups.
- Distribute the roles.

Do the following:

- Briefly review the instructions and timing for the exercise.
- Remind students to read the instructions and roles carefully and to take the necessary time to prepare their roles.
- Ask for and answer any questions about how to proceed.

2. Student preparation (10 minutes)

Working in their small groups of three to seven participants, students should decide, without looking at the roles, who will play the manager and who will play the waitperson. All others will be observers. They should also select a spokesperson for the group who will report to the rest of the class.

Optional Curve Ball

Try the following curve ball at this point in this exercise:

After the roles have been distributed, meet with all those who are to play the manager's role in a place that is out of earshot of the rest of the class. Tell half of the managers that they do not have to listen to anything Mickey says since they are "the boss." Ask the other managers to be very understanding and listen attentively. While this set-up may become obvious as the groups report out, try having the autocratic managers' groups report out alternately with the others to point out the differences in reactions.

3. Role play and small group debrief (30 minutes)

During the role play, flag two time periods:

- After 12 minutes, signal that there are 3 minutes left to reach resolution or stop.
- After 15 minutes, signal that role play should stop and discussion begin.

After the role play, the manager and the waitperson should describe to their small group how they felt during the role play and in what ways they acted differently from their usual behavior in the face of conflict.

Next, the observers should report what they observed, using specific information, and make suggestions for what could be improved. It is important for all members of the group to give input at this stage. Try briefly visiting each group to be sure that there is full participation. It helps to ask the quieter students to give their impressions during your brief visit.

During this time, again give a 12 minute time signal.

4. Class discussion (full class: open-ended)

After each spokesperson has reported his or her group's findings, using the "Observer Sheet" as a guide, ask participants to discuss larger lessons learned.

The discussion might include or focus on:

- parallel personal experiences of students, good and bad.
- difficulties in coping with emotional reactions to confrontation.
- how students might use confrontation techniques in their personal lives.

5. Part 2 (50 minutes)

Follow the steps in Part 1 above.

Part 2 of this exercise gets at issues that arise when people fail to confront one another directly, instead preferring to take their issues elsewhere in an effort to avoid confrontation.

The manager in this role play usually reports feeling betrayed by Mickey, especially since the manager feels that she or he has dealt effectively with the issues presented in Part 1. Include in the discussion of this part of the exercise issues about power, avoidance of confrontation, and chain of command.

Conclude the discussion of both parts by stressing the organizational and economic benefits of managing conflict effectively, including avoidance of stress; time and productivity savings; and even the avoidance of costs of possible official and/or legal actions should conflict become heightened.

62

FIVE CONFLICT MANAGEMENT ROLE PLAYS

Group Size: Any size group.

Recommended Time: Minimum 90 minutes; 10 minutes for set up and reading roles, 10 minutes per role play, 10 minutes debrief per role play, process repeated two more times.

Provided: Instructions.

Also Required: No other materials required.

Facilities: One large room. Two moveable chairs for role players.

Objectives

- To consider the components of conflict
- To examine personal styles of reacting to conflict
- To explore ways of finding mutual interests in conflict situations
- To practice the skills of conflict resolution

Background

This exercise offers five role plays, each with a conflict scenario that is either vertical (between two persons of differing positions and power) or horizontal (between peers with roughly equal power). They are based on typical conflicts that most people encounter many times in their lives. Characters in these conflicts confront one another over differences of opinion, needs and concerns, and objectives.

Before using this exercise, be sure students are familiar with role plays, the skills of managing confrontations, and the skills of active listening, described in the "Methodologies and Skills" section of the student edition.

The emotions of the role players are not clear in the role descriptions. Ask students to project their own feelings and emotions into the situation presented.

Each role play should be repeated at least twice (for a total of three times) with different players. Discussion should follow each round and should include an exploration of what the role players did well and what they might have done differently.

This is a good exercise to use periodically throughout the semester, selecting a different role play each time, to explore the ways students have come to better understand their personal styles and responses and have developed their conflict management skills.

Suggested Outline and Timing

1. *Set-up (full class working individually: 5 minutes)*

   Ask students to read both roles of the role play you have selected and to make notes about what they see as the areas of disagreement and how they might feel about each role should you ask them play one of the characters. For example, in the role play between parent and teen, students should think about how they would feel if they were the parent and how they might feel if they were the teen. Use the "Questions for Discussion" as a guide.

2. *Role play (10 minutes)*

   Select two people at random to play the given roles in front of the entire group. After 10 minutes, stop the role play whether or not a resolution has been reached. The object of the role plays is to examine the components of conflict, ways to find common ground, and practice the skills of conflict resolution. The object is not necessarily to resolve the conflict.

   During the role plays, observers should make notes as to what the role players are doing well and what they might have done differently.

3. *Debrief (full class: open-ended)*

   Using the "Questions for Discussion" as a guide, explore what the role players did well and what they might have done differently to bring about a different resolution.

4. *Repeat the role play with new players, as above. Consider how each round improves as the players come to learn from the previous players mistakes.*

Questions for Discussion

1. Were the role players able to state their interests clearly? What else might they have said, and how might they have said it?
2. Did the role players listen to one another? If not, what kinds of static got in the way? Include in this a discussion of the emotions that were displayed and how the display of those emotions impacted the ability of the role players to reach resolution.
3. What did the role players do well in bringing about a meaningful resolution? What might they have done differently? If no resolution was reached, what might the role players have done to come to an agreement?
4. In the repetition of the role play, what traps did role players appear to have avoided by having seen the previous role play(s)?

63

A PLACE OF YOUR OWN: A NEGOTIATION ROLE PLAY

Group Size: Any number of groups of four to six.

Recommended Time: 60 minutes (may be more depending on the number of groups and the length of the discussion): 10 minutes to set-up; 20 minutes for role play; 10 minutes for small group discussion and observer feedback; 20 minutes (minimum) report out and group discussion.

Provided: All roles, instructions, and Observer Sheets are in the student edition.

Also required: No additional material is needed.

Facilities: Large room with moveable chairs.

Objectives

- To give participants practice in negotiation skills
- To give participants practice in making their needs and desires understood
- To give participants practice in active listening

Background

All of us begin to develop negotiation skills well before we are forced to use them in business settings. An infant, for example, learns that screaming will bring food and attention, while a parent, wanting to work out an amicable solution to mutual distress, will likely offer the child what is wanted. The child, in turn, stops screaming, thus giving the parents what they want. When the child's demands begin to feel extreme to the parents, they may react by requiring the child to postpone gratification or by giving attention but not food. In time, the child may learn that smiling will bring more food than screaming, and so it will go, as parent and child learn what will fulfill one another's needs. This is a simple negotiation.

In negotiating, it is important to go beyond the surface demands to understanding the underlying interests of both parties. It is also important to recognize what alternatives exist that can meet those underlying interests. For example, a child may demand ice cream, but the underlying interests may be to stop the discomfort of hunger, be able to sleep, and even to stay alive. Carrots or other food may meet the child's underlying interests as well as the ice cream.

This exercise gives students a chance to practice their negotiation skills around an issue with which many may be familiar. Encourage them to project themselves into the roles and make their needs and interests clear. The more carefully students prepare their roles, particularly in determining what they see as the negatives and positives to the student's moving into a coeducational house on fraternity row, the more effective the role play is likely to be.

One idea that students will likely focus on is saving money by moving into a group house. Note that the case states that housing will be approximately 20 percent less than the room and food plan together at the dorm. Parents are likely to be concerned about the extra costs of food, but more important, they are likely to be concerned about general nutrition and the student's ability to prepare and eat a healthy diet. Among other parental concerns will be the division of the three bedrooms among five students of different genders; the ability of the student to study in an unsupervised setting; the temptations of parties on fraternity row; safety and security; provisions for equal sharing of financial obligations, e.g., whose name will appear on the lease; the extra distance to school, and so forth. If students who are to play the roles of parents get bogged down in preparation for their roles, suggest that they consider what their parents or their friends' parents might feel about the proposed situation.

Suggested Outline and Timing

1. *Set-up (full class: 10 minutes)*

   Divide students into groups, and briefly review the instructions. Students should decide within their groups who will play each role. Remind students of the importance of role play as a learning tool and of how much more successful they are likely to be if students take them seriously. Finally, ask students to review the instructions, decide who will play the roles, and spend time preparing for the roles they are to play.

2. *Role play (small groups: 20 minutes)*

   During this time, it is useful to observe each group briefly.

3. *Small group discussion (10 minutes)*

   Stop the role play after 20 minutes, and ask the observers to discuss with their groups what they saw, using the "Observer Sheet" as a guide. Ask role players to reflect on what they felt as they played their roles.

   Ask groups to select reporters to report their process and outcome to the rest of the class.

4. *Report out and discussion (20 minutes minimum)*

   Have each reporter describe their process and outcome. If time is short and there are many groups, ask one group to begin the report. Then ask if any other group had a different process or outcome.

   Hold a full class discussion, using the Observer Sheets as a guide. One useful way to begin the discussion after the report out is to note, e.g., "Group 1, I saw you do.... How did that work for you?

64

RABBIT FEVER*

Objectives

- To demonstrate and practice the skills of a distributive negotiation
- To practice the skills of establishing a reservation price in a negotiation
- To examine the significance of a zone of agreement
- To demonstrate the skills in achieving win-win resolutions

Background

"Rabbit Fever" is an example of a *distributive negotiation*, in which two parties deal with a single issue: the amount to be paid for a car. If the purchaser's reservation price (the most she or he is willing to pay) exceeds the seller's reservation price (the least she or he is willing to accept), a zone of agreement exists, and it would be inefficient for the parties to fail to reach agreement.

On the other hand, any contract within the zone of agreement is efficient. In distributive bargaining there is a fixed amount of surplus (the difference between the two reservation values), and the only question is how that surplus is to be shared.

Of course, the buyer would prefer to pay as little as possible—only a penny more than the very least the seller would accept—and the seller would like to extract the most that the buyer would be willing to pay.

This tension is usually manifested in attempts by each, both to conceal the true value of their reservation prices and to set a personally favorable tone to the negotiation. These actions can result in a failure to reach agreement, even though, by definition, the existence of a zone of agreement means that *both* parties are better off reaching accord anywhere in the zone than in ending the negotiation without an agreement.

The Reservation Price

Try the following exercise to demonstrate the importance of selecting a reservation price based on the negotiator's no-agreement alternative. Divide the class into four equal-size groups in preparation for a series of short two-person negotiations. In the first negotiation, the individuals in Group A will negotiate, one-on-one, with those in Group B, while Group C

* These notes were written by Morris Raker.

will divide up for one-on-one negotiations with Group D. In the second round, Group A will negotiate with Group C, and Group B with Group D. Each round should be limited to 6 minutes, but the first round should be preceded by about 10 minutes preparation time.

General instructions are that each dyad has been awarded $100 by a mysterious benefactor. However, the award is subject to the condition that the pair be able to reach agreement on how to share the money. Confidential instructions should also be given (preferably in writing) to each of the participants. Instructions to Groups A and B—"You should try for as large a share of the $100 as possible, and you may make up any story you want to substantiate your position."—should be exactly the same, but the members of the groups should not be aware of their instructions being identical.

Your instructions to Group C should be "Consistent with standards of fairness and equity, try for as large a share of the $100 as possible. You may make up any story you want to substantiate your position."

Your instructions to Group D should be "You should try for as large a share of the $100 as possible, and you may make up any story you want to substantiate your position. In no event are you to accept less than $60. If you do, you will forfeit the amount you accepted, plus $50."

Some of your students are going to be uncomfortable with having to make up stories about why they need a large share of the money. You might find it helpful to anticipate this in their confidential, written instructions by asking them to go along with this situation and pointing out that they will not be involved in making up things in future negotiations.

After the two rounds of negotiation have been completed, take about 30 minutes to debrief, focusing mainly on the three considerations that apply to virtually all negotiations: the importance of reaching a fair result; the importance of ethical behavior in negotiations and the differences of opinion on the point at which conduct becomes unacceptable; and the importance of basing one's reservation price on the no-agreement alternative.

It is interesting and instructive to see how many negotiators decided that fifty-fifty was fair, and accordingly, $50 was the least they would accept. Question their no-agreement alternative, and ask why they thought it was better to get nothing than, say, $40, or even $10. Would they have acted differently if the amount being split was $100 million? If so, why?

"Rabbit Fever"

In "Rabbit Fever," the value of the no-agreement alternative is a bit fuzzy. The seller can assign probabilities, but has no way of knowing whether a new buyer will shortly appear willing to pay $X, another new buyer might pay $Y, and so on. The seller's reservation price—his or her alternative to not reaching an agreement in the current negotiation—is the expected value of this lottery.

Debriefing can be very informative for each of the negotiations. To be sure there is going to be adequate time for this analysis, you may want to assign the actual negotiations as out-of-class exercises.

If you take this route, it is important that students not share their results with others who have not yet completed their negotiations. As noted above, there is no single correct result;

any contract within the zone of agreement represents an efficient result. However, information about another team's agreement is likely to be given undeserved weight, causing a distortion in the later negotiation.

Absent these distortions, most teams will probably reach agreement, but that is where the similarity is likely to end. The range of results, when charted on the board, can be an interesting point of departure for discussions concerning reservation prices and negotiating tactics.

Many negotiators fail to appreciate how large the zone of agreement might be and are too willing to accept agreement at or very close to their reservation price. These students might find it helpful to focus their negotiating tactics—opening bid, counter bid, and so forth—on a "target price," while retaining the flexibility to retreat as far as their reservation price, should that become necessary.

The wide range of results will also mean that several students who had been perfectly happy with their agreements will become very unhappy when they learn that others playing the same role ended up with much better deals. In most business negotiations, this type of comparison will not take place. Nevertheless, the comparison is helpful in a classroom setting, both to illustrate opportunities for improvement and to identify those situations, if any, where one of the parties profited from questionable behavior.

If some negotiators distorted the facts in their confidential instructions, this should be discussed during the debriefing. Every culture has its own ethical standards for negotiators' conduct, and it is critical that students be aware of the standards against which their conduct will be judged. Exceeding these bounds might be beneficial in the short run but will almost always be counterproductive over the long term. This will certainly be true in the context of the intracompany negotiations in which managers are continually involved.

Distributive negotiation, what we have been discussing so far, is often referred to as win-lose bargaining. There is a fixed surplus to be shared, and each additional dollar received by the seller represents an additional dollar's cost incurred by the buyer.

In contrast, *integrative negotiation* involves multiple issues and the opportunity to expand the amount of surplus to be shared by the parties. Under these circumstances, most agreements reached through negotiation turn out to be inefficient because the negotiators have failed to maximize the surplus.

The parties to a negotiation are seeking, through joint action, benefits greater than those available by acting alone. As a result, they tend to gauge the acceptability of a proposed agreement against the minimum standard of the no-agreement alternative, rather than on the basis of what is optimally possible. Furthermore, most negotiators impose barriers, often without realizing it, that preclude achieving optimal results.

In integrative bargaining, efficiency depends on the successful creation of joint gains—often referred to as the process of enlarging the size of the pie. Thus, a logical objective of any course in negotiation should be to gain an understanding of how joint gains are produced.[1]

1. See David A. Lax and James K. Sebenius, *The Manager as Negotiator* (New York: Free Press, 1986).

One of the issues in "Rabbit Fever" is how to deal with the missing boot. The buyer might argue for a price reduction of, say, $250 to pay for a replacement boot, while the seller might contend that a replacement would cost only half that amount and that this amount was taken into account in fixing the asking price.

The buyer could respond that she or he will agree to a price, $X, subject to the understanding that the price will be reduced, dollar for dollar, to the extent that a replacement boot costs more than $125. If the parties really believe what they have been telling each other, the buyer will view this agreement as costing $125 less than the seller thinks he or she is being offered. Thus, the differences in perception of the cost of replacing the boot result in improving the value of the deal for both parties. This is an example of win-win negotiation.

Buyer's Confidential Instructions

You and your spouse are expecting your first child in about three months. Your car is an old two-seater sports car that both of you agree is not going to be practical once the baby arrives. It will not be easy to part with the two-seater, but both of you think that a sporty convertible would be an acceptable compromise.

You live on Beacon Hill in downtown Boston. Street parking is hard to find and can be hazardous for the vehicles. From experience, you have learned that soft tops are regularly cut to steal radios. You have removed the radio from your MG and intend to do the same with the new car.

You have an engineering degree and have worked in technical sales for six years. In 1989, you and three partners started your own business. It has been going reasonably well, but controlling spiraling overhead costs may be critical to the company's survival.

You have an appointment in 15 minutes to see a yellow Rabbit convertible that was advertised for $4,900. That sounds a bit high for a 1988, but it is within your budget of $5,000. You also know that it's the middle of winter, and it won't be until at least May that you'll be able to put the top down.

You began looking at used cars a few weeks ago. Rabbit convertibles are fairly rare and tend to hold their value well if they're in good condition. Unfortunately, the ones you have seen within your price range have been badly abused. The description of this one sounds good to you, except you were disappointed to learn that the boot is missing.

Seller's Confidential Instructions

You purchased the Rabbit convertible new in December 1987. Mileage is low because it has been used as a second car by you and your spouse. It has also been used by your teenage daughters, but they have been away at school over most of the past five years and have used it only during school vacations.

The car has been easy and inexpensive to maintain. Your principal incentive to sell relates to your having moved from the suburbs into Boston's Back Bay in September 1996. You have rented a parking space for your other car and have been parking the Rabbit on the street, but finding street parking is increasingly difficult, particularly during the winter months.

You and your spouse barely make use of one car, let alone two, now that both of you are able to walk to work. It makes sense to you to sell the second car and use a taxi on those few occasions when one car will not be sufficient.

You badly want to sell the Rabbit before year-end in order to avoid having to renew the insurance. You have been running the newspaper ad for more than four weeks and have begun to kick yourself for waiting so late in the year to try to sell a convertible. You're concerned that there might not be much interest in convertibles until April or May. Avoiding that delay, coupled with the expense of reinsuring and maintaining the car over the winter, might be worth close to $1,000.

Before placing the ad, you checked with a computer-based service of *Consumer Reports* that claims to have area-specific current values on used cars. They gave you a retail value of $4,600 for a low-mileage car in showroom-perfect condition. However, the same car in only ordinary condition and with 75,000 miles was said to be worth $4,200. You know the car isn't perfect, but you think it's a lot better than "ordinary" condition.

For the first time, someone responding to the ad has made an appointment to see the car. The prospective buyer is due in about 15 minutes.

You have washed the car, and it really looks good. You are concerned about the broken tape deck. A replacement radio/tape deck from Volkswagen would cost over $500; you're not sure what it would cost to repair the tape deck. You're also annoyed that the boot was mistakenly left behind when you moved. On the other hand, it was forgotten because no one had ever bothered to use it.

65

THE CRAIG MIDDLE SCHOOL: PART A*

Objectives

- To provide experience in defining a problem and its causes
- To analyze the management and implementation of a change

Background

Managing change is an important skill for managers in today's fast-paced world. One aspect of managing change is the ability to define and resolve problems that occur during the implementation phase. This case allows students to develop their skills in defining a problem and its causes. It can also be used in a more general way to examine the management of change.

Problem Solving

There are numerous models that describe the problem-solving process. Most begin with an analysis of the situation, i.e., problem definition. On the surface, it would appear to be simple to analyze a situation and define the problem. Unfortunately, this phase of problem solving is often marked by errors that can have serious consequences.

Problem definition should focus on the visible signs of distress. Problem solvers should ask what is not happening as expected or desired that affects the achievement of the organization's goals. It is important to avoid defining problems that do not directly affect the organization's goals. This will help eliminate defining causes or solutions as problems. For example, while Ms. Carole may indeed be causing teachers to call in sick, defining the problem as her behavior does not describe a problem directly affecting the achievement of the school's goal to educate children. Absenteeism, however, directly affects the education of the children. This problem definition does not preclude Ms. Carole from being examined as a possible cause. It does, however, keep open the possibility that there are other causes.

Consequences of Incorrectly Defining a Problem

One obvious consequence of an error in problem definition is that the problems causing the greatest loss of effectiveness will not get addressed. When this happens, managers are always putting out fires. They spend most of their time resolving the most pressing issues without understanding why these "fires" are constantly being lit. As a result, a manager may success-

* These case notes were written by Steven B. Wolff and Maida Williams. Used with permission.

fully resolve a particular issue but never address the underlying problem that caused the issue to surface. For example, the principal of the Craig Middle School notices the increase in absenteeism. This is a "visible sign of distress" that needs attention. Yet, the problem is often defined as Ms. Carole's aggressive style or the extra work required of teachers. These are possible causes of the absenteeism, not "visible signs of distress," i.e., a definition of the problem. As is seen in part B of the case, these are not causing the bulk of the absentee problem. Focusing attention on these issues probably will not significantly lower absenteeism and may lead to another negative consequence of incorrectly defining a problem—creation of a self-fulfilling prophecy.

Many managers are quick to attribute problems to employees. When this happens they may actually create a problem where none previously existed. Ms. Carole is a hard-working teacher who expends much energy for the students. While some teachers said they wish she were less bossy and disruptive, no data suggests that this has become a demotivating factor for them. They may very well recognize the energy Ms. Carole devotes to her work and have high respect for her even though she is deemed to be overzealous at times. If it is assumed that Ms. Carole is the cause of the absenteeism, then not only will the problem not be resolved, but Ms. Carole may become resentful and demotivated. This may result in a loss of energy and an increase in her absentee rate, thus exacerbating the problem that we are trying to solve.

Human Factors Leading to Incorrect Problem Definition

Defining a problem is often hindered by the human tendency to try to fit a current situation into experience. While past experience is certainly useful in understanding many situations, it cannot bring to light an understanding of the unique aspects of a particular problem. People will examine their memory for similar situations and attribute causes or solutions from that problem to the current situation. The result is that problems are often defined in terms of a cause or a solution. For example, instead of defining the problem as an increase in absenteeism, it might be defined as Ms. Carole's aggressiveness (a possible cause), or the need to make participation in the after-school program voluntary (a possible solution). When a problem is defined as a cause or solution, it prevents the exploration of alternative causes or solutions. If the problem is defined as absenteeism, then Ms. Carole might be one possible cause, but adherence to a problem-solving process would require looking for other possible explanations. Alternatively, if the problem is defined as Ms. Carole, the cause of increased absenteeism may never be found.

The Rest of the Problem-Solving Process

Once a problem is defined, it is important to collect data that specifically describes the problem. Often this will help in the next step, which is to define possible causes. In the Craig case, the data has been collected on the absentee rates by grade and by day of the week. Although this should give away the definition of the problem, many students will still avoid defining the problem as absenteeism. It is important to stress that a full understanding of the problem generally requires collection of information.

After defining the problem, possible causes must be considered. There are usually multiple causes to any problem. It is important to consider as many as feasible and avoid jumping to conclusions. Data should be collected to determine how much each cause contributes to the problem if at all. This is the stage at which Part B of the case ends.

The remaining stages of the problem-solving process are to develop, implement, and monitor solutions. When the most probable causes have been determined through careful examination of the data, solutions can then be devised to address them. An implementation plan should be constructed, keeping in mind the various constituencies affected by the solution. This will determine who must be involved in the planning, who must be sold on the idea, and who must be kept informed. When the plan is put into practice, it must be monitored to ensure its effectiveness. Areas where the plan is not working can then be defined as problems, and the process repeated.

Managing Change

Managing change is very similar to the problem-solving process. Once the need for a change is recognized (problem definition), a plan must be devised and implemented (solution implementation). The implementation must be monitored and adjustments made to the plan as necessary; this is the phase of the change process that characterizes the Craig Middle School.

One aspect of managing change that is not addressed in the problem-solving model is resistance. Resistance to change can occur for many reasons; a major reason is a perception that something of value will be lost, such as stability when the outcome of the change is unknown and thus more uncertain; a feeling of competence when the change requires new skills; or economic security when the change may result in lower compensation or new work rules requiring more energy for the same pay.

Each of these possible resistances is potentially present at the Craig Middle School. The teachers will be implementing new programs but cannot know if these will be better than the current methods until they have been tried. Teachers are being asked to teach in new ways. The methods they have been comfortable with may have to change. They are also being asked to invest more time and energy, especially in the after-school program.

Resistance to change may be overcome using a variety of methods. Education concerning the reasons for change can help people realize that it is necessary to do things differently to cope with new environmental demands. People will be less hesitant to change if they understand the need for it. Involving people in the change process can increase understanding and buy-in. We may become invigorated by changes done by us but resist changes done to us. Ms. Smith's effort to involve the teachers in making changes has led to the participation of most teachers in decision making and planning.

It is also important to provide support and coaching to those going through a change. If people feel they are being helped to develop new skills and are allowed to make mistakes as they try them out, they generally will be less resistant to change. Ms. Smith has been providing support that is appreciated by the teachers and serves to reduce resistance.

Discussing the Case

The case can be used to discuss the problem-solving process or to analyze change at the Craig Middle School. If you want to focus on problem solving, assign Part A as preparation for an in-class discussion. If you want to focus on change, hand out Part B, and have the students read both parts of the case and answer the questions regarding change at the end of Part B. This can be done as a written assignment or as an in-class discussion.

Problem-Solving Discussion

Using this case to discuss problem solving helps students develop the critical skills of defining a problem and its causes.

The case presents much circumstantial data about problems and their causes at the Craig Middle School. In a real situation, much information must be processed and filtered before a problem can be defined. The additional data presented in this case is intended to simulate this condition and lead the students into making some of the common mistakes that are made in defining a problem.

Students should first focus on defining the problem. If you develop a list of problem definitions on the board, it most likely will have many perspectives. Many will be causes, and others will be solutions. You might get items such as teachers being overworked, Ms. Carole's behavior, the old building, the need to make the after school program voluntary, and teacher absences. Point out that a good problem definition should focus on the visible signs of distress that affect achievement of the organization's goals. Also point out that there may be multiple problems, and these must be prioritized. Ask, "Which problems can we do something about, and of those, which will have the greatest impact on organizational goals?" With this in mind, go through the list of problems generated, and help the students weed out those that are not within the school's control. Ask students to consider the following:

Issue: Teachers being overworked

Response: This only affects the education of students through some behavior. If teachers are calling in sick because they are overwhelmed, then being overworked is a cause of a problem. By defining the problem as teachers being overworked, the focus is shifted from absenteeism, which may have other causes.

Issue: Ms. Carole's behavior

Response: This is also a potential cause of some other behavior that might directly affect student education. See the first discussion. Defining the problem this way may cause other problems such as a decline in Ms. Carole's performance. This is one reason the problem definition is so critical. It is often possible to create more problems than are solved when personnel are incorrectly implicated.

Issue: The old building

Response: It could be argued that the poor condition of the building affects the ability of the teachers to provide a good education. Ask whether this is something that can be addressed at this time. The case states that a renovation is scheduled in two years.

The implication is the problem has been recognized and addressed. There is probably nothing that could be done at this time. You might also ask whether this is the highest priority problem at this time. Are there other problems, such as absenteeism, which have a more immediate affect on student education?

Issue: The need to make the after-school program voluntary

Response: This is a solution stated as a problem. Ask the students why this necessary, and the answer is likely to be to lower absenteeism. Point out that the need to make the after-school program voluntary is not a visible sign of distress. It is a solution to another problem. By focusing on the solution, other possible causes of absenteeism may be overlooked.

Issue: Teacher absences

Response: This is a visible sign of distress that affects the education of students. This should be one, if not the only, problem left on the list when you are through examining all the items. If there are other legitimate problems, have the students prioritize them. Absenteeism should be close to the top of the list. The remainder of the case assumes absenteeism is the main issue. For purposes of the case discussion, explain to the students that you would like to focus on absenteeism.

Once the problem has been defined, stress that additional information, such as the data on absences in Part A, should be gathered to help further define the situation.

When sufficient data has been collected about the problem, possible causes can be suggested. Ask students to brainstorm possible causes of absenteeism. After generation of many possible causes, ask them what their next steps would be. These should be to collect data to determine which cause is contributing the most to the problem. Because the reason for the bulk of the absences is purposely not readily apparent, you can emphasize human tendency to jump to conclusions. Students are likely to have missed the major cause altogether. Unless the causes have been researched and properly defined, it is likely that much time and energy will be wasted on solutions that do not address the problem. It is also likely that attacking the wrong causes will create more problems than are solved.

At the end of Part B, students have enough information to know that the major cause of absences is the research being done by the eighth grade teachers. There is not enough data to suggest that resentment is causing the bulk of the problems. The data suggest that even though there is some resentment, the teachers are professionals and hesitate to take sick days.

At this point you should ask the students what their next steps should be. It is important to examine whether the eighth grade teachers account for all the additional absences. While it is likely that they account for the bulk, there may be additional causes that must be examined. Perhaps some teachers are indeed unhappy with the changes. While this is not the major cause of the increase in absences, it may become the highest priority problem after the main cause is found. Students should not assume the problem is solved because they have found the major contributing factor. Doing so may mask additional problems that need attention.

Alternative Problem-Solving Discussion

A powerful way to illustrate that our personal preferences will affect the definition of a problem is to have the class discuss the case in groups. Before the class, have students fill out the "The X-Y Scale" that appears on Pages 239-240 of the student text, and turn it in with their name on it. Group students according to their scores. You should have a Theory X group, a Theory Y group, and a range of groups in between. Don't tell the students how the groups were formed until the debriefing session.

Ask students to do the following in their groups:

1. Define the problem at the Craig Middle School.
2. Describe the causes of the problem.

Give the groups about 30 minutes for discussion. When time is up, have a reporter from each group put their answers on the board on a matrix, with one column for each group and a row for each question.

The usual outcome is that the Theory X group tends to define the problem in terms of people, i.e., Ms. Carole, and the Theory Y group tends to avoid people in the definition of the problem. This provides a powerful example of how people's perspectives affect the way they define problems and causes. Use this to discuss some of the consequences of defining the problem inaccurately. For example, if Ms. Carole is defined as the problem or its cause, it is likely that confronting her will create additional problems.

Although there is usually a clear distinction in the way groups define problems and causes, this is not a foregone conclusion. If there are no major differences, you can congratulate the students on their ability to maintain a balanced perspective in their definition of the problem regardless of their personal inclinations. You can still make the point about perspectives affecting problem definition by referring to our observations that there have been differences among the groups in all but one class where we have used the case in this manner.

Choosing this alternative does not preclude you from holding the discussion as described in the previous section of these notes. It only adds the possibility of additional understanding regarding the influence of personal perspectives in defining a problem.

Managing Change

At the Craig Middle School, teachers have been asked to try new programs and teach in new ways. They have been asked to give up habits, develop new skills, and put in additional effort, the outcomes of which were uncertain.

At this point, the Craig Middle School has gone through the stages of change as described in Greiner's six step model or Lewin's unfreezing, change, and refreezing. Monitoring and reevaluating, the steps that begin the change process again—change being a continuous process—are now taking place.

Over the past two and a half years, Ms. Smith's management style has been helpful in overcoming some of the resistances that are naturally found when an organization goes through the kind of changes that have been brought about at the Craig Middle School. While little change seemed to have come about under the aegis of the previous parade of principals, one wonders just what it is that Mrs. Smith did right.

To begin, Ms. Smith communicated with and educated the staff about the need for change. The after-school program, suggested by parents was explained to the staff at a meeting at which the entire faculty and some parents were present. Next, Ms. Smith involved the teachers in planning and decision making. After selling the after-school program, Ms. Smith gave the teachers the final say on whether the program would be adopted and then involved them in planning the implementation. Her management style encourages communication and involvement. She has an open-door policy and encourages teachers to express their concerns. Ms. Smith also provides support and encouragement to her staff. This can be seen in her approach to mainstreaming the SPED (special education) students.

At the end of Part B, the school is well into the implementation phase of the change process. It must now reassess its change programs. It should examine some of the issues such as absenteeism and possible feelings of teachers being overwhelmed.

THE CRAIG MIDDLE SCHOOL: PART B

As you studied the pattern of teacher absenteeism at the Craig Middle School, you began to share some of Ms. Smith's concerns. In your capacity as a consultant, you decided that you should do more research to find out just what was going on.

Over the past several days, you have talked with a number of teachers to find out how they feel about the changes that are taking place in the school. Some said they feel overwhelmed, but many also said they are very pleased. They told you that they like the additional freedom and enjoy the new challenge at the school. The eighth grade teachers, for example, said they are very excited about the opportunity to revamp their reading curriculum. This is something they had wanted to do but hadn't previously felt they had the authority or permission to do. Although it meant working some extra hours, they said they didn't mind because they enjoyed the challenge.

Entrepreneurial in their approach to devising a new curriculum, the eighth grade teachers said they realized that it would be beneficial to visit other schools with innovative programs. Unfortunately, visiting schools meant they would have to be out of the building during the school day, and they had heard that there was no money in the budget for additional substitutes. One eighth grade teacher had the idea to write a grant to provide money for coverage, but the grant was not funded. The alternative, they decided, was to take sick days so they could visit the other schools. They knew an excellent substitute who had worked well with their classes in the past. Since he was available only on Fridays, they arranged their school visits to coincide with his availability.

Other teachers were clearly not as energized by the longer hours and extra work needed to revise their curriculum, so they continued to follow their old ways. They were doing a good job, but they said they didn't like the subtle pressure from the principal to be more proactive in their teaching. One seventh grade teacher who had been out more than usual said she had thought about taking extra sick days but would never do it because it would hurt the children. You still wondered why she had been out so much, but you didn't ask because you didn't want to come across as if you were conducting an inquisition. You remembered someone telling you that her mother had been sick, and you figured that perhaps this was the reason for her absences. In any case, after a few more interviews, you recognized that there was some resentment about the changes in the school, and you wondered if this could be the reason for the higher than normal absentee rates. As a very astute and thorough consultant, you want to ensure that this is not a trend that might continue to increase and become more serious in the near future.

Questions for Consideration

1. Based on the information in Part B, what do you believe is the major reason for teacher absenteeism?
2. When you brought your findings to Ms. Smith and the school council, they questioned you closely as to whether there were other concerns they should look at as well. What did you tell them?
3. This case involves the management of change. Using the Continuous Change Process Model [see Moorhead and Griffin, Organizational Behavior, 5th ed.(Boston: Houghton Mifflin, 1998) Chapter 19], or another accepted model, determine where The Craig's change process is on the model. Explain.
4. What do you see as some of the reasons that the teachers might be resistant to change?
5. What has Ms. Smith done to help reduce resistance to change?
6. Using the model as a guide, determine and describe your next steps. Be specific.

66

DISABILITY SERVICES DISABLED*

This case demonstrates the problems inherent in making changes that require buy-in without soliciting and using input from those whose buy-in is required. Students should utilize aspects of organizational behavior such as leadership, sources of power, organizational culture, and communication in their analysis.

Leadership

The Hersey-Blanchard Life Cycle Model is probably the most applicable leadership theory. Ethel is using a telling style of leadership, which is not appropriate given the situation and the level of the people with whom she is working. In a situation where changes are being made and the employees are experienced, she should be using a participating leadership style.

Sources of Power

Ethel is essentially using her legitimate power to do things her own way, regardless of whether her way is the best. She fails to take into account the expert power of her colleagues, which serves to anger and alienate at least one (Clara) and causes her to lose the support of the others. In addition, she assumes an expert power based simply on the fact that she is disabled, rather than on actual knowledge or expertise. Finally, Ethel fails to take into account Clara's referent power with her colleagues.

Organizational Culture

Clara states repeatedly that decisions at Turnerville are made by consensus; in fact, this was one of the primary reasons she chose to work there. By not using participative management and forcing changes that people feel are going to cause difficulties, Ethel is violating the norms and culture of the organization, both of which are very important to Clara.

Communication

There is definitely a breakdown in communication that has occurred between Ethel and Clara. Ethel has misinterpreted the message that Clara has transmitted to her, as is evidenced by her comment that she and Theodore will continue making changes. Also, Theodore uses one-way communication and then leaves, giving no one the opportunity to provide feedback or ask questions.

* These case notes were written by Gail E. Gilmore.

Managing Change

To regain the support of the coordinators, Ethel needs to manage change in a way that will encourage acceptance rather than resistance. As this is a situation in which employees have valuable information and input to give and have considerable power to resist any changes with which they do not agree, an approach incorporating participation and involvement should be used. Ethel needs to meet with the disability coordinators to discuss both the types of changes they would like to see made and what the most feasible ways of implementing these changes may be. In addition, factors which might make the proposed changes difficult to implement should be considered (a Force Field Analysis could be useful here).

Whatever changes are decided upon, the coordinators must be active participants in determining how these changes will be implemented. Given the organizational culture of Turnerville, it would probably be helpful to establish committees to work on various aspects of the change process.

Ethel also needs to realize that having a disability does not make her an expert on the needs of all disabled students. Her coordinators are all experienced at their jobs, and Clara is considered an expert in her field. It is important that Ethel understand that the coordinators may be more knowledgeable in certain areas and may have better answers than Ethel when it comes to what is appropriate for the specific student populations with which they work.

Theodore should plan to meet with the coordinators along with Ethel and also plan to meet with each coordinator individually to determine how he can be more flexible and receptive, as some of the coordinators have experienced difficulty in working with him. He also needs to recognize their expertise and use it to his advantage. Finally, he needs to improve his communication style; using two-way communication instead of one-way communication would be an excellent first step.

67

THE BUREAUCRACY GAME*

Group Size: Groups of twenty to fifty.

Recommended Time: At least 60 minutes (10 minutes for set up; 15–20 minutes for planning and strategizing; 45–60 minutes for exercise; remainder for report out and discussion).

Provided: Instructions, background, and proposal form in student edition. Roles for photocopying and distribution follow these notes.

Also Required: No additional materials required, although three color markers and five sheets of newsprint per group are recommended.

Facilities: One large room.

Objectives

- To examine the effects of bureaucracy on productivity, morale, and decision quality
- To explore the limitations on innovation imposed by bureaucracies
- To explore methods for overcoming the limitations of bureaucracies

Background

This exercise gives students a taste of how hard it is to be innovative when forced to go through the official channels of an impersonal bureaucracy. The exercise provides experiential learning that corresponds with the theoretical concepts of organizational structure and the organizational life cycle.

Roles for this exercise should be photocopied for distribution. A handful of made-up words have been included in the text—for example, *fritillated*, *metallizing*, and *polymerized*. They have no known meaning and are used only to suggest futuristic high technology.

Suggested Outline and Timing

1. Set-up (full class: 10 minutes)

After assigning roles to various groups and individuals, ask task team members to leave the room for a few minutes to work on their initial product proposal. In their absence,

* These case notes were prepared by Scott Weighart and Janet W. Wohlberg. Used with permission.

instruct the rest of the class to act as bureaucratically as possible—for example, never give their names to task team members, just their job titles; when asked by task team members to bend or break the rules, refuse to compromise and respond with one of the following: "There are certain procedures that must be followed," "I'm just doing my job," and "If you don't like it, you'll have to speak to one of my superiors."

In addition to playing various roles, everyone except the task team should also keep notes on their observations of the proceedings. Ask them to think about the following questions while they watch:

- What effects does bureaucracy have on productivity, morale, and decision quality?
- What tactics did the task team attempt to use to get the proposal approved (that is, persuasion, logic, threats, compliance with rules—no matter how absurd)? What tactics worked best?

Remind students that everyone will be asked to make a comment after the exercise.

2. *Exercise (60–90 minutes, depending on time availability)*

Ask student groups to spend their first 15–20 minutes reading the necessary background information and preparing their roles. Signal a start to the action at the end of this time period.

If no agreement has been reached at the end of 60 minutes, end the game and debrief.

Generally, students enjoy playing the parts of bureaucrats; most relish the opportunity to be the naysayer, probably because most have more often been on the receiving end of a bureaucratic tussle. There will be many humorous moments as the inherent catch-22s between departments emerge and the task team starts to become frustrated.

3. *Debrief (open-ended)*

When the proposal finally gets approved, or when time runs out, wrap up the experience by asking the students the following question in addition to those suggested above:

- If bureaucracies are so frustrating, impersonal, and dehumanizing, why do large organizations operate this way?

In answering this question, you may find it useful to explore the concept of the organizational life cycle. According to Quinn and Cameron (1983), organizations go through four stages: entrepreneurial, collectivity, formalization, and elaboration. A bureaucracy is only appropriate in the last two stages. As the task team found out, it's very difficult to try to be entrepreneurial in an atmosphere of formalization.

According to Richard Daft (1989), bureaucracy is also not appropriate when any of four conditions are present:

- Small size does not call for bureaucratic procedures. Rules and paperwork are not necessary because of the relatively high amount of personal contact.

- Professional employees do not require close supervision and rigorous rules and regulations. In fact, their performance is typically worse in such environments.
- An unstable environment is also a mandate for a nonbureaucratic organization. Flexibility is vital in such a situation; red tape cannot be tolerated.
- When nonroutine technology is involved, requiring frequent adjustment and sophisticated, nonprogrammed decision making, nonbureaucratic methods work best.

It is important to note that bureaucracies are not "bad" per se, but they are appropriate only in specific situations. Most recent literature suggests that large organizations are more productive than smaller ones. Bureaucratic methods provide the coordination and control needed to maximize the benefits of the resources available to them.

Research and Development Department

Everyone in the research and development department (R&D) has at least one role. If there aren't enough people in the group, individuals may play more than one role.

Role 1: Research and Development Manager

You assign the five roles below to the people in your department. Make it clear to your group members that any task team manager must be referred to you first upon arriving at your department. You must also have full agreement from each department member before approving any proposal. Whenever a task team member comes to you with a product proposal, please refer him/her to your corporate relations specialist.

Role 2: Corporate Relations Specialist

Your job is to check carefully the task team's written product proposal. If you do not see a signature next to the line reading "Approved by Production Department," tell the task team member that the production department's approval must be given before your department will even consider it. If questioned further, tell them that there is no point to designing something that can't be produced.

Role 3: Design Specialist

As far as your department is concerned, the task team can have the design of its choice, as long as the choice is a plain silver CD with black lettering. Other colors are a headache to design.

Role 4: Sound Quality Engineer

To guarantee acceptable sound quality, you will not approve any CD with a running time of more than 48 minutes. Longer CDs are more likely to skip, leading to more customer returns.

Role 5: Packaging Designer

As far as you're concerned, the only acceptable form of packaging is cardboard, which is easy to work with. You will reject any other material.

Role 6: Engineering Cost Specialist

Realistically, a CD's production cost will be at least $4.95. Making CDs any cheaper by cutting corners will greatly increase defects. Reject any proposal that calls for a lower cost.

Production Department

Everyone in the production department has at least one role. If there aren't enough people in the group, individuals may play more than one role.

Role 1: Production Manager

You assign the roles below to the people in your department. Make sure everyone agrees before you sign any product proposal. When a task team manager brings you a proposal, please refer him or her to your corporate relations specialist.

Role 2: Corporate Relations Specialist

You are the first to inspect the product proposal when it comes to your department. To avoid the anticipated bickering between production and R&D, check the proposal to see if R&D has approved it. If they haven't, you must reject it. After all, there is no point to agreeing to produce something that can't be designed. You can also reject a proposal if it is messy or has crossed-out words.

Role 3: Color Specialist

Due to recent capital investments, you can produce virtually any color label, except for lavender or purple. You are eager to experiment with the new possibilities.

Role 4: Sound Reproduction Expert

You are proud of the machine you personally developed, a device that makes it possible to produce CDs with up to 70 minutes of music. As such, you will reject any CD that runs less than 50 minutes.

Role 5: Packaging Clerk

You want cardboard. The various plastics produce unpleasant fumes when they are molded, and you are concerned about your health.

Role 6: Production Cost Specialist

Realistically, you can produce a CD for as little as $3.75. Making CDs at such a low price will please your best friend, who works in finance, since this will increase profit margins.

Marketing Department

Everyone in the marketing department has at least one role. If there aren't enough people in the group, individuals may play more than one role.

Role 1: Marketing Manager

You assign the roles below to the people in your department. Make sure your whole group is in agreement before approving and signing any product proposal.

Role 2: Label Assistant

Your job is to approve only disc designs that call for colorful labels, since they catch the eye of consumers. Your rule is that labels must be purple, red, pink, gold, or kelly green.

Role 3: Customer Satisfaction Monitor

Since your surveys show that customers want value for their money, you will approve of no CD with less than 50 minutes of Nuclear Lunchbox's music.

Role 4: Environmentalist

Your careful monitoring of national trends has led you to believe that consumer groups may boycott CDs in cardboard boxes, which are ultimately harmful to the environment. Accordingly, you will only approve of packages made of recyclable fritillated plastic.

Role 5: Pricing Manager

You will only approve proposals that call for a production cost of less than $5, so savings can be passed on to consumers. You will "nuke" any other ideas.

Role 6: Brainstorming Expert

Your mission is to try to interest the task team members with an endless barrage of ideas. Basically you'll try to test the diplomacy—and patience—of the task team member: Suggest as many far-out ideas as you can—for example, packaging the CDs in miniature lunchboxes with a free can of Jolt soda inside, starting an ad campaign called "Nuclear Lunchbox Is Radio-Active" to get the attention of FM stations, and so forth. Eventually give in and approve whatever proposal they have, but only if they promise to at least consider your ideas in the future.

Finance Department

Everyone in the finance department has at least one role. If there aren't enough people in the group, individuals may play more than one role.

Role 1: Finance Manager

Assign the roles below to the people in your group. Make sure your whole group agrees before you sign any product proposal. Refer all task team members to your procedural assistant first.

Role 2: Procedural Assistant

Your job is to enforce the department's rules about the appearance of product proposals. You will not approve a proposal unless all colors are written in capital letters (e.g., BLACK) and all numbers are written out as words (e.g., SEVEN DOLLARS AND FIFTY CENTS). Incorrect spelling is also unacceptable to you.

Role 3: Purchasing Agent

Due to high materials costs, you will only accept a proposal that says packaging will be made up of inexpensive polymerized plastic.

Role 4: Production Cost Analyst

You would like to see production costs no higher than $4.50 and feel you can defend this because a friend of yours in production assures you this is possible.

Role 5: Resource Allocation Manager

Any compact disc with a running time of more than 44 minutes is unacceptable to you because you don't want to be blamed if additional time makes the project's budgeted costs run higher than expected.

Role 6: Color Specialist

Due to the prohibitively high cost of metallizing CDs with assorted colors, you will only approve of a CD that is plain silver or purple.

Task Team

Upon receiving this memo, your group will leave the premises to prepare your first product proposal.

Your job is crucial to the future of the Wildcat Compact Disc Company. You will have only a limited amount of time to get the approval of four departments and the CEO. If the Nuclear Lunchbox CD is not released soon, other punk-rap-classical groups may capture the market. Your mission is to make sure that Nuclear Lunchbox is a radiation sensation across the nation.

Use any tactics you think will be useful in getting a product proposal approved. Maybe charm and diplomacy will do the trick; maybe a sound and rational argument will help.

The following rules must be followed:

- If two departments have rules or procedures that contradict each other, you may submit a written memo to the executive board requesting a rules change. The board has the authority to accept or reject a rules change based on how wise and plausible it appears to be. If a rules change occurs, it must be initialed by the managers of each department, including your own, before it goes into effect.
- No more than two group members at a time are allowed to walk freely around the room to meet, negotiate, or communicate with members of other departments. Other group members should listen carefully to their negotiations, taking notes and preparing memos for the executive board if necessary. Every minute counts!

It is your job to make initial contact with each of the departments.

Executive Board

It is best if at least two but no more than three people comprise the executive board.

The executive board has chosen the task team to complete the difficult task of getting input from all departments. Since the Nuclear Lunchbox CD will be the first major release by Wildcat, a timely and qualitatively sound decision is of crucial importance.

The board will review any memos from the task team and determine if any companywide rules change is necessary. Only memos that truly justify the proposed rules change should be approved. If a memo says nothing more than, "Can we make a rule that allows us to have a CD that runs 55 minutes?" it should be rejected in a written memo that requests additional information. The board will decide if the task team has good reasons for requesting a change, reasons that are consistent with the company's overall goals of quality and profitability. Be tough, but be reasonable—especially given the tight deadline.

The board members will have a quick meeting when any memo is received. Everyone should be allowed to voice his or her opinion until a consensus is reached.

Upon agreeing to a rules change, the board members will write a memo that must be initialed by a board member, a task team member, and all four department heads.

The board members will also be the last to review and sign off on a product proposal. Feel free to ask the task team to defend each choice they have made. Once you are satisfied, sign the proposal accordingly.

68

THE DAY CARE RESOURCE AND REFERRAL AGENCY* PARTS A, B, AND C

Background

The Day Care Resource and Referral Agency (DERRY), based on an actual entity and a situation it encountered, requires students to consider issues of managing change, how to constructively work with an organization's culture, how to determine who is best qualified for a position, and whether determining in advance that the ideal candidate for a position is one of a particular gender or race is discriminatory towards candidates who may be otherwise highly qualified.

Part A

Part A asks students to consider the changes DERRY has gone through, the role each of its leaders has played in those changes, the kinds of changes that now need to take place, and how best to implement the desired changes. Students should recognize that DERRY has not only undergone major structural changes, but has gone through changes in organizational philosophy as well. DERRY has grown from a two-person organization to a social services agency with a president, board of directors, and more than two dozen employees. The philosophical emphasis of the organization has evolved as well; rather than existing primarily to serve the employment needs of area factories, the organization now also focuses on providing jobs and careers for welfare recipients in the Brighthaven community.

Each of DERRY's leaders has played a role in the metamorphosis of the agency. Connie Donovan recognized that the demand for day care was greater than the supply, and she instituted training programs that enabled potential day-care providers to be licensed. She was instrumental in helping the agency grow to its present size. She also set the stage for trouble by hiring Tom Lichtenberg, an outsider and a male, as her replacement, thus angering and alienating the primarily female minority employees who comprised the organization.

Tom Lichtenberg, because of his management training, recognized early that the records were a mess and that Bertha was not qualified for her job. He felt that changes had to be made to ensure the fiscal soundness of the agency, and one of these changes was replacing Bertha with a computer. Although the board agreed that changes were necessary, it also recognized the high degree of referent power possessed by Bertha and the extent to which she was an informal leader. The board recognized that attempts to eliminate Bertha would wreak havoc within the agency. Although Tom quit without making any concrete changes, he nonetheless pointed out problem areas in the operations of the agency and made the board aware of the need for some very important changes.

* This case is presented in three parts, A, B, and C. Case "C" appears in the *Instructor's Resource Manual* only—at the end of these notes—and may be removed and freely copied for class distribution.

Andrea Chierico, while remaining true to the organizational philosophy, allowed the agency to continue its downslide by permitting herself to be manipulated by Bertha. The result is that she is unable to see that the agency is being run inefficiently until the fundraiser and business liaison point it out to her in no uncertain terms. Although she agrees to talk to Bertha, the conversation does not go well. Rather than "tough it out" and try to make some real changes, Andrea elects to leave. This provides DERRY with the opportunity to assess what it wants and needs in Andrea's replacement, what kinds of changes need to be made, and how best to implement them.

Change

When asked to identify changes that should take place at DERRY, students should cite most of the following, though they will probably come up with other suggestions as well: the new director should come from within the community and be able to relate to the employees; staffing and structural changes will need to be made; unqualified and nonproductive employees will need to be trained or terminated; salaries either need to be restructured or the higher-paying positions need to be more gender-balanced; and amends will need to be made to corporate sponsors and positive professional relationships reestablished.

Students should find virtually any theory of managing change useful in setting out their plan for implementing the necessary changes; organizational development process, Lewin, and Greiner would all work well here. The most important thing is that the plan relates to the changes the students have identified as needing to take place, and that the steps are carried out in the order described by whatever theory the student has chosen to use.

Part B

Part B asks students to analyze the résumés and interviewers' notes for several job candidates, determine the strengths and weaknesses of each candidate, determine who will be best equipped to carry out the changes that need to be made at DERRY, and consider the difficulties that may arise when the changes are implemented. Before doing this, however, students are asked to consider the traits and characteristics of the ideal candidate, to write a job description, and to write the copy for an ad for the job.

The new director will need the support of the employees if changes are to be made successfully. It is important, therefore, that the person selected be able to win the employees' trust. The ideal person will probably but not necessarily be female, a minority, and from the Brighthaven community. Bilingual capability, particularly in Spanish, would also be helpful. In addition, the person selected will need to establish contacts in the community and mend fences with angry customers. Therefore, the person should also have community contacts, experience in running a similar agency (or other relevant experience), fundraising ability, and excellent conflict management skills. Supervisory experience and the ability to successfully institute change will also be important traits, as will a commitment to diversity.

The actual job description should include a specific listing of the person's duties as well as of the goals and expectations that the board has established. In addition, minimum qualifications and preferred qualifications should be stated. The ad copy should be a succinct version of the job description. However, in writing the copy, students need to be careful not to use phrases that are discriminatory and/or illegal. While a job ad cannot specifically state the gender or ethnicity of the preferred candidate, it is perfectly acceptable to include a statement such as "women and minorities are encouraged to apply."

After analyzing the strengths and weaknesses of all candidates against the job description and organizational goals and objectives, Rosa Gonzalez-Bueno is probably the most supportable candidate for the position. While Melvin Baker is well-educated, has strong negotiation skills, and seems committed to making a social contribution, he is also a friend of Clark Donovan's (which may give the appearance of nepotism), has no community involvement or connections, is not bilingual, seems to have no supervisory experience, and has no other relevant experience. He is also male.

Sarah Penniman is a more suitable candidate than Melvin. She has relevant work experience, is interested in biculturalism, comes from Brighthaven, and has work experience with women and minorities. However, she has no management experience to speak of, may be viewing Brighthaven according to "old stereotypes," has no apparent community involvement or connections, and has only held one full-time job.

Linda Spiers has good qualifications as well: hiring and supervisory experience, fundraising and development experience, public relations experience, some community involvement (though not in Brighthaven), and has done some relevant research. However, she is an outsider with no community connections, does not speak Spanish, has no direct agency experience, and may be a bit too assertive for the population with which she would be working.

Rosa Gonzalez-Bueno, while not as highly educated as the other candidates and with less relevant work experience than at least one of the candidates, nevertheless brings more useful qualifications to the job than any of the others. She has had extensive community involvement in Brighthaven, has many connections, is familiar with the community, is a female and a minority, speaks Spanish, has excellent fundraising skills, does not back away from conflict, has a solid employment history and, having struggled to get to where she is, is someone her employees and others in the community can relate to and look up to—she is a "success story." This is the decision the board made in the actual situation on which this case was based—and it has turned out to be a good one.

The main problems Rosa will be likely to have when attempting to implement change will be with DERRY's employees, particularly Bertha. Because Bertha has a high degree of referent power and is an informal leader among the employees, she has the power to resist changes with which she does not agree and to encourage other employees to resist as well. Rosa will either have to convince Bertha to make the changes necessary for DERRY to recover, or she will have to fire her. Rosa will need to form alliances with other employees. This will be particularly important if she has to let Bertha go. In the actual agency's situation, Bertha and several of her cronies were dismissed in a massive reorganization.

Change will need to be managed through education and with input from the employees. Because previous hiring practices brought in employees not entirely qualified for their jobs, training will be an important part of any structural or operational changes. Education and training are also important for employees who are likely to feel threatened by changes.

Rosa may also experience difficulties with regaining the trust of DERRY's corporate sponsors. An important first step will be to make realistic promises and then keep them.

Part C

Part C asks students to consider the basis for the board's decision to hire Rosa, to think about whether or not they agree with the board's decision, and to ponder some of the broader social implications of making hiring decisions based on criteria that take into account an organization's culture and the community the organization serves.

For the necessary changes to happen, employee acceptance of the executive director is crucial. Someone who is "one of them," connected to the community, an activist, and able to relate to employees and corporate sponsors and clients alike is certainly the best choice and the person most likely to succeed in the position.

Students may raise issues of reverse discrimination in the job description and hiring of Rosa. They will need to consider whether anyone but a minority woman would have been able to succeed in this position, given both the changes that needed to be made and the organizational culture. It is also important to understand that as long as the person hired is the person best qualified for the job, discrimination probably has not occurred.

Finally, in considering some of the social implications for hiring decisions based on DERRY's criteria, students should examine issues such as the shifting balance of power that would most likely begin to occur as more minorities assume positions of power in organizations, what actually constitutes discrimination, and whether hiring practices such as these are more effective than traditional hiring practices.

The Day Care Resource and Referral Agency: Part C

After two weeks of deliberation, the board decided that the new executive director should be both a woman and a minority: They hired Rosa Guarino-Bueno. In slightly more than six months, Rosa, with the board's support and some trepidation, had trimmed the workforce at DERRY by almost one-third. Among those let go were Bertha, Ella, and Josie.

Concerned about being sued for discrimination and wrongful dismissal, the members of the board held their breath. Months went by and nothing happened. In the meantime, Rosa instituted office systems, including computerization of financial and other functions. She trained a number of lower-level but talented employees to do more sophisticated jobs and made several promotions from within. Working with a team of employees, she developed an organizational chart and a book of clearly delineated job descriptions. In addition, she brought Al Hawkes, who had started his own firm to consult to day care agencies and programs, back as a part-time consultant supported by two bright and hard working full-time DERRY employees.

Today, about a decade after its founding, DERRY is considered a model for many other agencies across the country.

Questions for Consideration

1. Why do you feel the board made the decision to hire Rosa? Do you agree with their decision? Why?
2. What do you think about the legal, moral, and ethical implications of the basis for their hiring decision?
3. What are the broader social implications of making hiring decisions based on the criteria set by the DERRY board?

69

PLAYING FOOTSY WITH THE FAMILY BUSINESS

Upon the death of Joseph Savenor, founder and patriarch of the family-held Savenor Shoe, Inc., he leaves his son-in-law, Abe Seiler, as essentially titular head of this manufacturing company. The founder's four children own 80 percent of the stock, the remainder having been divided among long-term employees and retirees. Recognizing the unfavorable future for shoe manufacturing in the United States, Seiler decides he wants to move out of production and wholesale sales and into import and retail outlets. Well-entrenched norms, loyalties to workers who are seen as extended family, and other rational and emotional concerns, all spell potential resistance to Seiler's plan. This case contains enough organizational and family dynamics to support lengthy discussions and written analyses.

Teaching Objectives

This case can be used to explore the issues of managing change, leadership styles, inter- and intragroup conflicts, stages of group development, group cohesion, norms, uses and abuses of power (French and Raven), ethics, and leadership. Students should also recognize that not all business decisions can realistically be made using rational processes that fail to consider sentiment and emotion.

Students should identify and analyze the various stakeholders and what their resistances and interests are likely to be. Students must move beyond thinking that the only parties involved in effecting change in organizations are those in whom power is centralized and legitimately held. Therefore, students should recognize that Seiler's proposal is likely to impact not just the stockholders, but workers, retirees who don't hold stock, members of the family whether they hold stock, and various individuals and groups who make up the concentric circles of the world in which the organization does business.

Case Approach and General Discussion

Students will probably find it useful to create some organizational charts of the old board, the new board, the company hierarchy and the stock distribution, as well as of the Savenor family, in addition to the usual preliminary steps of character analysis and chronology. In order to analyze the dynamics in this case, students will need to understand the role, authority and decision-making power of the board, the stockholders, and other relevant stakeholders.

The next most useful step is to do a Force Field Analysis (Exhibit 1), a good tool for dissecting the case and for developing recommendations. Force fields generate the most effective recommendations when restraining forces are described concretely rather than broadly.

Possible recommendations for how Abe might reduce restraining forces include hiring a strategy consultant to work with the board on long-term strategic issues, with all members having input (in order to reduce resistance and increase commitment to any changes); adding some outside directors to the board; selling Jeffrey on the new vision [thereby increasing support on the board (through Malcolm) and among stockholders] by offering to send him for a marketing degree and promising him a future role in retail; trying to garner support from Eleanore, who has the greatest referent power among employees and retirees (but who probably will be very difficult to win over); trying to keep Eleanore from becoming the next chairperson; persuading stockholders (including retirees) of what they will gain financially if the business changes; developing early retirement, retraining, and relocation incentives for employees; offering college scholarships to employees' children and retirees' grandchildren for careers in retail; and memorializing Joe Savenor and the company's history through the new retail stores' marketing, name, and image.

There are many opportunities for intergroup conflicts. For example:

- Family members versus employees and retirees of the company
- Siblings versus nonsibling family members (Abe, Anne, and Jeffrey)
- Family subgroups (e.g., Malcolm, Anne, and Jeffrey) versus other family subgroups
- Traditionalists (Eleanore, Harold, Susanne, and the retiree stockholders) versus less sentimental, more bottom-line thinkers (Abe)
- Some people may be especially susceptible to intergroup conflict since they are members of both factions. For example, Susanne has membership in her married family (so she's allied with Abe) and in her family-of-origin (so she's allied with his adversaries).
- Between retirees (who might gain financially from changes) and current employees (who could lose their jobs)

Group cohesion is seen within the Savenor Shoe Company, reflected in the long-term (multigenerational) employee membership, geographic proximity, homogeneity (for example, attending same church), clear norms, low turnover, and low conflict. The Savenor family business also has enjoyed stable membership and leadership, low conflict (as far as we know) and clear boundaries. What makes this group less cohesive now, however, is the geographic dispersion; the lack of clear, common goals; the leadership vacuum; and the uncertainty that old norms still hold (for example, that stock dividends will continue to be generous and that the directors' meeting will serve only ceremonial purposes). There is a potential for high cohesion if Abe's adversaries close ranks in order to thwart his new plan.

In terms of group development, both the stockholders' group and the board have reentered an early stage: students might support a diagnosis of either forming or storming (B. W. Turkman).

This case offers an interesting look at informal leadership versus formal leadership. (Joe was clearly the most influential person even after he handed over the reins to Abe, and Eleanore may be viewed by employees as his true heir.)

Sources of Power

Organizational charts should be used as a framework for an analysis of sources of power (French and Raven) and their relative strengths: Abe has legitimate power in the company but is equal to other board members; his expert power may or may not be valued by others and his reward and coercive powers are tempered by the board's. Eleanore, on the other hand, has referent power with employees and retirees, legitimate and expert power within the company, and "blood" power, if you will, as a family insider and close associate of her father. In playing out the options now available to Abe, it would be a disastrous misuse of legitimate power for him simply to impose his plan upon the others.

Ethics

Ethical considerations spring from the company's implicit (but not legally binding) contract with its employees that, in return for their loyalty, lifetime employment, productivity, and resistance to organized labor, the company will employ them and their relatives, offer stock after 20 years, provide emergency financial assistance, and treat them as valued family members. How long should this commitment be upheld? And at what cost? Students should go beyond easy answers here: Is it worth losing the business to save these jobs for a few more years? Students may try to sidestep the issue of laying-off workers, but they should not. It's unlikely that Savenor's can convert its entire manufacturing workforce to retail sales, or that long-time North Deighton residents will all pull up stakes and move.

This case can also be used to explore the process of managing change, and it is here that the Force Field Analysis is especially useful. Students must grapple with several important issues: the relative power and authority of the CEO, president, board, and stockholders; the informal influence of family; and the interplay of emotional issues and rational reasoning. Using the Force Field Analysis, students can direct their efforts in developing a well-focused plan of action for Abe to follow.

Playing Footsy With the Family Business

Goal: To move from manufacturing to retail shoe sales

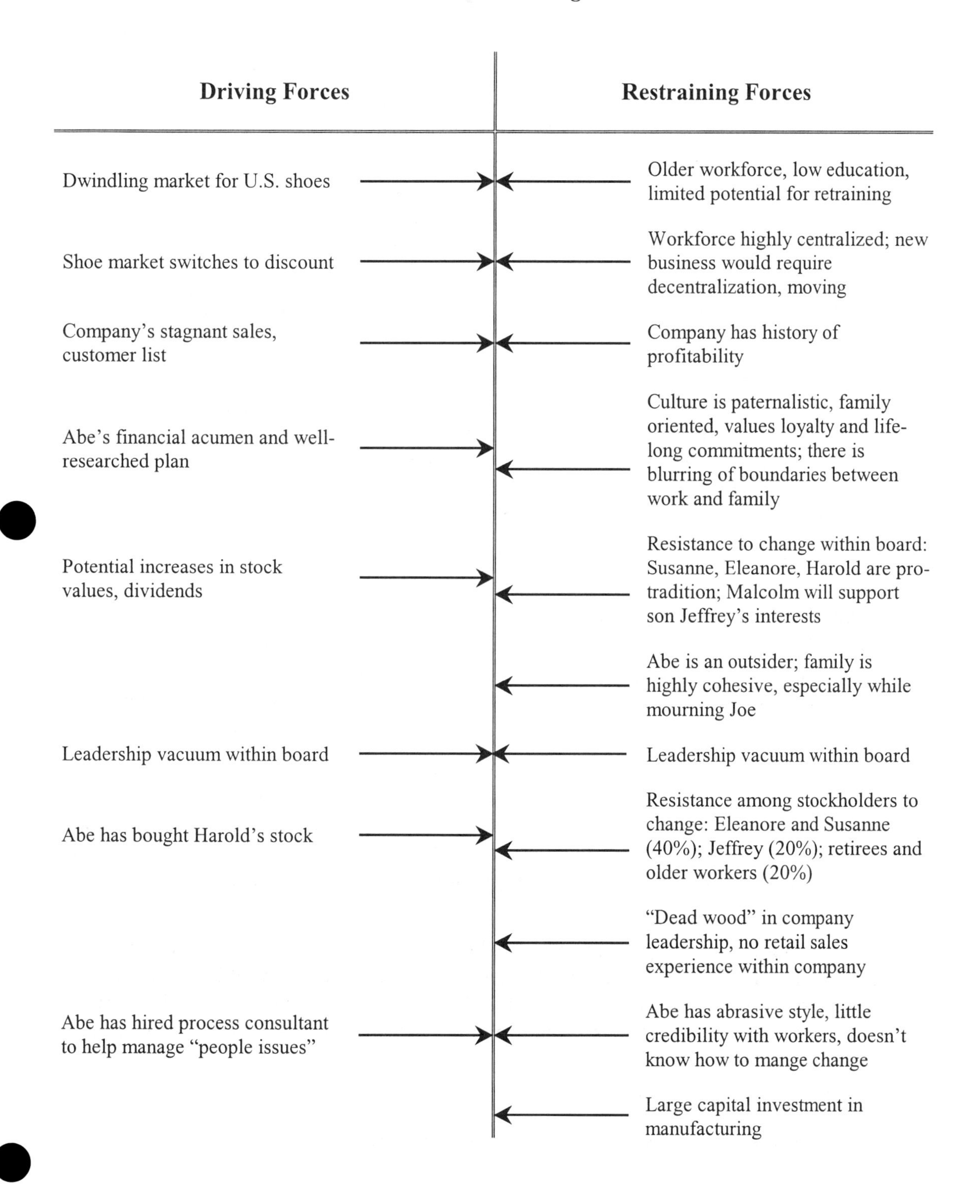

70

THE PROVIDENCE PRIVATEERS*

This case demonstrates the ripple effect a major, strategic organizational change will have on a variety of stakeholders both within and outside of the organization planning the change. I have used this case in my classes for many years. It has been popular with students and has usually generated a rich and multi-layered discussion.

Key issues that appear in most discussions of the case are:

- Who are the stakeholders, and what are their issues?
- **Industrial issues:** How does this proposed change impact other organizations in the industry (major league baseball)? What is their reaction likely to be? What should the Privateers do to plan for this reaction?
- **Community issues:** Most discussion here centers around community issues in Providence, such as the loss of a tax base, job loss, loss of sense of community, etc. Thoughtful groups will also identify issues in the receiving community (Jacksonville) as well. There will be inevitable resistance to this change in the Jacksonville area from those who see this altering the nature of the community they have come to know. Other issues attendant to the building of a new state of the art stadium and the disruption and possible destruction of community neighborhoods will also arise. How do the Privateers manage this?
- **Associated organizational issues:** What are the issues for organizations directly affiliated with the Privateers, such as the Parking Authority, food service providers, security personnel, subcontractor employees such as ticket takers, ushers, etc., local television and radio stations that broadcast the games, and city bureaucratic offices associated with the Privateers lease on the city-owned stadium? What should the Privateers do, if anything?
- **Non-associated organizational issues:** Organizations with secondary and tertiary interests in the Privateers will be affected by this move. Local restaurants, hotels, souvenir shops, independent peanut and hot dog vendors, local police (decrease in overtime associated with games), among others, number among those who will see their interests diminish in this move and will likely resist the change. How should the Privateers plan to handle this?
- **Employee issues:** Aside from the baseball players, managers and coaches (who expect to move often in their careers, and are well compensated as a result), what internal issues exist for the Privateers regarding their office and administrative staff regarding this move? Does the organization provide assistance in relocation, such as real estate services in selling one house and buying another? Moving assistance? School information in the new

location? Assistance in finding spouse/significant other employment in the new location? For those who opt not to go to Florida with the team, should the team provide outplacement assistance; if so what should the extent of it be?

- **Corporate social responsibility/ethical issues:** Many of these are embedded within this change. What should the Privateers do about them? Inevitably, there will be some free-marketers in the room who will argue that the Privateers are simply following the dictates of the marketplace and owe nothing to the people of Providence. An interesting discussion can be had around what is the nature of corporate social responsibility beyond simply earning profits and providing employment. If this organization has been a part of the fabric of this community for over 100 years, do the Privateers owe the community something for the impact they will have by moving the team? If so, what? If not, why not? What of the disruption to the community in Jacksonville where the new stadium will be built? Do the Privateers have a corporate social responsibility for any actions there? If so, what? If not, why not?

- **Marketing perspectives:** Should the team change its name, logo, or team colors?

  An interesting discussion can be had linking marketing issues to organizational culture, public image, and strategic change management. Should the Privateers change the venerable team colors of puce and magenta to something more tropical such as teal and burnt sienna? Should they become the Jacksonville Barracudas rather than remaining the Privateers? How would these changes diminish resistance to change? How might they help the healing process in Providence?

- **Other constituent organizations:** What others can the Privateers tap for assistance in managing this change? How might the city of Jacksonville, State of Florida, Major League Baseball, etc., provide services/assistance to the club in planning and managing this move? How can the hotel, restaurant, tourism, television, and radio industries in Jacksonville be of assistance?

- **Creative options:** Students can come up with some very creative options in helping the Privateers with this move. Some of these have included putting the Privateers' top minor league team into the newly abandoned stadium in Providence with the old team name and colors, running charter "sun and fun" weekend trips down to Jacksonville at very low rates for die-hard Privateer fans, and special cable TV packages from Jacksonville for broadcast of team games, among other creative options. The key point to explore is what needs are being addressed by these efforts, and why is the organization trying to address those needs.

A few words about process:

I divide the class into groups of 3 to 5 people (5 to 7 if it is a larger class) and after a brief discussion of the case where I introduce myself as the owner of the team, I send them to various corners of the room, hallways, lounge areas, breakout spaces, etc., with newsprint, markers and masking tape, and instruct them to tear the case apart and return at an appointed time with their 5 to 7 minute presentation on the case. I usually flit from group to group during their deliberations, playing intellectual gadfly and trying to spark new directions in thought. The presentations and resulting debrief are usually very textured and stimulating.

71

THE SEATTLE FERRY COMPANY

Klaus Wade is asked to spy on the company in which his stepfather is somewhat of a silent partner. While at the outset he isn't clear on the reasons for "keeping his eye open," the problems soon become evident—not just to Klaus, but to the immediate world. Changes have to be made if the company is to continue to operate.

Sources of Power

Jack Daniels, Derek, the owners, and Robert all have various sources of social power as described by French and Raven. All use them or fail to use them in different ways. As mate, Jack Daniels has legitimate power which he exercises selectively. The most notable use is to enforce his coercive power by prohibiting the deck hands from leaving the ship on washing days. He uses reward power negatively by yelling at the hands and telling them they are lazy. Daniels seems to have little referent power with his subordinates; the deck hands seem to hold him in low regard. Those above him, however, keep him on the job and seem to believe he is doing a good job. His prior job as a member of the Coast Guard may give him expertise, but he does not appear to use it as a social power.

Derek, the deck hand to whom Jack has passed his responsibilities, has legitimate power over the other deck hands by virtue of his informal position, as it has been granted to him by a higher authority. As he seems to know what needs to be done, he appears to exercise some expert power. However, the case states, "He wasn't particularly thorough...." It is unclear whether he has coercive power over the deck hands, despite his responsibility to monitor their behavior, e.g., when they arrive at work late or hung over. In this example, one might conclude that he has responsibility without authority. He has and exercises reward power in making out the "days-off" schedule. (Some students will question, rightfully, if he then actually has legitimate power.) "Taking care of his friends" may indicate some referent power.

The owners certainly have legitimate power; however, they appear to do little to exercise the powers that go along with their positions, that is, reward and coercive. They appear to have authority while turning responsibility over to those who work for them. Robert, who is granted the legitimate right to run the ferry line on a day-to-day basis, also appears to do little to exercise his other powers, although he apparently has reward and coercive powers by dint of his position.

Students should recognize that the abdication of many of the social powers by those who have them is a key factor in the Seattle Ferry Company's present problems.

Managing Change

Managing change at the Seattle Ferry Company cannot come without a real analysis of the changes that have to be made and the resistances that are likely to be encountered in doing so. Clearly the Seattle Ferry Company is going to need more time and commitment from those in charge. Necessary changes are going to mean exercising more control over those who now have power, and there will surely be concerns about resource allocation.

Necessary changes include proper disposal of trash and sewage; institution of better accounting systems to avoid blatant theft of such things as food, beer, and cash receipts; more appropriate use of personnel; better supervision of employees; more control over hiring; institution of reward systems, and so forth. This will mean threatening the existing status of individuals such as Jack, Robert, Derek, the deck hands, Valdez, and even the owners, all of whom will likely resist such change. Students should be able to give examples of each of the resistances, for example, the deck hands who now get a free case of beer for cleaning the bar will likely resist the change that deprives them of that perquisite, and chart at least some of this out on a force field. Using Lewin's change model, students should walk through the steps of unfreezing, changing, and refreezing.

The case text makes clear that firing employees is not an option, although it might appear that some selective use of coercive power might be in order. Such recommendations, however, must be carefully supported.

The final question of the case calls for opinion, but, as always, opinion must be supported by rational, meaningful arguments. Klaus has a fringe role in this family, and it is unclear to whom he owes allegiance, if anyone. This is particularly true with regard to his protection of Robert at the potential expense of his stepfather.

72

DALE'S HEALTHY SNACKS: A CASE OF FOOD FOR THOUGHT

Background

This case presents an organization whose business is changing as a result of market forces. Dale's Healthy Snacks is changing its distribution system from using a network of independent distributors and direct shipment to a fully in-house sales and distribution. Dale's currently has a force of route service representatives (RSRs) who are responsible for ensuring accurate and timely delivery of healthy snacks to a wide range of customers, including diet and nutrition centers, health clubs, and retail stores. As Dale's changes to a fully in-house distribution system, the nature of the RSR's job will change. RSRs will now become route account managers (RAMs) responsible for taking and processing orders, rotating inventory, delivering and building displays, selling in promotions, and educating customers as to the benefits of their products.

Some RSRs have embraced the change and see it as a challenge, while others are not sure that they have the time or the skill to successfully perform the new duties. Dale's managers must decide how to implement the change in a way that motivates RSRs to take on the new challenges. The case, therefore, can be used to examine motivation as well as the implementation of change.

Change

As managers implement the changes at Dale's, they must unfreeze the system and be aware of possible sources of resistance. Many RSRs have been in their positions for a long time. They have become entrenched in the routine of delivering products without providing any additional service. They are now being asked to change the habits that they have formed, which is likely to meet with resistance. Potential economic factors may cause resistance as well, as RSRs wonder if they will be able to perform at their new jobs. Sales positions are typically associated with commissions, and the RSRs may worry that their income will be reduced because they cannot make the necessary volume. Fear of the unknown may also produce resistance, and this change involves much uncertainty. RSRs are uncertain about the exact skills they will need to be successful. They are not quite sure what the new job entails, what is expected of them, and whether this is the latest company fad that will eventually go away.

As the company attempts to unfreeze, RSRs must be educated about the need for change. Most of them are unlikely to be aware of the many changes that are facing the industry as a whole. This would also be an excellent opportunity to educate the RSRs about the company's heritage and traditions so that they can use this information during their visits to customers.

Dale's has begun providing training in merchandising and selling, however, there is little indication that the organization has attempted to help the RSRs understand the necessity and urgency of this change. Furthermore, the district managers do not seem to have a consistent and well thought-out plan of action. Pat wants to take a hard line, while Martine is more inclined to give the RSRs time to see how easily they will be able to perform their new jobs.

The district managers (DMs) must also communicate more clearly about the nature of the RAM job. Currently, much of what is known about the position is through the rumor mill. The DMs should clearly define the roles and responsibilities of the new job and explain what will be expected as well as what the pay structure will be. Without this information, the RSRs will likely fill in the void with their own worst fears and be more likely to resist the change. The DMs have an excellent opportunity to share information and reduce fears by bringing in RAMs from the successful test markets to tell their story. This has the benefit that RSRs are more likely to believe their peers.

Another means that can be used to reduce resistance is to include the RSRs in the process of defining the transition into their new jobs. It is difficult know the fears and concerns of each RSR. By involving them in the change process and providing the necessary support for them to make the transition, their resistance will be reduced. In addition, each RSR is likely to have a different confidence level in his or her skills to do the new job. A flexible training program can be implemented that allows the RSRs to take advantage of the portions they need and avoid the others.

Motivation

This case may also be used to discuss motivation. Some of the RSRs are clearly motivated by the change, while others are not. One way to explain this is through expectancy theory. Steve is worried that he will not be able to perform at a level that will gain him the outcomes he desires, whereas Jim believes that "once you have the system down, the biggest challenge of the day is finding a new store that you've never been to before." Expectancy theory suggests that people must believe their efforts will result in a desired outcome. Jim clearly believes this is the case whereas Steve does not.

Management Styles

It is also possible to examine the likely effects of Pat's and Martine's different management styles. Pat appears to be a Theory X manager, while Martine seems to be more Theory Y. To wit, Pat sees the resistance as an indication of a lack of desire to take on new challenges, while Martine appears to believe that people need to get accustomed to their new jobs and will eventually realize that they can easily perform them. Her concern is only that people will attempt to "go too far too quickly." The two styles are each likely to create their own self-fulfilling prophecies. Since RSRs are likely to be motivated by safety needs, as they fear they may not have the skills required to maintain their jobs, Pat's strategy of telling them to "shape up or ship out" is likely to thwart the satisfaction of safety needs and demotivate those who are feeling insecure.

73

THE DEEP-WATER HARBOR

Group Size: Any number of groups of six or more.

Recommended Time: 60 minutes (5 minutes for set up; 5 minutes for students to read and assess role; 5–10 minutes for students to share their positions; 15–20 minutes to identify driving and restraining forces; remainder for report out and discussion).

Provided: Instructions and information forms in student text, roles for photocopying and distribution following these notes.

Also Required: No additional materials required. However, if you wish students to create a graphic force field analysis, two to three sheets of newsprint and two markers are recommended for each group.

Facilities: A large room with moveable chairs.

Objectives

- To explore the role of stakeholders in resisting and driving change
- To practice identifying driving and resisting forces to change
- To practice using force field analysis to assess and plan change

Background

This exercise has been developed to give students practice using force field analysis in the management of change. Each role includes somewhat transparent driving and restraining forces that students should quickly recognize as they go through the role play.

The proposed change, from a shallow harbor used primarily for recreational use to a deep-water harbor to be used by commercial shipping, is largely driven by economics. The town has been in decline, due to a decrease in the timber industry—which probably places this town somewhere on the West Coast, possibly in Oregon or Washington—and needs new job opportunities for its residents. A local fish-packing plant, while important, simply cannot support a community of 750,000. Neither, most likely, can the two-months-a-year summer tourist industry. Yet the loss of either or both of these could mean further devastation.

Also entering into the picture are environmental and aesthetic concerns. Industry isn't pretty, and it is almost always in direct opposition to keeping the environment pristine. While students may want to debate the need for environment versus industry, the town has already made its decision by voting to dredge. Therefore, you can move the discussion directly into the management of the proposed change.

Forces driving the change include:

- providing more jobs
- potential for bringing more industry into the area
- enhancement of general economy
- increased tax base
- avoiding the loss of the fish-packing plant
- increasing demand for property and thus increasing values
- potential to decrease trucking through residential neighborhoods
- ability to use an unused resource—railroads

Forces resisting the change include:

- cost of dredging
- imposed time limitations
- appearance—during dredging
- appearance—of more industry
- appearance—of sludge site
- environmental issues—sludge dump, disruption to harbor, and so forth
- noise
- possible loss of leisure areas—beaches, safe and quiet harbor for small boats
- loss of summer tourist trade
- costs of moving the fish-packing plant

Students also may want to complete a separate force field analysis for the fish-packing plant.

Some of the forces for resisting the change of moving to a new location include:

- cost of moving
- restraints on growth from present situation
- need to hire and train a new workforce at a new location
- resistance of current plant manager
- poor public relations from closing plant
- need to relocate executives

Some of the driving forces include:

- costs of maintaining current system

- ability to grow and expand in new location
- ability to operate in a healthier economic environment
- lack of a deep-water port in current location

The fish-packing plant seems to have more reasons to stay than to go, but the reasons for leaving appear to be overriding if dredging is not carried out. However, what this second force field may reveal is that there may be some negotiating room in terms of time demands for completing the dredging and that the plant may also be willing to allocate at least some of the funds necessary for the project. These directly relate to at least two of the restraining forces on the town's list. Therefore, part of the plan for implementation may include participation by the plant managers to diminish the strength of these forces.

Suggested Outline and Timing

1. *Set-up (5 minutes)*

    - Explain the exercise to the students, reviewing the learning objectives.
    - Distribute the roles.
    - Answer any questions.

2. *Exercise (30–40 minutes)*

3. *Report-out and discussion (open-ended)*

    If you have asked students to complete graphic force field analyses of this problem, ask them to present them at this time.

Restaurateur

You are the owner of a very successful seafood restaurant on the shore of the harbor near the fish-packing plant. Thanks to the many customers you get from among the plant's employees and visitors to the plant, you do a very brisk lunch business almost year round. There are no other restaurants in this vicinity. During the summer, sailors who keep their boats in the harbor and people with summer cottages along the water frequent your restaurant for dinner.

You have somewhat mixed feelings about the plans for dredging the harbor. Right now, the view from your restaurant's windows is picturesque. During the dredging, however, diners will probably look out at cranes and other industrial equipment. You're also concerned that the barges, noise, and general disruption to the harbor will drive the leisure sailors and tourists away during the process.

Lawyer

You were one of the prime forces in getting the town to accept the deep-dredging plan for the harbor. The owners of the fish-packing plant have been your major clients, and you are aware that, without the dredging, the plant probably will be moved more than 100 miles away. The plant owners have given the town six months to complete the project, although they are pushing to have it done sooner.

Recently, you got a couple of feelers from executives of major store chains. They are looking for sites for distribution centers that require ports accessible to container ships. There is a reasonable chance, you believe, that at least one will want to locate in your town once the deep-water harbor is complete. This, of course, will mean additional jobs and economic opportunities for the area.

Sailor/Accountant

You are a 56-year-old private accountant who moved with your spouse into a luxury 48-unit condominium—twenty-seventh floor—that overlooks the harbor on one side and the proposed site for the harbor sludge dump on the other. While harbor sludge, the material that is removed from the harbor floor by dredging, is rich and may eventually provide a fertile base for the growth of such seaside vegetation as beach roses, heather, and various flowering vines, it is ugly and emits an unpleasant odor when first removed. On a hot day, the smell can be really offensive. You think the fish-packing plant already smells bad enough.

In addition to your annoyance over the sludge dump problem, you and many of your friends are concerned about the costs of doing the dredging, the potential loss of summer boating facilities, and the possible threat to the small white sand beach on the condo property.

Contractor

You are a local contractor who is hoping to get the dredging contract. You believe that you can complete the dredging in about eight months, just two months beyond the schedule requested by the owners of the fish-packing plant. You don't have the equipment needed for doing it much faster than that, however, so if the six months is a mandate, the contract will probably have to go to a larger contractor from out of state. You believe you can do as good a job at a substantially lower price if given enough time.

Personally, you are also concerned about the proposed sludge dump. You're an environmentalist, and you know that the site is now home to thousands of marsh birds and small animals. You're willing to haul the sludge out to be dumped at sea if the town is willing to pay your costs—you're not interested in making a profit on this part of the job.

Property Owner

You own a number of summer cottages along the harbor's rim, and you depend on the income from renting these during the summer months. Although the cottages are winterized, in recent years there has been a decreasing demand for them during the rest of the year. Unhappily, the lack of commerce in your community has been steadily driving the value of your properties down.

If the dredging is done during the summer, you are concerned that the noise and general disruption will keep people away. You're also fearful of potential damage to the beaches from the increased shipping.

Manager, Blue Marlin Fish Cannery

You are head of the fish-packing operation, a subsidiary of a larger food-processing company located elsewhere in the country. Clearly you have an interest in the dredging being carried out in a timely fashion. You and your family have come to love the area and all that it offers. You don't want to move if it can be avoided.

From a business perspective, the costs of moving will be considerable. While you think you might have some leeway in terms of timing, each day that boats are unable to come into the harbor to unload at the plant is costly. At present, boats are being unloaded 100 miles to the south, and the fish are brought by refrigerator truck to the processing plant. More than 30 trucks a day are brought into town, driving through residential areas to reach the plant.

Your orders from the national office are either to push for the dredging or move. You know that there are substantial costs to be incurred from moving, and you think you can convince the national office to come up with some money to subsidize the dredging operations if doing so will prevent having to move.

74

ISSUING A BLANKET STATEMENT

Despite having watched their possessions burn, students at a college insist they have a right to keep appliances in their rooms and use them. The ultimate confiscation results in student anger and protests, as well as considerable consternation on the parts of the older—and perhaps wiser—residence staff.

The students seem to be stubbornly resisting doing what is good for them, but "what is good for them" has been decided by outside forces. There has been no education and no negotiation; the students have not been included in the planning and decision making at any level. From what we know about decision making, in situations that require high levels of acceptance and compliance, involvement of those people who must carry out the decisions is crucial.

A Force Field Analysis is useful here: Forces driving the change to enforcement of the no-appliance rule include danger of fire, potential loss of personal property, potential inconvenience of having to move to temporary quarters, potential loss of life, costs to school, potential for having dorms closed for noncompliance with code or heavy fines levied, loss of fire insurance coverage, and so forth.

As you can quickly see, students would be likely to consider most of these driving forces to be remote possibilities at best, not to be weighted as heavily as their most immediate needs, i.e., the sources of resistance. Forces resisting the change include food facilities closing too early, inconvenience of having to order out, cost of having to order out, institutional food is unappealing, loss of "rights," only one week to remove appliances, and feeling that students are being treated like children.

If the students are allowed to participate in finding ways of reducing resistance, they will be far more likely to comply with the rule. Among possible solutions generated by our students in analyzing this case have been giving the students more say in what gets served in the cafeteria; getting a student committee to be in charge of late hours at the snack bar; supplying small dorm kitchens that can be used after hours; a longer period for getting rid of the appliances, perhaps to the end of the semester, when students can take them home instead of shipping them; a packing-and-shipping day run as a party, with the students collecting shipping boxes and the school supplying tape and snacks and arranging for pickup; and so forth. The list goes on. As you work through the case with your students, they will most likely add to it considerably.

In addition to the Force Field Analysis, students should talk about the ways they would involve students in the decision-making process. The mandate has been received secondhand. Perhaps the school president should meet with the students initially to voice his concern, doing so without issuing any mandate other than, "We have to work together to find ways to ensure one another's safety and the availability of school facilities. We hope you'll help."

Residence staff, who were told to carry out this mandate—also without having been involved in the decision—need to meet to talk about their role. Next, residence staffers might do well to form student committees to look into each of the resistances to find ways of reducing them. As with any total quality improvement plan, communication must flow through all parts of the organization, from the top down, across all departments and levels, and back.

Students should be able to use one or more of the models for managing change in dealing with this case, and should also consider how to keep the problem from recurring as new waves of students enter the school.

75

INSUBORDINATION OR STRUCTURAL CONFUSION AT OMEGA HOUSE?*

Background

Ellen, the program director of Omega House, a hospice, was wondering how to deal with the new development officer, George. He reports to her and is also part of a cross-program task force on fundraising within the Social Action Consortium (SAC), the umbrella organization for a variety of service agencies located in the Midwest. Ellen is accustomed to working in a team and finds George's non-communicative approach disconcerting. She is puzzled as to how to deal with the situation and wonders whether the problem with George is structural rather than individual. George's job seems unclear, with him reporting both to her and the SAC development office chief who heads the task force. Thus, she asks herself, "Is the problem George's irresponsible and non-communicative behavior, is it confusion over who is to direct his efforts, or both?"

Questions for Discussion

1. What organizational factors appear to be influencing the relationship between Ellen and George? In responding to this question, consider organizational factors at both SAC and Omega.

   The umbrella organization, SAC, appears to be highly autocratic. While the case doesn't state it, it is likely that Ellen has been taught to manage in hierarchical settings, such as hospitals, as well. In such settings, physicians tell nurses what to do and, based on their internal hierarchy, nurses then tell one another what to do. Thus the suggestion that Ellen is a team manager may not be wholly accurate. Certainly her approach to George suggests autocratic rather than collaborative behavior. In addition, the kind of ideologically-driven managers one is likely to find in a hospice setting may sometimes be autocratic because they feel the mission to be all important and the people working for them less so. Because of the emphasis on hierarchy in autocratic systems, fiefdoms tend to develop. Ellen seems somewhat unaware or unsympathetic to the cross-program needs that require George's attention.

2. In what ways do you believe the problems with George are personal and in what ways do they appear to be structural? Why?

   George does not seem to have role clarity, but his approach to this confusion appears to be defensiveness rather than openness to exploration and discussion of how he might better answer the needs of his supervisors. From Ellen's perspective, and the story is told very much from her point of view, George is putting the umbrella organization's interests well before the needs of Omega. Her objections are legitimate given the stated source of George's salary. It in unclear, however, whether the grant against which his services are charged is one which has been raised by SAC and merely assigned to Omega's budget. If this is the case, SAC may have some rights to George's time, and it may be in Ellen's interest to be more aware of and respectful of George's efforts to raise funds for SAC. The argument over who is rightfully entitled to scarce resources in the kind of cross-program organization described is understandable, particularly in this setting in which programs sometimes suffer due to seemingly arbitrary decisions by SAC's autocratic leader. The various stakeholders in this organization would do well to make every effort to explore their mutual and exclusive interests and come to an understanding.

3. If you were Ellen, what would you do next? Why?

   Ellen needs to work with George to get him to embrace the mission of Omega House and understand the need for their own fundraising efforts as well as those of the cross-program of SAC. She should try to find ways to support him and draw him out. It might be wise for her to be more sympathetic to his dilemma as she works towards making him an ally.

   In addition, Ellen should work with the leader of the cross-program task force at SAC to clarify George's role there as well as make her own needs explicit. Such confusion is common when subordinates divide their loyalties between two bosses, in this case, Ellen, the program head, and the cross-program task force leader.

4. If you were George, what would you do next? Why?

   George's dilemma needs clarification. He would do well to request, even demand, a written job description to better understand what his duties are, how he should be dividing his time, and to whom he is answerable. Should no job description exist, George might consider meeting with his supervisors, discussing with them how they see his job, and writing a job description himself. This could be presented to his supervisors at a collaborative meeting in which they then fine-tune what George has come up with. Without clarity of his job situation, his days at SAC and Omega might well be numbered.

   George might also request a performance appraisal as a way of clarifying those expectations that he is meeting and not meeting on the job. It is likely that Ellen will tell him that she finds it difficult to communicate with him, etc. This will then give George specific performance areas in which to concentrate his efforts.

Exercise*

(60 minutes or more)

1. *Divide the class into three parts, or divide the class into a number of small groups divisible by three (e.g., three groups of five students each).*

   Assign one-third of the class or groups the role of Ellen, one-third the role of George, and one-third the role of SAC's development chief.

2. *Ask each group or third of the class to write a brief job description for George as they believe their assigned character might write it.*

   Students should include in the job description:

   - A short list of what they believe George's duties should be.
   - A clear statement of who George's employer is.
   - A break-down of how they believe George should divide his time.
   - A brief description of how often and in what format George should report his activities to his superior(s).

   Students should also explore what they believe George's responsibilities should be with regard to attending meetings and developing relationships with donors, and include a brief explanation of this in the job description.

3. *Report out*

   Ask students to describe the various aspects of their job descriptions. Record these on separate flip-charts or blackboards for each of the characters.

4. *Discussion*

   Explore the differences among the three job descriptions, and consider how these differing perceptions might lead to the problems described in the case.

   Consider how a coordinated job description might help George do his job more effectively.

* This exercise was written by Janet W. Wohlberg.

76

THE JOB REFERENCE: AN ETHICAL DILEMMA

Group Size: Individual

Recommended Time: 60 to 180 minutes (5 minutes to set up; ten minutes for completion of survey; 10 minutes for individual reading of case; 10 minutes for presentation of case; discussion open-ended).

Provided: All instructions, descriptions, and forms

Also Required: No additional materials required.

Facilities: Case format classroom.

Objectives

- To help students recognize opinions about others' ethical behavior
- To recognize the possible lax awareness of one's own ethical behavior
- To encourage students to consider the implications of their behavior
- To provide an opportunity for discussing relationships between personal behavior and professional responsibility
- To provide a vehicle for discussing theories of ethical behavior

Background

Ethics is the study of what is "right" and "wrong" in decision making. It involves beliefs, morals, attitudes, and actions. The discussion of ethics is particularly germane to organizational behavior and management education. "The Job Reference: An Ethical Dilemma" including "My Friend Pat" is an exercise to stimulate classroom discussions on ethical reasoning and decision making. The exercise is adaptable to many classroom situations.

Introduction

The discussion of ethics in management and organizational behavior classrooms is commonplace. Stimulated by American Association of Collegiate Schools of Business (AACSB) requirements, increased emphasis has been placed on ethics in management education within business schools. Some colleges of business include an entire course devoted to the coverage of ethics in their curricula.

Although the necessity for ethical decision making cannot be disputed, resources for instructors are limited. Journals and textbooks have few exercises for demonstrating ethical decision making. In a review of the *Journal of Management Education*, only three business ethics exercises have been published in recent years (Collins, 1999; Dennis and Stroh, 1997; Mallinger, 1997). These exercises are more applied and interactive than the discussions offered in textbooks. Textbooks typically offer case scenarios and questions for discussion, but they are surprisingly similar in that they each pose an ethical dilemma and ask students to answer questions regarding the situation. This type of exercise remains detached from the students, and it can be particularly difficult to bring the discussion to life for students with limited work experience.

"My Friend Pat" will help instructors create fun and interesting ethics discussions. The exercise can be used in conjunction with discussions on theories of ethical decision making. As a teaching tool, it is simple to use and produces interesting and lively discussions.

The Case

"My Friend Pat" takes place in the sales department of a large corporation. The case places the reader in a dilemma. A friend has asked for a recommendation for a promotion. Although the friend is regarded positively within the company, she or he has occasionally engaged in questionable personal and professional behaviors. The reader is faced with the decision of whether or not to recommend the friend, Pat, for promotion.

During the case discussion, the instructor should ask students to explain why they would or would not hire Pat (Discussion Question #8). This discussion can then transition into theories of ethical reasoning and decision making. A brief review of theories that can be incorporated into the discussion follows.

In using the case in an MBA class, I observed a sharp demarcation between foreign and American students. Foreign students were more accepting of Pat's behaviors while American students were more critical of Pat's behaviors. There may also be cultural or religious differences that could affect responses. It is important to remind students of their own ethical behavior (from the survey) and that often there can be inconsistencies between our self-concept and our actual behavior.

Underlying Theories

Management textbooks by Daft (1991); Daft and Marcic (1998); Jones, George, and Hill (1998); and Robbins and Coulter (1999) all have chapters dealing with ethics that focus primarily on the model put forth by Cavanaugh, Moberg, and Velasquez (1981). Cavanaugh et al. (1981) present three models of ethical decision making: utilitarian, moral rights, and justice. The utilitarian model is concerned with outcomes or consequences and the greatest good. The moral rights model is concerned with protecting the rights of individuals. The justice model is concerned with equitable and fair distribution.

Daft (1991) and Daft and Marcic (1998) also draw on Tulega (1987), Longnecker, McKinney, and Moore (1988), Kekes (1988), and Wiley (1995). Both Daft (1991) and Daft and Marcic (1998) discuss individualism which states that decisions that promote the individual's best interest will also, in the long run, promote society's best interest. Robbins and Coulter (1999) introduce Donaldson and Dunfee's (1994) integrative social contracts theory that suggests we make ethical decisions by comparing reality with the ideal.

Donaldson and Werhane (1996) cover three theories of ethical reasoning: (1) consequentialism (ethical egoism and utilitarianism); (2) deontological (Kantian and contractarian); and (3) human nature. Consequentialism focuses on the consequences of the action and whether or not a particular behavior will lead to a desired outcome. Consequentialism is further divided into ethical egoism and utilitarianism. In ethical egoism, one seeks to do what is best for oneself. In utilitarianism, one seeks to do what is best for the overall good. Deontological decisions focus on following rules of behavior. Deonotological decisions are of two types, i.e., Kantian and contractarian. Kantian deontology suggests that it is an individual's duty to behave appropriately regardless of the behavior or the consequences. Contractarian deontology suggests that social principles should govern all people's behavior. Human nature ethics supports the notion that all individuals are inherently good, that we strive for self-actualization, and that behavior should be consistent with this goal.

Yet another approach for discussing ethical decision making is to follow: Argyris and Schon's (1974) espoused theory versus theory-in-use. A person's verbal account of how they would behave under a set of given circumstances is termed his or her espoused theory. Espoused theory is what is generated from most ethics case discussions provided in textbooks. However, a person's actual observed behavior is termed his or her theory-in-use. Argyris and Schon (1974) point out that a person's espoused theory and theory-in-use may be contradictory, and that a person may not even be aware of the inconsistency. Using this framework to discuss the case may help students become more mindful of disconnects between their espoused theory and theory-in-use.

Questions for Discussion

1. What responsibilities or obligations do the reader and Pat owe to themselves, the organization, their profession, their peers, and the business community?
2. What are the implications of their behavior and decisions?
3. Does a company have the right to be interested in employees' off-work behavior? At what point does personal life spill over into work life?
4. Would the type of job make a difference in your recommendation (i.e., an international assignment)?
5. Should those in leadership positions be role models for subordinates?
6. Should friendships in the workplace influence decision making? Should Pat have asked for the recommendation?

7. How is Pat any different from you or me or the person sitting next to you? What is the implication in judging others when we may be guilty, too?
8. Finally, would you or would you not recommend Pat? Why?

Suggested Outline and Timing

1. *Set-up (full class: 5 minutes)*

   Go over the learning objectives, background, and instructions. Be clear that the self-assessment will not be collected and is only for each individual student's use.

2. *Individual completion of survey (10 minutes)*

3. *Reading the case (10 minutes)*

   Ask students to also review the "Questions for Discussion" and make any relevant notes.

4. *Case presentation (10 minutes)*

   Ask a student to present the case in brief format, highlighting the relevant issues.

5. *Discussion (open-ended)*

   Use the "Questions for Discussion" as a guide. Ask students, from time to time, to consult their self-assessment answers to compare the differences in the standards they have set for themselves as opposed to those they have set for others.

References

Argyris, Chris and Donald A. Schon (1974). *Theory in Practice: Increasing Professional Effectiveness*. San Francisco: Jossey-Bass, Inc. Publishers.

Cavanaugh, Gerald F., Dennis J. Moberg, and Manuel Velasquez (1981). "The Ethics of Organizational Politics," *Academy of Management Review*, 6(3), 363-374.

Collins, Denis (1999). "The Dollar Game: Questioning the Ethics of Capitalism and Bargaining," *Journal of Management Education*, 23(3), 302-310.

Daft, Richard L. (1991). *Management*, 2nd ed. Chicago, IL: The Dryden Press.

Daft, Richard L. and Dorothy Marcic (1998). *Understanding Management*, 2nd ed. Fort Worth, TX: The Dryden Press.

Dennis, Leslie E. and Linda K. Stroh (1997). "A Little Jeitinho in Brazil: A Case Study on International Management," *Journal of Management Education*, 21(2), 255-261.

Donaldson, Thomas and Thomas W. Dunfee (1994). "Toward a Unified Conception of Business Ethics: Integrative Social Contracts Theory," *Academy of Management Review*, 19(2), 252-284.

Donaldson, Thomas and Patricia H. Werhane (1996). *Ethical Issues in Business: A Philosophical Approach* (5th edition). Upper Saddle River, NJ: Prentice Hall.

Jones, Gareth J., Jennifer M. George, and Charles W. L. Hill (1998). *Contemporary Management*. Boston, MA: Irwin McGraw-Hill.

Kekes, John (1988). "Self-Direction: The Core of Ethical Individualism" in Konstanian Kolenda (Ed.) *Organizations and Ethical Individualism*, New York: Praeger Press, pp. 1-18.

Longnecker, Justin G., Joseph A. McKinney, and Carlos W. Moore (1988). "Egoism and Independence: Entrepreneurial Ethics," *Organizational Dynamics*, Winter, 64-72.

Mallinger, Mark (1997). "Decisive Decision Making: An Exercise Using Ethical Frameworks," *Journal of Management Education*, 21(3), 411-417.

Robbins, Stephen P. and Mary Coulter (1999). *Management*, 6th ed. Upper Saddle River, NJ: Prentice Hall.

Tulega, Tad (1987). *Beyond the Bottom Line*. New York: Penguin Books.

Wiley, Carolyn (1995). "The ABCs of Business Ethics: Definitions, Philosophies, and Implementation," *IM*, February, 22-27.

77

PRICE FIXING AT ADM*

Overview

This is a two-part case. In Part I, Mark Whitacre, a successful vice president of Archer-Daniels Midland, has excellent career potential, with the possibility of being promoted to the position of president. He begins to wonder if he should stay with the company when he hears rumors of illegal price fixing activity in other divisions. As the head of a new division, he fears that he may be required to participate in this illegal activity as well. When the FBI comes to ADM to investigate another matter, his superior asks him to lie to the FBI or at least not to disclose some information that may alert them to the illegal activity. Mark Whitacre must decide how much he will tell the FBI.

In Part II of the case, Mark tells all that he knows to the FBI, including his fears and the rumors he has heard about price fixing. As ADM continues to move closer to requiring Mark to participate in illegal price fixing activities, he must decide whether to stay with ADM, quit, or help the FBI put a stop to this kind of activity.

Objectives

- To help students understand what whistle blowing is, why it happens, and what the risks are
- To assist students in learning and applying Kohlberg's levels of moral development
- To help students see that well-intentioned individuals can find themselves in positions of having to make difficult ethical decisions
- To illustrate the strength of organizational pressures and how they can influence an individual's lapse in moral reasoning
- To illustrate the application of an ethical guide or framework to assist in making difficult decisions that have the risk of a moral lapse
- To illustrate that the consequences of doing something that you believe to be right can still be painful and can be compounded by a false naiveté, i.e., the belief that you will be appreciated for what you are doing

Teaching Approach

This case can be broken into two parts, with a discussion about whether or not Mark should blow the whistle on his company taking place prior to having students read Part II. Most students think Mark should not do more than answer the specific questions that the FBI representative asks. However, both Part I and Part II can be discussed together. The most interesting discussion generally takes place after Part II when Mark Whitacre has talked to the FBI, and Brian Sheppard has outlined several alternatives to Mark. The primary choices for Mark Whitacre are clearly outlined in this case: 1) to quit and get away from it all, 2) to help the FBI, and 3) to continue working at ADM. This third alternative is generally considered unfeasible by most students.

The rationale behind why the decision is made is important to illustrate Kohlberg's three levels of development. Table 1 outlines possible reasons why someone might make one choice or the other and where the rationale would fall within Kohlberg's framework. One caution: As you ask students about why Mark Whitacre might choose to either quit or help the FBI, it is helpful to keep this a general discussion speculating about how and why Mark might make his decision. As you explain how the different reasons for making the choice apply to different stages of moral development, it could embarrass a student to have their personal reasons for choosing to either quit or work with the FBI publicly listed at the lower levels of moral development.

In Part II, the impact of ADM's culture hits Mark full force. Not only does Mark Cheviron, the head of security, accompany Mark to his first meeting with the FBI, but his presence actually influences Mark to comply with his superior's wishes and not be candid with the FBI. This is a good time to emphasize to students exactly how the organizational culture outlined in Part I influences Mark. Group pressures to conform, such as in Asch's conformity experiments, are strong, especially when top executives of the company are exhibiting the unethical behaviors. When the illegal or unethical behavior is coming from such a high level, pressures to conform can blur the boundaries of what is and is not appropriate behavior even for those of the strongest moral character (Miceli and Near, 1992). In addition, Mark's ambition and desire to see the division become profitable influence his decision to remain at ADM. This is why using a decision framework, such as the one included in this case, as a guide in making ethical decisions can be valuable.

As Mark changes his mind and tells Shepard his concerns, remind the students of Kohlberg's stages of moral development. Has Mark shifted to another level of reasoning? Kohlberg (1981) found that ethical decision making and ethical behavior tend to increase as individuals operate in higher stages of moral reasoning.

The negative implications of complying with the FBI's request should be discussed because many whistle blowers never realize the personal consequences of their actions. Mark himself, as quoted in the epilogue, naively says that he truly thought he would be praised by ADM, even though the wrong-doers were the chairman, vice chairman, and president. He never considered the personal hardships or accusations that he might face.

Portions or all of the analysis section that follows can be used as a set of mini-lectures to introduce the case, or this information can be integrated into the discussion of the questions. The epilogue can be handed out after the discussion is over or summarized for the students. It can also be used as the basis for more discussion on the ethical issues raised. Be aware that when students learn the information contained in the epilogue, they may be left feeling "cheated" by Whitacre. This may generate some additional discussion.

Analysis

This case follows an individual through his decision to blow the whistle on his company's illegal and unethical practices and can be used to examine several issues related to ethical behavior in the workplace. Some of these include ethics, moral decision making, and organizational culture. The case offers students a chance to see how one individual grapples with organizational pressure to violate his personal ethical standards.

Whistle Blowing

Mark Whitacre blows the whistle on his company by telling the FBI about ADM's price fixing activities. Whistle blowing is defined as an employee informing the authorities of the wrongdoing of his or her company in order to preserve ethical standards and protect against wasteful, harmful, or illegal activities (Schermerhorn, Hunt and Osborn, 1994). While employees are expected to show loyalty to their organization, there can be situations in which their managers engage in unethical or illegal activities and pressure employees to do the same. Whitacre, we discover, succumbs to these pressures but still feels he should report the illegal activity. Employees must decide where organizational loyalty ends and what they should do to protect themselves, if anything. Whistle blowing is one option that employees have when they are pressured to act unethically or illegally. Whistle blowers are advised to air their concerns internally before going to an external source (Miceli and Near, 1992). However, Mark's orders were coming directly from ADM's top tier. When internal pressures are strong and come from upper management, many times the whistle blower has no choice but to elicit help from someone outside the company.

Whistle blowers can be perceived as either heroes or traitors. For a whistle blower to be perceived as a hero, the magnitude and severity of the wrongdoing must be seen as very high (Laframboise, 1991). But if the whistle blower is seen as blowing the whistle for either personal gain or as an act of revenge, he or she is unlikely to be seen in a positive light. In this case about ADM, no personal gain or revenge is apparent from Mark Whitacre's description of the story, and his perspective is the one this case takes. This is a useful perspective for students to step into and grapple with Whitacre's tough choices.

ADM's version of the events implies that Mark Whitacre was not purely altruistic. They accuse him of diverting millions of dollars in company funds into a Swiss bank account ("ADM Whistleblower," 1995). After the epilogue is presented, this perspective changes, and you can discuss Mark's motive for whistle blowing in light of the new information. One cannot ignore the possibility that Mark Whitacre acted in his own self-interest when he informed the FBI. He may have done this because he was disgruntled about Terry's involvement, because he was disappointed with the progress at his plant, or perhaps to protect himself. However, the actual case focuses on Mark's perspective in order to offer students a picture of an individual struggling with organizational pressures to behave illegally.

Ethical Theories

This case can be analyzed from several perspectives. Students should be provided with a brief overview of the three ethical theories primarily in use in the United States (Cavanagh, Moberg and Velasquez, 1981). The case also offers insight into the individual- and organizational-level factors that impact ethical decisions. Finally, a framework for guiding individuals in making ethical decisions is offered.

The three main ethical theories found in the United States are utilitarianism, theories of justice, and theories of moral rights (Cavanagh, Moberg and Velasquez, 1981).

Utilitarianism: The goal of utilitarianism is to provide the greatest good for the greatest number of people. This view tends to dominate business decision-making and is consistent with organizational goals like efficiency, productivity, and high profits. But, a strictly utilitarian view can result in ignoring the rights of some individuals, particularly those that lack representation or "voice," in this case, ADM's customers. ADM's philosophy is strictly utilitarian. By fixing prices, appropriating technology, and having Mark lie to cover the trail, the company is striving to benefit itself and its stockholders by increasing profits. According to Mark, this philosophy runs counter to his beliefs.

Justice: Justice theories require decisions to be guided by the canons of equity, fairness, and impartiality. Justice theories emphasize the protection of the interests of those who may be underrepresented but can also encourage a sense of entitlement. In this case, ADM could argue that it was fair for them to make a profit because they had such a large investment in building a plant. Customers could argue that price collusion was unfair because it circumvented free market forces.

Moral Rights: The theory of moral rights asserts that individuals have certain basic rights that apply to all decisions. In the United States some of these rights are protected by the Bill of Rights and should be respected in all situations. The Bill of Rights establishes that standards of social behavior are independent of outcomes. The framework for moral decision making, discussed later, originates from this stream of reasoning. Each of these perspectives may be used in discussing the implications of the case with students. Conclusions can be drawn from each perspective about how to make decisions when experiencing organizational pressure.

Kohlberg's Levels of Moral Development

Kohlberg's levels of moral development can be introduced with this case (see Table 1). They offer insight into how individuals make ethical decisions and how individuals may experience a lapse in their moral reasoning. Kohlberg (1981) suggests that there are three levels of moral development, each level having two stages. Level one is referred to as the self-centered or pre-conventional level. Decisions are made based on obedience, the avoidance of punishment (Stage 1) and satisfying immediate interests (Stage 2). Right and wrong are based on whether an action will be rewarded or punished.

Level two is referred to as the conformity or conventional level where decisions are based on what is expected either by those close to you (Stage 3) or by society (Stage 4).

At Level three, the principled level, individuals become aware that there are many values competing for attention (Stage 5), and they begin to choose their own ethical principles to follow (Stage 6).

Research has shown that most people make decisions at one dominant stage; however, they may occasionally move above or below that stage (Kohlberg, 1981). For instance, Mark may appear to be working at Stage 4. He sounds as if he has a law and order orientation, focusing on what is right for society and the importance of doing his duty to uphold those laws. However, his initial decision to lie to the FBI could be seen as a lapse in moral reasoning. He appeared to be influenced by the norms of his organization and his close peers to act in accordance with their wishes (Stage 3) or because he wants to protect himself or his position in the company (Stage 2).

The Rationale for Mark's Decision Based on Kohlberg's Levels

Kohlberg Level	Quit	Work With the FBI
1. Self-Centered or Pre-Conventional		
Avoidance of Punishment Orientation	"ADM might find out. The consequences could be bad."	"The FBI might accuse me of price-fixing if I don't help."
Personal Reward Orientation	"It would be too dangerous to stay at ADM."	"It sounds fun to work as a spy for the FBI."
2. Conformity or Conventional		
Good Boy-Nice Girl Orientation	"My wife couldn't handle the stress if I worked for the FBI."	"I owe it to my wife and family to do what is right by the law."
Law and Order/Authority Orientation	"I was taught never to lie."	"It is my duty to help—law-breaking should be punished."
3. Principled		
Social Contract Orientation	"There might be something others know about this situation that I don't fully understand, so I'll quit but allow it to continue."	"Perhaps the FBI can illuminate the situation to help others see."
Individual Principles	"Purposeful deception is always wrong."	"The world will be a better place if I assist in catching criminals."

Table 1

Organizational Culture

In addition to an individual's personal level of moral development, the situation or organizational culture can play an important role in determining ethical behavior. The culture at ADM seemed to encourage unethical behavior. The case provides information on some of these activities such as the rumors about Terry Wilson's involvement in price fixing; the attempts to purchase proprietary information from the Japanese engineer; the request to lie to the FBI; and ADM's past implication in an illegal technology purchase. In addition, both the company and Chairman Dwayne Andreas have been implicated in rather questionable practices in the past.

The following information was not inserted into the case because its negative implications might overshadow the struggle that Whitacre faced: Both Ralston Purina and Ajinomoto (the company involved in the alleged price fixing discussed in this case) have sued ADM in the past for alleged technology theft. Also, ADM was accused of artificially inflating the price of sugar in order to make its substitute, high fructose corn syrup, more competitive (Kilman, Ingersoll and Abramson, 1995). However, this information can be shared later as organizational influences on individual behavior are discussed.

ADM Chairman, Dwayne Andreas, has been involved in rather questionable practices as well. In 1972, a $25,000 check from Mr. Andreas found its way into the bank account of Watergate burglar Bernard L. Barker. Additionally, Mr. Andreas delivered $100,000 in $100 bills to Nixon's secretary, Rose Mary Woods. In 1973, Andreas was charged with illegally contributing $100,000 in corporate funds to Hubert Humphrey. In 1993, he was fined $8,000 for exceeding the limit on political contributions (Kilman, Ingersoll and Abramson, 1995).

With these leadership precedents from both the chairman and the company, even seemingly simple decisions can become very difficult. ADM's actions blurred the boundaries for its employees between right and wrong. According to Mark Whitacre, fixing prices, appropriating technology, and peddling influence at the government level was the way ADM chose to do business. In organizations where unethical behavior is common, it is much easier for employees, even those with a strong sense of their own values and ethics, to begin to rationalize behavior that they previously felt was questionable (Miceli and Near, 1992). An organization's culture defines the way people should and should not behave, what is right and wrong, and how situations are dealt with. "The key to understanding behavior is that once one is socialized into a culture, these definitions are also accepted and one behaves in accordance with them" (Bluedorn, 1995, p. 178). One could argue that ADM's culture affected Whitacre's perceptions, defining his reality in a way that made it easy to rationalize unethical behavior. Because of the strong impact that organizational culture can have on individual behavior, it is helpful to have a guide to maintain a sense of ethics in such a turbulent environment. The "MORAL Decision Framework" discussed next offers individuals a guide for making difficult decisions in the presence of outside pressures.

MORAL Decision Framework*

This case offers an excellent opportunity to introduce the idea that having a framework to assist in making ethical decisions can be valuable, especially if a decision must be made under pressure. There are several frameworks or series of questions that can be used to assist individuals in making ethical decisions and avoiding moral lapses when they are under pressure. The MORAL framework is an example of one that was designed specifically to help in these situations.

The MORAL framework for ethical decision making comes from the moral rights stream of reasoning and uses the acronym M.O.R.A.L. to make it easier to remember. It assists individuals in examining the issues with an underlying belief that there is a right and a wrong answer when faced with an ethical dilemma.

The MORAL decision making framework is as follows:

- Make the decision. Then ask the following questions:
    - Other people—If the decision was viewed from another person' perspective, would it make a difference? E.g.; If my decision and subsequent action were made public, i.e., printed in the newspaper, or if my mother knew, would it make a difference in my decision?
    - Reversibility—If the situation was reversed, would this decision still feel right to me? E.g.; If I were an ADM customer or an ADM competitor, would that make a difference in how I think the decision should be made?
    - All—If everyone made the same or similar decisions, would the world be a better place?
    - Leadership—Will my leadership impact others? I.e.; Will this decision set a positive or negative precedent for others to follow?

The discussion questions that follow can lead the students through a discussion of Kohlberg's stages of moral development and the use of a framework for decision-making.

Discussion Questions and Answers

1. Which stakeholders could be affected by the decision to participate in illegal activities such as price fixing?

   The stakeholders to consider, in addition to Mark and his potential criminal liabilities if he participates in illegal activities, include:

   - ADM and its employees—severe fines and penalties can be imposed if they are caught and found guilty.
   - The shareholders of ADM—stock prices could fall both as a result of the scandal becoming public and the fines and penalties imposed if convicted.
   - The customers will be hurt by higher prices if ADM raises prices in collaboration with their competitors.

2. What values come into conflict as Mark grapples with this decision?

   Mark's terminal values, such as achievement and self-respect, along with instrumental values, such as honesty, responsibility, and ambition, conflict with his values of loyalty to the company, job security, and obedience to authority. Milgram's studies can be referred to here to illustrate the strong societal norm of obeying authority figures.

   Even though Mark feels uncomfortable lying to the FBI, he feels a strong commitment to the company and his superiors. Additionally, he is very committed to making his division a success. These strong forces make it more difficult for Mark to make an ethical decision.

3. What are the pros and cons of each of the Mark's choices? What would you do if you were Mark? Why?

   Students may think that Mark should quit his position and simply walk away from the situation. Yet, it is important to highlight how difficult this will be. Mark has really become involved in his position and enjoys the challenge of his job. He has a chance to be promoted to president, and the company has made his life very comfortable. Additionally, his family is used to a certain lifestyle, and he may feel pressured to continue to support them at this level. He may be able to find these opportunities elsewhere eventually, but it will be difficult on short notice. He has several years invested in this operation and may feel a strong desire to see his lysine plant become successful. The decision to quit is likely to be difficult considering Mark's commitment to the company, to his project, to his family, and also to his prospects.

   These questions can be used to address the issue of moral development and specifically address how different rationales indicate different levels of moral development. Table 1 outlines examples of possible student responses for why someone like Mark might choose to quit ADM or work with the FBI, and how these responses fit within Kohlberg's framework.

   Initially, when Mark meets with the FBI agent, he complies with his company's request. This act could be considered a lapse in moral reasoning, as Mark is obeying his company and living up to what is expected by his superiors and peers. When Mark decides to tell the truth, he may be working within Stage four of Kohlberg's model (1981) of the levels of moral reasoning if he is focusing on what is expected by him not just from the company but also by society. He could feel that it is important to uphold the law, and one very important aspect of that is to be truthful to authorities. Both of these stages are within Level two, the conformity (or conventional) level.

When he decides to lie to the FBI, Mark is conforming to the desires of those around him (Stage 3); if he decided to be truthful to the FBI, because he was conforming to the values of society and his duty to obey the law, this would be Stage 4. It is helpful to walk students through the decision rationale at each level of moral decision making, showing how either decision can be found at any of the levels but the key factor is why individuals make their decision.

4. Under what circumstances might you consider blowing the whistle on an employer if you were aware of an illegal or unethical practice?

This is a good thought question for students. Some factors they might consider include: whether they had a family to support; whether they had tried to work from the inside first; or how serious the problem was, e.g., was it just a financial issue or were there safety issues or even lives at risk?

5. What organizational influences may be affecting Mark?

The organizational culture that Mark is facing appears to condone behavior that is unethical. From the rumors of price fixing to Mark's own personal experiences with Terry and Mick, it is obvious that these beliefs are held at the highest levels of the organization. Even the most moral person could be affected by the strong organizational influences that support unethical behavior. For instance, Mick Andreas, the one who first approached Mark, is the vice chairman and son of ADM Chairman Dwayne Andreas. Terry is the president of the corn division. The rumors that Mark has heard since he started with the company point out how the practice of price fixing seems accepted at the company. Additionally, the phrase "the competitor is our friend, the customer our enemy" seems strongly ingrained in the company's value system. All of these organizational influences are working against Mark, who may be struggling with his own values of honesty, integrity, and accomplishment.

The case does not focus on the many illegal or unethical allegations that are previously discussed in the "Analysis" section. This gives students an opportunity to experience Mark's conflicts between his desires and ambitions and his sense of right and wrong. Once students have developed a sense of Mark's conflict, then this information can be offered to show just how institutionalized unethical practices appeared to Mark at ADM.

6. What kinds of questions could Mark ask himself to help think through his decision and avoid an ethical lapse?

The questions in the framework for MORAL decision making introduced in the "Analysis" section can be introduced here if students do not generate many of their own questions. These questions might have given Mark the opportunity to seriously consider the consequences of his actions. If he decides to lie to the FBI, he could think about how the decision would look from the perspectives of the FBI agent, of Ajinomoto, and of

ADM's customers. If the company goes through with the price fixing or makes further attempts to purchase technology illegally from competitors, students can use the framework to consider the consequences for the company, the competing companies, and also for the customers purchasing the product. At ADM, "the customer is our enemy." Mark should consider what would happen if everyone acted in the same way. The issues facing Mark are difficult, but using the MORAL framework can help him to bring the issues into focus and avoid a lapse in moral reasoning.

On Page 310 is the epilogue that describes what actually happened to Mark Whitacre and others at ADM. The "Epilogue" may be removed, photocopied, and used for additional class discussion regarding the consequences the company and its employees faced for their illegal activity as well as the behavior of Mark Whitacre.

Archer-Daniels Midland pleaded guilty to fixing the prices of lysine and citric acid and paid a record fine of over $100 million (*LA Times*, July 10, 1999). Dwayne Andreas stepped down as chairman in 1999 and was replaced by his nephew, Allen Andreas (Walsh, 1999). ADM employees Mick Andreas and Terrance Wilson were sentenced to two years in prison and fined $350,000 each for their role in the price-fixing conspiracy (Walsh, 1999).

Mark Whitacre, as it turns out, was no angel in white. Not only was the entire sabotage story a hoax (J.N. and J.F., 1999), he lost his immunity in the price-fixing suit (Eichenwald, 1999) when he pleaded guilty to charges of fraud. It appears that the rumors about embezzling money from ADM were true. He was also convicted of money-laundering and income tax evasion and is currently serving a 9-year prison term. He was ordered to pay $16 million in restitution (J.N. and J.F., 1999). And, when Mick Andreas and Terry Wilson were convicted of price fixing and sentenced to 24 months in prison, Mark Whitacre was also sentenced to 30 months in prison for his role in the price-fixing scheme (Walsh, 1999).

References

ADM whistleblower to plead guilty, report says. (1995, Sept. 27). *Columbia Daily Tribune*, p. B3.

Bluedorn, A.C. (1995). *Organizational culture*. In F. Luthans (Ed.) Management. NY: McGraw-Hill.

Burton, T.M. (1995a, October 9). Informant on Archer-Daniels-Midland is named CEO of biotechnology firm. *The Wall Street Journal*, A4.

Burton, T.M. (1995b, October 17). ADM's chairman says auditors found no improper payments to executives. *The Wall Street Journal*, A3.

Cavanagh, G.F., Moberg, D.J., and Velasquez, M. (1981). The ethics of organizational politics. *Academy of Management Review*, 6, 363–374.

Eichenwald, K. (1999, July 13). Clues to sentencing mystery in the Archer Daniels case. *The New York Times*.

Greenwald, J. (1995, August 28). The spy who cried help. *Time*, 48–49. Kilman, S., Ingersoll, B., and Abramson, J. (1995, October 27).

How Dwayne Andreas rules Archer-Daniels by hedging his bets. *The Wall Street Journal*, A1, A3, A8.

Kohlberg, L. (1981). *Essays in moral development: The philosophy of moral development* (Vol. 1). New York: Harper & Row.

Laframboise, H.L. (1991). Vile wretches and public heroes: The ethics of whistle blowing in government. *Canadian Public Administration*, Spring, 73–78.

Lublin, J.S. (1995, October 11). Archer-Daniels Midland is drawing fire from some institutional holders. *The Wall Street Journal*, B3. Miceli, M.P. and Near, J.P. (1992).

Blowing the whistle: The organizational and legal implications for companies and employees. New York: Lexington. N.J. and F.J. (1999).

The mole who cracked a conspiracy. *Maclean's*, p. 49. Schermerhorn, J.R., Jr., Hunt, J.G., and Osborn, R. (1994).

Managing organizational behavior (5th ed.). New York: Wiley.

3 sentenced in price-fixing plot at Archer Daniels. (1999, July 10). *LA Times*.

Walsh, S. (1999, July 10). 3 former officials at ADM get jail terms; Price-fixing plot was global in scope. *The Washington Post*, E1.

Whitacre, M. and Henkoff, R. (1995, Sept. 4). My life as a corporate mole for the FBI. *Fortune*, 52–62.

Appendix 1
List of People in the Case

Dwayne Andreas	Chairman of ADM
Mark Whitacre	Vice President of ADM
Asian Operations:	
Terrance (Terry) Wilson	President Corn Processing Division
Michael "Mick" Andreas	Vice Chairman of ADM
Jim Randall	President of ADM
Mark Cheviron	Head of ADM Security
Brian Shepard	Head of FBI in Decatur, Illinois

Epilogue

Mark Whitacre decided to help the FBI. For three years he worked with the FBI, meeting with them several times a week. Mark knew that Mick Andreas, the vice chair, and Terry Wilson, a division president, were the main actors involved in the price fixing scheme. He taped many meetings in which they reached agreements about worldwide volume as well as prices.

Mark knew the FBI was going to raid ADM before it actually happened. The FBI arranged to interview Mark and take papers out of his office during the actual raid just like everyone else so that he would not be suspected as the informant. The FBI warned Whitacre that he would need an attorney who was not connected to ADM to advise him in this situation. But Mark didn't heed that warning. Following the raid, he spent several hours discussing his situation with an attorney hired by ADM who promised that he wouldn't tell anyone at ADM about his real role. By Mark's account the next morning, someone called him and said, "Hey, Dwayne (Andreas, the chairman) told me the attorney just told him that you're the mole. You're the one who caused all this." (Whitacre and Henkoff, 1995, p. 62)

Soon after, the character assassination began. Company employees said that Mark Whitacre was not a good manager. Rumors flew that he had been caught price fixing and had been forced to cooperate with the FBI in order to lighten his own sentence. He was accused by company officials of stealing $2.5 million. Mark replied that he had received bonus payments of that amount, but that the company had insisted on the method of payment, which was to use an invoice scheme and pay off the invoices. Mark was fired from Archer-Daniels Midland in August of 1995.

According to *Time* magazine's report (August 28, 1995) the discovery of Whitacre's role made him a villain and a prisoner in his Decatur, Illinois, home, also the home of ADM. Distraught over his firing from ADM, being branded as a traitor, and the accusations by company officials that he had stolen millions of dollars from the company, Mark Whitacre attempted suicide on August 8, 1995. Mark naively thought ADM officials would thank him for his participation in the FBI raid. "I really believed I was doing a good deed. I still think that. I won't ever regret that part. I think I did a good thing. The consequences, however, are a little different from what I expected. I thought I'd be able to fix the problem and stay with the company." (Whitacre and Henkoff, 1995, p. 62)

PRICE FIXING AT ADM*
Part II—The Pressure Builds

Mark Cheviron, head of ADM security, accompanied Mark Whitacre to the meeting with the FBI. Whitacre told the whole story just as Mick Andreas had requested, including the two lies, i.e., that Ajinomoto's engineer had contacted him concerning the technology purchase and that the conversations had taken place on a company phone line.

After the meeting, Mark agonized over his decision to go along with Mick's request. He was uncomfortable lying to the FBI. He felt he would have told the truth if Mark Cheviron hadn't been there. Whitacre suspected that Cheviron was sent along to ensure that he complied with Mick Andreas' requests.

"I tell you what, I would have told him the truth at his office this afternoon if Mark Cheviron hadn't been there." (Whitacre and Henkoff, 1995, p. 56)

Brian Shepard, the FBI agent, made arrangements to visit Mark Whitacre's house later that night to install a recorder on the company phone line. In the meantime, Mark decided that he was going to tell Shepard the truth, correct the misinformation he had given earlier, and also share his fears about price-fixing. He was uncomfortable about Terry's involvement with the lysine association, and although no crime had yet been committed, Mark did not want to lie to the authorities. Mark was also worried that he would be caught in his lie once the wiretap was installed.

Brian Shepard impressed Mark as being a trustworthy person, and this reinforced his decision to tell the truth. At their first meeting, the two seemed to hit it off well and talked for four hours that first night in November 1992. Mark found it a relief to air his concerns and fears to someone with a receptive ear. He relayed the rumors about price fixing that were circulating within the company and his concerns regarding Terry's involvement in the lysine division.

As months passed, the pressures at work mounted. It became apparent that ADM would actually attempt to fix lysine prices with their competitors. Mark had voiced his concerns to an ADM attorney, but the attorney was not receptive. Mark felt there was no way to fix the problem internally; it went too far up the corporate hierarchy. After all, his orders came from the CEO's son, ADM vice chairman Mick Andreas.

Mark knew if he continued in his position, there would soon come a day when he would actually have to participate in illegal activities. He trusted Shepard and his other FBI contacts; in fact he began to trust those he worked with at the FBI more than he trusted those he worked with at ADM. Mark was facing one of the most difficult decisions of his life. His company was about to require that he participate in an act that was not only illegal but that also went against his personal work ethic. The FBI pointed out that he had to make some choices. He could stay with the company and break the law, or he could quit and walk away from the project he had worked so hard to develop.

Mark had not yet participated in any illegal price-fixing activities, but if he stayed with the company it would be a matter of days before he would be forced to do so. The FBI offered Mark a third choice, to continue with the company and assist the FBI in their attempts to catch ADM in the act of fixing prices. The FBI asked Mark to carry a concealed tape recorder and record conversations with Terry and other high-ranking ADM executives that might involve discussions about price fixing. The FBI made a strong argument regarding the service he could provide by cooperating with them to stop this serious crime.

Mark had to decide what to do before he found himself in an untenable position.

Questions for Discussion

1. Which stakeholders could be affected by the decision to participate in illegal activities such as price fixing?
2. What values might come into conflict as Mark tries to make this decision?
3. What are the pros and cons of each of the choices Mark has? What would you do if you were Mark? Why?
4. Under what circumstances might you consider blowing the whistle on an employer, if you were aware of an illegal or unethical practice?
5. What organizational influences may be affecting Mark?
6. What kinds of questions could Mark ask himself to help think through his decision and avoid an ethical lapse?

78

MAKING THE IDEAL JOB COME TRUE

Objectives

- To give students a chance to reflect on short- and long-term career aspirations
- To help students assess the skills they now have and those they will have to acquire in order to achieve their career aspirations
- To give students a chance to explore their role versus the role of their employers in developing their careers
- To give students the opportunity to practice skills in human resources management

Parts A and B

The first two parts of this exercise are for students to work through on their own. They give students an opportunity to reflect on the various aspects of career aspirations and the fit between career and self with regard to skills, abilities, values, and temperament. Students should complete these parts of the exercise prior to using Part C as an in-class exercise.

Part C: Role Play

1. *Set-up (full class: 5 minutes)*

   Review the objectives of the exercise. Tell students that they are to select a partner. One member of each dyad should play a manager or human resources professional, the other an employee.

2. *Role play (dyads: 20 minutes)*

   Dyads should review the material that the employee has detailed in response to Parts A and B of the exercise. The manager should help the employee to clarify how best to go about achieving his or her five-year career goal. Asking students to create timelines for achieving their goals is useful.

3. *Role play (dyads: 20 minutes)*

   Dyads should reverse roles and proceed as above.

4. *Discussion (full class: open-ended)*

   Discussion should focus on the ways in which the manager was able to help the employee focus on and better define career goals and paths.

79

TED JOHNSON: PARTS A AND B*

Ted Johnson: Part A

The "Ted Johnson" case touches on a number of issues especially relevant to undergraduate students. The first part of the case focuses primarily on self-assessment and provides an introduction to career exploration. Students will need a general familiarity with the terms of self-assessment to understand Ted's findings.

Among the problems Ted faces are that his parents want him to return to Nebraska and that his mother has definite ideas about what his career should be. This provides an introduction to issues that will be central to the second part of the case.

One useful way to present the case is to have students read it thoroughly once or twice and take note of any kind of skills and interests evident in the case. Point out that Ted has completed some of his own self-assessment, and ask students to list the courses he enjoyed and his personality type. This should be helpful when considering potential careers for Ted. Students also may list possible occupations that would appear to satisfy Ted's interests and values. After students have completed this on their own, list their ideas on the board or other visible place.

The importance of values and a preferred work environment should not be overlooked when discussing the case. It is clear that Ted is not interested in a highly structured office job. Values evident in the case include a need to achieve, autonomy, curiosity, closeness to family, and so forth. A brief discussion of what Ted's parents want can lead into a consideration of decision making and how to deal with significant others. This topic can be expanded upon in "Ted Johnson: Part B."

Ted Johnson: Part B

In this part of the case, Ted has continued to explore careers and has identified a possible career to pursue—that of a claims adjuster. Students should recognize the role that career exploration has played for Ted. He has arrived at this tentative decision through a process of self-assessment, informational interviewing, and the use of what amounts to an internship.

In identifying Ted's major issues, students generally will sympathize with the difficulty of choosing a type of work. Have students look at Ted's interests, skills, and values to decide if being a claims adjuster would be an appropriate match. Ted's decision of where to live may be impacted by his choice of work, though it appears entry-level jobs are available in a number of locations.

* These notes were written by Bruce Leblang. Used with permission.

A major part of the discussion should touch on the issues of how to make decisions and prioritize. In addition, students should consider just how much significant others, such as parents and friends, should influence these decisions. Here, students also need to consider the role peer pressure should be allowed to play in their career decisions. One question might be, "If you were Ted, would your ego allow you to do what you want to do, even if it was something your peers considered to be beneath you?"